RED DWARF

PROGRAMME GUIDE

RED DWARF

PROGRAMME GUIDE

by
Chris Howarth & Steve Lyons

Virgin

This edition published in 1995 by
Virgin Books
an imprint of Virgin Publishing Ltd
332 Ladbroke Grove
London W10 5AH
First published in 1993

Reprinted 1993 (twice), 1994 (twice) updated (1995)

Photos 1, 2, 5, 6, 14 and 16 by Peter Walsh
Photos 17, 20 and 21 © BBC TV
Photos 4, 7 and 19 by Steve Lyons
Photo 8 by Peter Wragg
Photos 15 and 22 by Mike Vaughn
Photo 18 © Robert Llewellyn
Photo 3 by Paul Grant
Design Sketches (9 to 13) by Alan Marshall

Typeset by Mark Stammers Design, London

Printed and bound in Great Britain by
Cox & Wyman Ltd, Reading Berks

ISBN 0 86369 682 1

CONTENTS

For Liz Guest

ACKNOWLEDGEMENTS

The Authors would like to say a great big thank you to the following:

Rob Grant and Doug Naylor.

Charles Augins, Chris Barrie, Suzanne Bertish, Mel Bibby, Stephen Bradshaw, Mike Butcher, Ed Bye, Craig Charles, Paul Cornell, Kate Cotton, Matthew Devitt, Andy de Emmony, Howard Goodall, C. P. Grogan, Hattie Hayridge, Jonathan Head, Graham Hutchings, Kathleen Hutchison, Danny John-Jules, John Knight, Andrew and Catherine Liddell, Denis Lill, Robert Llewellyn, Norman Lovett, Mac McDonald, Keith Mayes, Jim Marshall, Chrissie Moses, Helen Norman, John Pomphrey, David Ross, Gary Russell, Lisa Wardle, Peter Wragg, and Sophie at Egmont, who's finally got around to watching an episode.

Oh yes, and thanks a bunch to all at Noel Gay Television.

SECTION ONE:

THE HISTORY

Rob Grant and Doug Naylor's science-fiction situation comedy *Red Dwarf* first appeared on our television screens in 1988, some four years after it was initially devised. The concept was in fact developed from Grant and Naylor's earlier creation 'Dave Hollins – Space Cadet', which featured as a regular segment on Radio 4's comedy sketch show *Son of Cliché*. The eponymous hero of the piece was the last human being alive (a sort of embryonic Lister), played by Nick Wilton, his only companion in the vastness of space the computer Hab, voiced by Chris Barrie.

The decision to turn 'Dave Hollins – Space Cadet' into *Red Dwarf* came about for two reasons. Firstly Grant and Naylor were keen to do their own television sit-com and secondly Rob in particular wanted to write science fiction. 'Hollins' was an obvious starting point for both ambitions. To make *Red Dwarf* a completely separate entity from its radio forerunner, Dave Hollins became Dave Lister and Hab transformed into Holly. It was clear from the beginning however that, if the transition into television was to be at all successful, it was necessary for the cast to be expanded. Rather than dilute the original premise, which required the pivotal figure to be the last human being alive in the universe, the extra characters were very intentionally non- human. Rimmer, the hologram of a dead man, was created first, followed by the highly evolved Cat. At this early stage, the temptation to include a robot in a central role was resisted as it was considered to be a standard science-fiction cliché.

The pilot script for *Red Dwarf* was written half way up a Welsh mountain in a cottage belonging to Doug Naylor's father; it was more or less completed in a week, but was subsequently re-written six times before it was perfected. With its lengthy gestation period it is not surprising that this script is not identical to the version that finally appeared on our television screens. There are several interesting variations contained in its pages; some of the differences are simply lines of dialogue, but other changes are more significant. The outline of Dave Lister is rather vague, but he is descnbed as being 41 years old and he was to have to have spent seven billion years in stasis – which makes the three million he did spend there seem like no time at all really. Holly, quite prophetically, is female at this early stage. In both these instances casting would be a contributive factor in dictating the need for alterations A less crucial, but nonetheless interesting, change is the choice of song selected for George McInttyre's funeral. Originally it was to have been 'Heaven is Ten Zillion Light Years Away' by Stevie Wonder, in the transmitted episode it was 'See Ya Later Alligator'; both songs are equally appropriate in their own ways. The only other diversity of note is the number of crew members aboard *Red Dwarf*; it was initially specified as 129 but increased slightly to 169. However, later on in the programme's run the number of crew members was expanded again, by a thousand. It is perhaps worth mentioning at this juncture that – albeit with occasional variations in the prefix – Lister's crew number is given as 169 several times throughout the series, suggesting that his is the lowest rank on the ship bar none.

Once completed, the pilot script was handed to producers John Lloyd and Paul Jackson – who between them were responsible for most of the alternative comedy programmes around at the time, including such classics as *Blackadder* and *The Young Ones* – both of whom were decidedly impressed with it. It even seemed likely, for a while, that they might work together on the project, but the proposed co-production was destined not to be; the task of selling the project ultimately tell to Paul Jackson alone. Jackson's initial attempts to sell the idea proved fruitless, possibly because of Grant and Naylor's insistence that – rather than lose valuable minutes of air time for the sake of a few commercials – the show must be made by the BBC. Their faith in the potential of *Red Dwarf* as a thirty-minute ongoing sit-com even led its creators to turn down an offer to include it as part of the highly respected Film on 4 series; the films produced by Channel 4 along with the ones made by the BBC are virtually all that now remains of the British film industry and naturally a large degree of prestige is involved in any such production. Ultimately, however, Grant and Naylor's confidence in their creation turned out to be justified, and eventually Paul Jackson did indeed manage to persuade the BBC to commission a series.

With the series accepted, at long last, by the Manchester based BBC North West (now simply BBC North), the next stage was to assemble a cast. Once again proceedings did not run entirely as planned. Rob Grant and Doug Naylor had always envisaged if not classically trained then, at the very least established 'legitimate' actors portraying their main characters and indeed legend has it that several high-profile people did audition for the lead roles in *Red Dwarf* but were quite unsuitable. What Grant and Naylor eventually got – and in fact selected themselves – were a poet, an impressionist, a dancer and a stand-up comedian. Despite the descriptions, which Grant and Naylor themselves applied to their choices, the casting was inspired; the performances of the regulars would prove to be as instrumental in the series' eventual success as the innovative scripts.

The first to join the cast was the comedian Norman Lovett who originally auditioned for the part of Arnold Rimmer, but was signed up as the ship's at this stage male computer, Holly. (It was in fact Lovett who later suggested that the computer's face should appear on screen rather than just be heard as a voice-over.) Danny John-Jules was the next to be enlisted; dressing as the Cat for his audition, he made a positive impression from the start. The important role of Dave Lister was given to Craig Charles, but Charles landed the part in a rather unusual manner. Paul Jackson was keen to ensure that there were no racist elements in the script. Why he considered that there might be is uncertain; perhaps he thought that having the Cat portrayed as a sharply dressed, cool black guy could be perceived as a racial stereotype. He sent a copy to Craig Charles for appraisal and then had the notion that Charles could possibly play the Cat. Perhaps not surprisingly, Jackson had second thoughts and decided that Charles would be better suited as Lister. Rob Grant and Doug Naylor met Craig Charles at this point and decided that Paul Jackson's recommendation was a good one. The line-up was completed with the addition of Chris Barrie as the hologram, Rimmer. Barrie – who had previously worked with Grant and Naylor on several series – seems such an ideal choice for Rimmer that it is perhaps surprising to discover that he did, in fact, also try for the role of Lister. The casting of people from the comedy side of the entertainment industry as the programme's mainstays also set a precedent for some of the guest stars featured in the show's six series run. These have included: Morwenna Banks, Tony Slattery, Tony Hawks, Craig Ferguson, Ruby Wax and Gordon Kennedy. The serious side of the profession has also been well represented by the likes of Jenny Agutter, Nicholas Ball, Frances Barber, Jane Horrocks, Ron Pember, Maggie Steed and John Abineri as Rimmer's father. His 'bitch queen from hell' mother, Mrs Rimmer, would also appear on a couple of occasions played each time by Kalli Greenwood, and Simon Gaffney featured in three episodes as the young Arnold Rimmer.

With the scripts finished, the cast assembled and the sets constructed at BBC's Oxford Road studios in Manchester, *Red Dwarf* looked set to take off. Unfortunately, although rehearsals took place in North Acton, an electricians' strike precluded any actual recording. Eventually season one had to be postponed. During this enforced respite it was feared that *Red Dwarf* might not happen after all. But, to the relief of all concerned, it did and around six months later the series was remounted.

The first episode of *Red Dwarf* season one, 'The End', was broadcast on BBC2 on 15 February 1988. It wouldn't be unfair to say that the series was not a massive overnight success, at least in the opinion of the press reviewers. Craig Charles himself was particularly hurt by the insulting comment in the Daily Mirror which suggested that the trouble with *Red Dwarf* was the little brown dwarf, Craig Charles. The early episodes were slower paced than now and concentrated more on the relationship between Lister and Rimmer. Viewed in retrospect – now that the personalities of the protagonists are familiar – season one is funnier and more entertaining than it might have seemed at the time. As Rob Grant and Doug Naylor feared, some of the production values were disappointing, the sets in particular looked cheap and tacky and the uniforms too were very basic, consisting of simple cotton shirts and trousers. Fortunately Peter Wragg's special effects and model shots were superb, the skill that would later win awards for the series very much in evidence. The original model of *Red Dwarf* itself was eight foot in length, though sadly this piece of television history no longer exists; it was irreparably damaged and consigned to the skip. Another early plus factor was Howard Goodall's music – especially the closing theme song which would be retained throughout the series' run. The singer of the theme was Jenna Russell, who has appeared more recently in an acting role in the situation comedy *On the Up*.

The first episode established the, now familiar, scenario: Dave Lister, a 21st-century slob and a third technician aboard a deep space mining ship, is sentenced to eighteen months in stasis for bringing aboard an unquarantined animal, specifically a pregnant cat. Three million years later he is brought out of stasis to discover that his shipmates are dead, killed by a radiation leak caused by a faulty drive plate. Holly, the ship's computer, resurrects Lister's unpopular shift leader Rimmer as a hologram, to keep him company and more importantly to keep him sane. Meanwhile the descendants of Lister's cat have evolved into humanoid form and one of them is still around. It was implied in this episode that Rimmer was, in fact, responsible for the accident that wiped out the *Red Dwarf* crew. This was amended later on in the series' run. 'The End' featured a guest appearance by C. P. Grogan as Kristine Kochanski (or Christine with a C as her personality disc would later imply) – as Clare Grogan she had been the lead singer in the group Altered Images before she turned to acting and appeared in the title role of the film *Gregory's Girl*. The change to C.P. came about because there was already another actress called Claire Grogan in Equity. Kochanski, who would return in a couple of other episodes, is included in the *Red Dwarf* saga merely as an icon – a romanticised ideal to provide Lister, along with his desire to return to Earth, with some motivation for living. Initially it was established that Lister had simply worshipped Kochanski from a distance and had never plucked up the courage to ask her out; later on this again was revised so that they had had a brief affair before she dumped him. Grant and Naylor's attitude to continuity within the series seems to be that if it's in the programme's interest to change something, then change it. The first episode also included in its cast Mac McDonald as Captain Hollister and Mark Williams as Petersen. The two of them would become very infrequent semi-regulars in the series – disappearing when the story lines referring back to the pre-accident days were dropped. Although Captain Hollister turned up in three episodes, Mac McDonald's scenes in 'Me²', were actually re-corded during the filming of 'The End'.

'Future Echoes', the second episode, gave Lister a few glimpses into his own future. As well as finding out that he's going to be around on *Red Dwarf* for at least another century he discovers that he is going to have twin sons, Jim and Bexley. With hindsight it seems as if the scene with the children was included intentionally to allow it to be followed up in later episodes. But in fact, at this stage, the writers did not have any specific notions about how they would go about introducing Lister to fatherhood, which perhaps explains why when the idea was eventually picked up, it was swiftly abandoned and subsequently ignored. The bread obsessed toaster with artificial intelligence was also introduced in the second episode, voiced in this, the first of three appearances, by John Lenahan. The story of the Cat People, evolved from Lister's pet cat Frankenstein, is revealed in some detail in the fourth episode 'Waiting for God'. Their God is none other than Lister himself; his apotheosis into Cloister the Stupid is explained in the Cat's bible. Noel Coleman appears in this episode as the blind Cat priest, the only other example of Felis Sapiens seen in the series so far. His death in the episode leads us to assume that, like Lister, the Cat is the sole survivor of his race (although a chapter dealing with the fate of the Cat People who left *Red Dwarf* would later be written for one of the novels but omitted before publication).

Although the opening episode of its introductory season achieved ratings of 5.1 million, coming in third on BBC2 that week, the series had lost 2 million viewers by its close. However, the BBC thought that *Red Dwarf* was worth continuing for two reasons: firstly they had received many letters and calls praising the series and secondly the Audience Appreciation Index (AI) was in the 80s (out of a possible 100). Reputedly at that time only the Queen's Coronation in 1954 had scored higher.

Season two debuted, later that same year, with the episode 'Kryten' broadcast on 6 September. The episode saw the introduction of the service mechanoid Kryten, discovered aboard the crashed spaceship *Nova 5*. Although the android, played by David Ross, would not reappear for the rest of season two, Doug Naylor was particularly keen on using the character as a regular and he somehow managed to persuade Rob Grant, who was initially dead set against the idea, that having a robot complete the team would be advantageous to the show's success.

Rimmer's father turned up in the second episode, 'Better than Life', or at least an illusion of him did, in the virtual reality game of the title. Much of this episode was filmed away from the studio.

Certain scenes were filmed in the Manchester hotel Sacha's, which would later play host to various conventions with a TV science fiction theme; including *Star Trek*, *Space 1999* and the extremely popular *Doctor Who* event 'Manopticon'.

The fourth episode, 'Stasis Leak', would be the last to concentrate on *Red Dwarf* before the accident. In it a bearded Dave Lister, from five years further in the future than the Lister we are familiar with, finds a way back through time and marries Kristine Kochanski. This occurrence served to wrap up any outstanding storylines without radically changing the set-up, or indeed changing it at all. This episode marked C. P. Grogan's last appearance in the series for several years; she did not appear at all in Kochanski's last scene, as the production team had let her go before realising she was required to appear in the final sequence, albeit without dialogue. Instead, assistant floor manager Dona DiStefano served as a stand in – wearing a large hat. The situation was hardly unique. In the previous episode, 'Thanks for the Memory', Mike Agnew had taken the place of the unavailable Craig Charles for one scene. Craig had been unavailable because at the time he was being rushed to London by taxi to be at the birth of his son Jack. Unfortunately he arrived twenty minutes too late.

The final episode of *Red Dwarf*'s second series, 'Parallel Universe', was shown on 11 October 1988. In it the crew of *Red Dwarf* are transported into a universe where, with the exception of the Cat, they all have female counterparts, even Holly the ship's computer, whose equivalent, Hilly, was played by comedian Hattie Hayridge. The female Lister and Rimmer, Deb and Arlene, were played by Angela Bruce and Suzanne Bertish respectively. During its early stages of development Rob and Doug had briefly considered using female leads in *Red Dwarf*, ideally French and Saunders. 'Parallel Universe' turned out to be Norman Lovett's last appearance in the programme. At the time, Lovett was living in Edinburgh, rehearsals were done in London at Acton and filming took place in Manchester. Consequently he was unprepared to do the amount of travelling that working on the show required. Lovett reluctantly – having greatly enjoyed his stint as the imbecile computer – chose to leave. Holly had shown, in the episode 'Queeg', that he was capable of changing his appearance. So, although it would be difficult to replace the highly popular Norman Lovett, recasting was not considered to be totally out of the question.

After the second series had been transmitted Rob Grant and Doug Naylor approached Penguin Books with a view to doing a *Red Dwarf* novel. The idea was accepted and the first book, *Red Dwarf – Infinity Welcomes Careful Drivers,* followed shortly thereafter.

It was just over a year after the end of season two that *Red Dwarf III* (this and subsequent seasons were numerically titled in the Radio Times and the press) hit the screens. It looked like a very different series; a fast-paced instrumental version of Howard Goodall's theme song accompanied the opening titles, which now culminated with a specially designed *Red Dwarf* logo, courtesy of De Wynters. The cotton uniforms and T-shirts were discarded in favour of specially designed space-corps outfits and plenty of leather. The old bunk room set had been vacated and the centre of operations switched to the more elaborately designed offficers' quarters. The reason for the changes is straightforward – between seasons Rob Grant and Doug Naylor had become involved in the production side of their creation. Although the budget had not significantly altered, careful spending made it look as if it had increased substantially.

As well as the look of the show the emphasis altered too: instead of concentrating on its own internal continuity the scope of the show broadened and other science-fiction concepts and themes were parodied. Events necessitated cast changes too. In the opinion of Rob Grant and Doug Naylor it might have been wise for them at the time to completely reinvent Holly. In the event replacing the computer proved not to be as big a challenge as was expected. Hattie Hayridge was available and, although she went through the auditioning process, she seemed to be the obvious choice – she jokingly claims to have been given the role simply because she has more hair than Norman Lovett. David Ross, though keen to return as Kryten, was busy in the theatre in *Flea in Her Ear* and consequently not available. So the mechanoid was reintroduced, complete with Canadian accent, in the form of Robert Llewellyn. Llewellyn had been spotted by Paul Jackson whilst playing a robot in the stage production *Mammon, Robot Born of Woman*. As if to consolidate all the changes and developments that had occurred between seasons, Lister and Rimmer were now said to have originally hailed from the 23rd century.

The last episode of season two had seen Lister – due to the differing laws of physics in the parallel universe – become pregnant by his female counterpart: the first episode of *Red Dwarf III* was originally intended to continue this storyline. The script, entitled 'Dad' – which would have properly resolved the sub-plot involving Lister's sons, who were first seen in 'Future Echoes' – was dropped, its content deemed not especially funny, and possibly offensive to women. The fate of Jim and Bexley plus the changes to the crew were explained in a *Star Wars* style roll past scroll at the beginning of the first episode. The twins, who had suffered from an accelerated growth rate due to being in the wrong universe, had been returned to their 'father' Deb Lister; the computer senile Holly had fallen for Hilly and performed a head sex change operation on himself and Kryten had crashed a space bike into an asteroid thus requiring extensive repair by Lister. The addition of Kryten as a regular cast member meant that the roles of Cat and Holly were diminished slightly although, because the parts were quite small to begin with, the change seemed radical. The android was now able to explain anything with a scientific basis – previously that task had fallen to Holly – and was also able to take part in any physical activity, whereas for the Cat to be bothered getting involved in anything requiring effort necessitated a detailed explanation of his motivation in the script. Robert Llewellyn probably didn't know what he was letting himself in for when he accepted the role of the service mechanoid; initially

Kryten's make-up took around five hours (nowadays the perfected process takes between one and a half to two hours). His first recorded scene (intended for 'Body Swap') took place in a sauna. As Kryten he was required to light two candles with his fingers and, because he was wearing full make-up and a costume that was wired up to produce the flames, a combination of water and sweat constantly caused Llewellyn to receive electric shocks. The scene, recorded at Manchester's Hotel Piccadilly, (the venue for Manopticon 2 if you're interested), was cut in editing.

Though *Red Dwarf III* was quite different from its predecessors the show subsequently stabilised in this format and it was this version that strengthened the series' status as a cult favourite, expanding the appreciative and loyal following it had begun to garner during season two. Much of the season opener, 'Backwards', was filmed in Manchester, with the northern locations masquerading as London or, more accurately, as Nodnol. This episode was bizarre even by *Red Dwarf*'s standards; the footage of the events set on Backwards Earth being shown in reverse. This gave some of the cast an unprecedented opportunity to utter a number of unprintable expletives, secure in the knowledge that a more innocuous version of the dialogue would appear in the subtitles. A printable example of transposed dialogue occurs when the bar manager, played by Arthur Smith, apparently accuses the *Red Dwarf* crew of unstarting a fight. He actually says (while pointing at Kryten), 'You are a stupidly square-headed bald git, aren't you eh? You, I'm pointing at you, but I'm not actually addressing you, I'm addressing the one prat in the entire country who's actually bothered to get hold of this recording, turn it round and actually work out the rubbish that I'm saying, what a poor sad life he's got.' The episode that followed 'Backwards' had had the working title of 'Men of Honour', but this was revised to the more catchy 'Marooned'. Keen-eyed viewers may spot a bit of a blunder as the insubstantial Rimmer can, at one point, be observed operating a radio. This episode is reminiscent of earlier shows in that it's a character piece; the old style script and new improved production values combined to produce a highly entertaining amalgam. However, Grant and Naylor were keen to introduce a host of threatening adversaries to face the crew of *Red Dwarf* and these foes would form the basis of many of the new-look episodes.

For the first, and so far only, time in the show's history a warning was given before the start of 'Polymorph'. However, it was actually a publicity stunt. With the episode being broadcast after the watershed time of 9.00 pm, a warning would not have been necessary even if the episode did contain scenes that were more frightening than usual.

Monsters like the Polymorph were not only a challenge for the crew of the mining vessel, but also for Peter Wragg's Acton based special effects team. They obviously faced up to it admirably, as *Red Dwarf* seasons three and four netted them the World Television Society award for their visual effects. Wragg and his department were asked to design a new shuttle craft to be used alongside *Blue Midget*. Selecting the drawing they preferred – of a ship called *Green Midget* – Grant and Naylor decided to re-christen it *Starbug*. Another of the shuttles designed, *White Midget*, was never used but is mentioned in the fourth episode 'Body Swap'. *Starbug* was destined not only to replace *Blue Midget* but *Red Dwarf* itself.

'Body Swap' has the distinction of being the only *Red Dwarf* episode not to be recorded in front of a studio audience. In order to gain an authentic laughter track it was shown to an audience at the Paris Radio Studio in London, coincidentally where 'Dave Hollins' had been recorded.

Ruby Wax put in a guest appearance in 'Timeslides', as American TV presenter Blaize Falconburger. Series director Ed Bye (Ruby's husband) admits that this piece of casting was 'an inside job'. Originally the part had been written for former *Monty Python* star Graham Chapman, who sadly died before shooting began, so Ed persuaded Rob and Doug to adapt the role to suit Ruby's individual style. Because of Ruby's late casting, member's of the 'Timeslides' studio audience were treated to an impromptu stand-in performance from the floor manager.

The third season concluded on 19 December 1989 with the episode entitled 'The Last Day'. Because the studio was closed down for refurbishment, it was the last season of *Red Dwarf* to be recorded in Manchester. Grant Naylor Productions moved south to Lee International's Shepperton studios, Stage G, for the making of *Red Dwarf IV*. Although, because of the fixed seating, the move prevented an overnight change round of sets for pre-recorded scenes, the nearby Stages E and F were utilised for this purpose when necessary, and the close proximity of Sunbury Pump-house also proved to be useful as the building served as a stand-in for various space ship interiors, etc. The move south was also a convenient one for the cast, as rehearsals were now able to take place on the *Red Dwarf* set itself. Because season four wasn't broadcast until February 1991 there were no new episodes shown in 1990. Disheartened fans were able to take temporary consolation from the publication of the second *Red Dwarf* novel *Better Than Life*.

Appropriately enough, season four opened on Valentines Day with 'Camille', an episode with love as its theme. Camille was a pleasure GELF, who appeared to the crew as the object of their desires. Appropriately enough, her Kochanski-like form was played by Suzanne Rhatigan – Craig Charles' real life girlfriend – and, not very coincidentally, Robert Llewellyn's better half, Judy Pascoe, also appeared as Kryten's favourite Camille.

The episode entitled 'DNA' on screen, though officially listed under its fuller title of 'Do Not Alter' gave Robert Llewellyn a much appreciated chance to appear without make-up, when Kryten became temporarily human. Llewellyn had already appeared briefly as 'himself' in 'The Last Day' playing Jim Reaper and would do so again as Bongo in the episode 'Dimension Jump'.

It was in the third episode 'Justice' that the continuity regarding the Cadmium 2 accident was changed. Rimmer is put on trial for causing the deaths of all but one of his crew mates (the number of fatalities, not counting Rimmer himself, now increased to 1,167). But Kryten argues, successfully, that he would never have been placed in a position responsible enough to have caused the tragedy.

The original Kryten, David Ross, made a brief return to the series in 'White Hole' playing Talkie Toaster. Although supposedly the same toaster as that which appeared in the first series, the infuriating appliance underwent a change in colour as well as voice. Ross is keen to return to the series again should the opportunity arise, but perhaps playing a character even more bizarre; he would not consider returning in the Kryten role should Robert Llewellyn ever leave the show.

The final two episodes of season four both featured different versions of the closing theme tune. 'Dimension Jump' featured a Hammond organ arrangement and 'Meltdown' had a spirited rendition from an Elvis Presley impersonator.

Interestingly, the order in which *Red Dwarf IV* was originally broadcast was rather different from the sequence as envisaged by Grant and Naylor – their preferred order was reflected in the 1992 repeat run of the series. Not only did the Valentines Day slot for 'Camille' affect the run of episodes but so too did the Gulf War. Both 'Dimension Jump' and 'Meltdown' were held back until hostilities ceased and, had the conflict continued, the two episodes would have remained unscreened. The BBC's objections to the heavily anti-war 'Meltdown' are perhaps understandable, but their insistence that 'Dimension Jump' be postponed merely because of the inclusion of macho pilot Ace Rimmer seems almost laughable. The episode did undergo some editing however. A scene in which Rimmer tries to dump a net full of kippers onto Ace was removed simply because it didn't work.

Filming for *Red Dwarf V* once again took place at Shepperton Studios, again in Stage G. Hilary Bevan Jones joined the team as producer. Ed Bye, who had directed every episode since the start of season one, left for other projects at the end of *Red Dwarf IV* and was replaced by Juliet May. Juliet's association with the series was short lived, however, and she left before the series was completed; the directorial chores for the remainder of the episodes were handled by Rob Grant and Doug Naylor themselves.

The fifth season saw the introduction of an updated, serif typeface logo. This wasn't the only change. Superficially *Red Dwarf V* was visually identical to its two immediate predecessors. But as far as the narrative was concerned, the balance between comedy and science fiction had been intentionally tipped toward the latter. Continuity too was observed more closely than it had been previously. The Inquisitor featured in the second episode was a simulant, the type of droid first introduced in the fourth season in 'Justice', and the Triplicator used in Demons and Angels' – which went under the apt working title of 'High and Low' – was adapted from the Matter Paddle as seen in 'Meltdown'. Rimmer's stint in the Samaritans is also mentioned, although the number of callers who committed suicide is reduced from five to four.

Customarily, the first episode of a programme to be broadcast is one of the strongest. 'Holoship', series five's opener, contained space ship model shots which must certainly rank among the best ever seen in a British made television show; the holoship, *Enlightenment*, designed by Paul McGuinness was a masterpiece in Perspex. Sadly the episode overran and needed eight minutes trimming, so some of the effects footage became a casualty of the editor's scissors.

The season concluded with an episode designed to keep the audience on the edge of their seats. Early on in 'Back to Reality' we were led to believe that the crew of *Starbug* had been killed and then we were persuaded that all of their previous adventures had merely been a video-game-induced fantasy and finally we saw our heroes at the brink of suicide. Grant and Naylor's ruse worked extremely well. But unfortunately for some of the more devoted fans, certain magazines aimed at them had given away too many plot details and spoiled the element of surprise. Once again effects work was deleted when the filmed Despair Squid model sequences were replaced in editing by a more subtle shadow of the creature.

With the editing of *Red Dwarf V* completed, Grant and Naylor flew to the United States to work on the pilot episode for a possible American series of *Red Dwarf*. Unfortunately the series never materialised (see Spin-offs section for details).

It would be quite a long wait for *Red Dwarf VI*. Initially Grant and Naylor's other work commitments prevented the series' go-ahead at the usual time. And even when production got under way – this time with director Andy deEmonny at the helm – they were forced to work on the later scripts right up until the day of filming. The season was completed and available for a spring '93 broadcast; however the BBC decided to hold it back until the Autumn schedule when it would reach a larger audience. Appropriately enough perhaps, when it eventually debuted on TV 200 years were said to have elapsed since *Red Dwarf V*. That was the least of the changes. . .

Thanks to the publication of the 'Psirens' script in *Primordial Soup* and news revelations in the Smegazine, the fact that *Red Dwarf VI* didn't feature Holly or indeed *Red Dwarf* didn't come as much of a shock to the series' hard-core followers. Nevertheless, these changes were rather drastic – especially the dropping of Hattie Hayridge. Rob and Doug had realised that as far as Holly and Kryten were concerned there just wasn't enough dialogue to go around. This factor coupled with their desire to make life more of a survival challenge for Lister and company led them to devise the theft and subsequent tracking of *Red Dwarf* which would provide the underlying theme of *Red Dwarf VI*. Not only would this sub-plot provide a convenient excuse to lose Holly for however long was required, but their favoured *Starbug* – with interiors redesigned by Mel Bibby – could logically be promoted to main ship of the series.

'Psirens' was perhaps most notable for its guest stars, in particular C. P. Grogan back as Kochanski (sort of) and Jenny

Agutter, whose appearance revealed the identity of Kryten's creator – Professor Mamet. Anita Dobson played Captain Tau, the name being an in-joke reference to the American pilot episode. Originally Rob and Doug had wanted Brian May to double as Lister's guitar playing hands and decided to ask for Anita while they were at it; they were quite surprised when she accepted such a small part.

While Lister and Kryten remained much as they were before, Cat was given nasal intuition, enabling him to detect danger. Rob and Doug had been concerned that Danny wasn't as much a part of the team as he ought to be and devised this ability in order for him to take a more active role. Rimmer too had been a problem to write for, being unable to touch and hold things; in the episode 'Legion' (working title 'Call Me Legion') the hologram is endowed with a solid light form, complete with blue costume. The change of costume resulted in a continuity error in 'Gunmen of the Apocalypse', where Rimmer is seen in a filmed sequence in his old red costume. Fortunately someone at the studio recording spotted this mistake and a line of dialogue was hastily added to the effect that he can use both forms.

Another error isn't as easily explained away: in 'Legion' Lister is seen to have his appendix removed, yet we all know from 'Thanks for the Memory' that he had it out years before (several million in fact).

If continuity had been observed in the previous season, *Red Dwarf VI* positively abounded with references. The hugely popular Duane Dibbley returned, as did a character who, although he strictly speaking wasn't Ace Rimmer, to all intents and purposes was a reprise for the macho pilot from 'Dimension Jump'. Along with new foes such as the gestalt being Legion, the season predictably featured more GELF and Simulant variants. One simulant in fact appears in two episodes; introduced in 'Gunmen of the Apocalypse' Liz Hickling reappears as the same character in 'Rimmerworld'. These episodes were filmed back to back but were separated by 'Emohawk' when broadcast.

The series ended with a bang – literally. 'Out of Time', originally titled 'Present from the Future', concluded with the deaths of all the main characters and *Starbug* being destroyed. The cliff hanger was actually a late decision taken during editing; scenes in which Rimmer saves the day by destroying the Time-drive and the crew celebrate with Margueritas were dropped, and replaced by the climactic explosion. Lister was also edited out of a time travelling scene in 'Rimmerworld' when someone noticed that this sort of linked with the last episode.

Presumably the series will be back as promised – Autumn '95 seems the most likely – and the crew will be alive thanks to Rimmer saving the day by destroying the Timedrive. In the meantime, the BBC has had the good sense to repeat the entire run of episodes beginning with 'The End'. And there was almost an early reunion for the team when BBC Radio commissioned a Licence Fee advert with a *Red Dwarf* flavour, which was unfortunately cancelled at the last minute.

SECTION TWO:

THE
CHARACTERS

LISTER

Full name: David Lister.

He picks his ears clean with tin-openers, he trims his toe-nails with his teeth, he thinks fresh vegetables are for health psychos and he sprays the contents of sugar puff sandwiches round his bunk room. A barely human, grossed-out slimeball, Dave Lister has the unearned distinction of being the last man alive in a Godless universe. Pity the universe!

Lister was born in the 23rd century – an Aries, if you must know – and was instantly dumped by his mother. He was found in a cardboard box, beneath the pool table of a Liverpool pub, and brought up by foster parents thereafter. Unfortunately, his stepfather died when Dave was a mere six years old. At the time, he was too young to fully understand what that meant, and he confesses that he saw the event primarily as a way of getting concerned relatives to contribute towards his Lego collection. He was told only that his father had gone to the same place as his goldfish, and as a consequence, the young Lister spent many fruitless hours with his head down the toilet, reading him the football results. Eventually, he was taken to see a child psychologist, who helped him to cope with the loss, but even now, he clings to the only photograph of the man that he ever had – and that shows only his leg, the focus of the picture being on his dog, Hannah.

From then on, Lister was brought up by his stepmother, and by his grandmother, a tough old lady who did little to increase his educational prospects by nutting his Headmaster when her grandson came bottom of the class in French. It is true to say, in fact, that Lister came bottom in most subjects at school, simply because he was totally unwilling to learn. In Biology lessons, for instance, the only task to which his skills were ever applied was to turn to page 47 of the text book and draw little beards and moustaches on all the sperms which were pictured there. And outside school, his 'education' was provided mainly by his friend Duncan, who taught him, for example, the art of using mirrored toe-caps to look up girls' skirts. Lister was deeply upset when, at the age of ten, Duncan and his family had to move to Spain because of his father's job – a bank job.

Even deprived of Duncan's tutelage though, Dave Lister had already realised one integral thing about himself – he hated working! He would much rather sit back with ten cans of lager and a curry, and he resented the intrusions of the more unpleasant realities of life. All he wanted from his existence was to just slob about and generally have a good time; while other twelve year-olds were busy considering which exams would shape their future, Dave Lister was busy going scrumping – for cars! – and losing his virginity to Michelle Fisher on the tenth hole of the Bootle Municipal Golf Course. He did make a token attempt to better himself, by moving to art college once school had finished, but even that didn't last. Having believed the option to be an easy one, Dave was appalled to learn that lectures regularly started first thing in the afternoon! Ninety-seven minutes after enrolling, he had had enough, and he left.

In the meantime though, Lister had actually managed to find himself a job. At the age of fifteen, he became a trolley attendant (presumably on a part-time basis at first) at a local supermarket. Low as the wages were, he managed to subsidise his income with what was now becoming his real love in life – his music. Author of such classics as 'Om' and 'The Indling Song', he was keen to put his talents to use, and saw himself as a future rock star. By age seventeen, he was the lead singer of a three-piece band called 'Smeg and the Heads', which even managed to earn itself a few gigs in local pubs. When he wasn't working or performing, Lister could often be found indulging in his all-time favourite hobby. He was a massive fan of Zero Gravity Football, supporting in particular the London Jets team, whose Roof Attack player, Jim Bexley Speed, was his absolute hero. He even managed to get his photograph taken with the player, who seems rather less than impressed in the shot.

Meanwhile, Lister's evenings were generally spent throwing his wages away at his local, 'The Aigburth Arms'. It was there that he turned his hand to pool, earning himself the nickname 'Cinzano Bianco' because, once on the table, no-one could ever get him off.

When he wasn't drinking, he was often out courting, although most of the girls he fell for were either heart-breakers or moral garbage on legs. Presumably falling into the former category, Lise Yates became the love of his life for a time, but he broke off the relationship himself when he felt she was trying to tie him down. He later regretted that move.

In the meantime, he had managed to put enough money aside to finally move away from home and get himself an unfurnished flat of his own. Financially, the move was probably quite an unwise one, but Lister solved some of his money problems by appropriating certain items from a nearby hotel. Not just the normal bars of soap and sachets of coffee, though. No, Dave Lister decided to go all the way – and, with a little help from his friends, he managed to lower the bed out of the hotel window.

All in all though, as his early twenties came and went, Lister was beginning to realise that he wasn't very happy with his life. Problem number one: He now knew that 'Smeg and the Heads' weren't going to become an international success, simply because they were totally crap. Problem two: Having spent ten years as a trolley attendant, he was beginning to worry about being tied down to a career! It was time for a change of direction.

For Lister, that change meant joining the Space Corps, and leaving Liverpool – and Earth – far behind him. So, by age twenty-five, he found himself assigned to the Jupiter Mining Corporation vessel *Red Dwarf*, as Third Technician David Lister, number RD52169. It was a post that he might have quite enjoyed (although, in keeping with his habitual aversion to work of any kind, he did request sick leave due to diarrhoea on no less than five hundred occasions during his eight months with the company), if not for the presence of one Second Technician Arnold Rimmer. Not only did he have to share a bunk room with Rimmer, but he also had to work for the man. Rimmer was in control of the ship's spectacularly unimportant Z Shift, the most important task of which was to ensure that the ship's vending machines didn't run out of Fun-Size 'Crunchie' bars, and life with him was not exactly Lister's idea of fun. The feeling was very much mutual.

For spick and span Rimmer, living with Lister was a nightmare. He sang, he clicked, he hummed, he deluded himself considerably about his guitar-playing abilities, and his chirpy, gerbil-faced optimistic approach to life drove Rimmer round the bend. Worse, he seemed to live on a non-stop diet of beer and vindaloos, and goodly amounts of these substances often 'decorated' his bunk-mate's meticulously crafted revision timetables. Breakfast for Lister consisted generally of last night's flat lager, sometimes in milkshake form, sometimes hot with croutons. And his clothes had to be seen to be believed. Lister's socks were capable of setting off the sprinkler system, and one of them was actually identified by the ship's computer Holly as a totally new lifeform. 'If you'd put Napoleon in quarters with Lister,' contended Rimmer, in defence of his own various failings, 'he'd still be in Corsica peeling spuds.'

The two were obviously not destined to hit it off, but for Lister at least, the Space Corps had its compensations, the biggest of which came in the form of Navigation Officer Kristine Kochanski. It was love at first sight – for Lister if not for his intended – and over the next few months, for the first time since his dreams of rock stardom had fallen down around his ears, he began to actually plan a future for himself. He would marry her, he decided, and they would have two sons, Jim and Bexley (both named after Jim Bexley Speed, of course). He would take her back to Earth with him, where they would start a farm on Fiji, breeding cows, sheep and horses. They would even open a chain of Hot Dog and Doughnut Diners, and they would certainly live happily ever after. Of course, he hadn't actually mentioned this glorious vision of the future to Kochanski yet – but he still had hope, even when a brief, three-week affair (during which they didn't even make love) ended with her throwing him over in favour of a catering officer.

There was, too, a very special place in Lister's dream for one other. Frankenstein was a pregnant cat he had picked up during planet leave on Titan, and which he had smuggled on board *Red Dwarf*. He kept her hidden in his quarters, away from prying eyes, feeding her with his regular milk ration, and bending her sympathetic ear with the intimate details of his wonderful plan, and of her position by his side when he achieved his ambitions.

The dream lasted no longer than eight months. It was then that Hollister, the ship's captain, discovered the cat's presence, and ordered Lister to hand her over. He refused. His punishment was to be placed in stasis for six months, until the end of the voyage – but as we all know, he actually remained there for slightly longer. Three million years later, Lister awoke to find himself the last human being alive – and the rest, as they say, is history.

Lister has precious little to remind him of his past now; just a few artefacts from the missing *Red Dwarf*, a tattoo on his inner thigh reading 'I love Petersen' (he doesn't – but that's what happens when you get drunk with your mates), a hologramatic reincarnation of his hated room-mate and a creature which evolved from Frankenstein's litter. Even his long dreamed of sons, Jim and Bexley, no longer see him, living as they do with their 'father', Dave's female equivalent in a parallel universe (and giving birth to them is an experience he doesn't wish to repeat).

You'd think, perhaps, that being cast adrift in space with no responsibilities would be an ideal situation for someone who proudly lists his occupation as 'Bum'. However, the opposite seems to be true. Placed in effective command first of *Red Dwarf* and later of the detached *Starbug* vessel, Lister has shown that he possesses strength, courage and even a lot more brain cells than he's been credited with. Of course, he still has grated onions on his cornflakes.

And when things are at their very worst, Lister still has the future to look forward to. Actually, he has several futures. In one, he and the rest of the crew become time-travelling epicures, although Dave accidentally loses his body in the process, becoming a talking brain in a dreadlocked tank. In another, his second son Bexley returns to *Red Dwarf* and dies in an explosion in the drive-room. A far more optimistic view of things to come sees a bearded, early-thirties Lister travelling back in time to marry Kristine Kochanski. Of course, she'll be wiped out three weeks later – but those three weeks will be brilliant! Perhaps best of all, future echoes have shown him that he might live to be 171 (although he'll pick up a cybernetic arm along the way). As for his long-stated objective, to return to Earth at last . . . well, only time can really tell.

CAST NOTES: Primarily played by Craig Charles, the role of Lister has also been enacted by Chris Barrie, in the episode 'Body Swap', and by Emile Charles (Craig's brother), who played his younger self in 'Timeslides'. An even younger self and a much older version were played by Duane Cox and Carl Chase respectively in 'The Inquisitor' (although Craig Charles himself played the older Lister seen in 'Future Echoes'), whilst Lister's female-dominated parallel universe equivalent was played by Angela Bruce. Jake Abraham acted as Craig Charles' stand-in for certain scenes in 'Demons and Angels', appearing also in 'The Inquisitor' as a Dave Lister who could have existed had the circumstances of his conception been different. John Sharian played a similar imaginary version in 'Back to Reality', and Production Manager Mike Agnew stepped briefly into the role in 'Thanks for the Memory', when Craig Charles was called away by the birth of his child. The switch is almost unnoticeable, due to the fact that Lister was wearing a space suit at the time – but if you watch carefully, you'll notice that his plaster cast disappears when the doppelgänger takes over. You don't need to watch at all carefully in 'Out of Time' to see that the future Lister is not portrayed by Craig Charles at all, but rather by a brain in a jar. However, as it retains Craig's voice, we won't count that.

RIMMER

Full name: Arnold Judas (not Jonathan, as he'd have us believe!) Rimmer.

Possibly the most apt description ever applied to Arnold Rimmer was when Kryten referred to him as 'an incompetent vending machine repairman with a Napoleon complex,' although the man's own view of himself as a 'Tosspot by Royal Appointment' comes pretty close to the mark, too. It says something about the state of Holly's logic circuits that he chose this sad specimen of humanity to resurrect in hologramatic form, to keep Dave Lister company. Originally a Class One hologram, sustained by a mobile light bee and a great deal of *Red Dwarf's* power supply, Rimmer has recently been converted to hard-light form by the gestalt entity Legion, allowing him at last the gift of touch. Alas, his characteristic make-up of arrogance and neurosis, coupled with enough charm to fill his little finger – almost – has remained absolutely unchanged.

Even when he had been alive, Arnold Judas Rimmer had not been the most ideal of room-mates. He was fixated with his ambition to become a Space Corps Officer, and even the tiny bit of power he enjoyed as the Second Technician in charge of '*Red Dwarf*'s' Z Shift was excuse enough for him to throw his weight around. Arnold Rimmer was destined for better things, he felt. After all, in a previous incarnation, he had even risen to the heights of being Alexander the Great's chief eunuch – or so Donald, his hypnotherapist, had claimed.

Unfortunately, it was getting to be a little late for Rimmer to achieve the fame which he felt he so richly deserved – hence the fact that his spare time was generally spent complaining about how unfair life had been to him. Incompetent though he knew himself to be, he would never dream of accepting re-sponsibility for his own constant failures. Instead, everybody around him became targets to be blamed.

Bad as that was, it certainly wasn't the worst that life with Rimmer had to offer. No, anyone unlucky enough to have to share their existence with Arnold Rimmer also found themselves the victims of his many other annoying habits. For one, he was the treasurer of the 'Hammond Organ Owners Society', and his unending recitals of Reggie Wilson 'classics' were more than any man could bear. He was also a great fan of twentieth-century telegraph poles and morris dancing, and when he waxed lyrical on his amazing 'Risk' campaign against Caldicott, his Cadet School Training Officer, the word 'boredom' took on a whole new meaning. As a confirmed slob, Lister was also less than happy with Rimmer's 'unhealthy' obsession with tidiness. Everything had to be kept orderly, he insisted – 'ticketty-boo' and 'licketty-split'. His over-starched pyjamas were always neatly folded, his nocturnal boxing gloves tidied away meticulously – even his underpants were kept on coat-hangers, and his ship issue condoms had name-tags sewn in each of them.

Rimmer never found the knack of making himself liked. He was the sort of person, according to Lister, who had to organise his own surprise parties. And his love life was just one disaster after another – from Sandra at Cadet School, to Carol McCauley (the recipient of his secret love letters) to a girl called Lorraine who, initially overwhelmed by the techniques Rimmer had learnt from his book on 'Picking up Girls by Hypnosis', eventually moved to Pluto to avoid a second date. For a long time, the nearest he got to a sexual liaison was with one Fiona Barrington, in his father's greenhouse – and even then, his illusions were shattered by the realisation that he had his hand in warm compost. In all of Arnold Rimmer's life, he only ever had sex once. The experience lasted for twelve minutes – including the time it took to eat the pizza – and was shared with one Yvonne McGruder, who has since dominated his dreams (usually clad in a skimpy peephole bra). As Lister is quick to point out, not only was McGruder the ship's female boxing champion, she was also concussed at the time, and she believed Rimmer to be somebody called Norman. Other than her, Rimmer's only 'intimate friend' was a blow-up doll called Rachel, and even she now has a puncture.

Still, as Lister has grown to realise, once you look under the almost unbearable surface, there is plenty about Arnold Rimmer with which you can't help but sympathise. Certainly, as a child, he was somewhat lacking in love and encouragement. Rimmer was the youngest and least able of four children, and was particularly despised by his elder brothers, John, Frank and Howard. When the Rimmer clan played at being the Three Musketeers, Arnold was always 'allowed' to be the Queen of Spain – and when the others weren't actively ignoring him, they were planning even worse fates for their kid brother. Arnold tried to turn a blind eye to their cruelty – even when they planted a landmine in his sand pit, he passed it off as a harmless practical joke gone wrong – but deep in his heart, he was beginning to realise that he wasn't exactly Mister Popular.

Neither was school any haven. Rimmer's nickname at Io House was 'Ace' – but no matter how many times he let the other boys beat him up, they would never use it, preferring instead to refer to him as 'Bonehead'. Indeed, in all of the school, Rimmer only ever had one person he could truly call a friend, and then, only if you ignored the fact that said friend, one Porky Roebuck, had once thrown him into the sceptic tank. In the end though, even that solid friendship was destined to come to an abrupt end. Its cessation occurred during a Space Scout camp, when Porky led a gang of boys in trying to eat the hapless young Arnold. His life was only saved by the timely intervention of the Scout mistress, Yakka Talla Tulla – and after that, relations between Arnold and Porky became somewhat strained.

Even animals never showed any friendship towards Rimmer. His favourite and much adored pet, a Lemming, sadly had to die when it bit him on the finger and refused to let go until he had smashed its brains out against the wall. The incident deeply upset young Arnold, primarily because of the severe damage which was suffered by his helicopter wallpaper as a consequence.

As unhappy as his life was, Rimmer received no encouragement or support whatsoever from his parents. His mother didn't suffer fools gladly – and Arnold was certainly that! Eventually, she gave up on him altogether, becoming more interested in keeping her numerous men-friends happy – and on the odd occasion that she did actually speak to him, she addressed him exclusively as 'Rimmer'. It says something about Mrs Rimmer's personality that, when a Psy-Moon gave form to Arnold's consciousness, it portrayed her as a huge, blood-sucking leech. Uncaring as she was though, she was nothing compared to Mr Rimmer Senior. Rimmer's father had been refused entry to the Space Corps because he was one inch below the regulation height. Frustrated at this failure, he was determined that his sons should pursue the career that he never could, and he followed this ideal even to the point of having them stretched on a rack. By the time he was eleven years old, Arnold's brother Frank was six foot five in height. Mealtimes too were a nightmare. Each night, Mr Rimmer quizzed his sons on Astro-Navigation theory. Only those who answered his questions correctly were allowed to eat – so naturally, poor Arnold nearly died from malnutrition.

Despite all this, Arnold Rimmer wanted nothing more than to please his father and to win the approval he had never had – but no matter what he did, it was never good enough. With all three of his brothers happily enrolled in the Space Corps Academy (his oldest brother, John, was a Test Pilot by the time Arnold was seven), he became nothing more than a bitter disappointment to both his parents. They let it show, too – particularly his father, who did nothing to ease Arnold's guilt at his failures by blaming him for the four strokes he suffered.

In the end, Rimmer could stand his home life no longer. At the age of fourteen, he took his parents to court and legally 'divorced' them. From then on, he rarely saw either of them again – although they had to pay him maintenance until employment age, and he did have access to the family dog every fourth weekend. It is not known exactly where Arnold resided at this time in his life, although he presumably stayed in the vicinity of both his home and his school. It was not until a few years later – at the age of sixteen, in fact – that he moved away from both altogether and attended Saturn Tech, where he took a maintenance course. He also found as many ways as he could to occupy his spare time; he took a film course at night school, and became a member of the Io Amateur War-Gamers, the Recreators of the Battle of Neasden Society and the Love Celibacy Society, plus of course, Cadet School and the aforementioned Hammond Organ Owners Society. He even joined the Samaritans, although his association with them proved to be extremely short-lived. All five of the people he spoke to on his first morning went on to commit suicide – and one of them was a wrong number, who phoned to check the cricket results! The event made the newspapers who, with their typical subtlety, christened the day 'Lemming Sunday', whilst Rimmer, disheartened, moved to pastures new.

In between all this, he had managed to keep in touch with his mother, albeit only by the occasional letter. As for his father ... well, the only link he had to him was the Javanese camphorwood chest which was the only thing, other than his disapproval, that he had ever given to his youngest son – and even that now has a guitar-shaped hole in it, thanks to a certain D. Lister Esq!

To give him credit though, Rimmer just kept on trying. Despite suffering a life which, in his eyes, was plagued by bad luck, bad company and the wrong sort of background, he clung to his ambition: to become a Space Corps officer and to make his father proud of him. When he was unable to gain access to the Space Corps Academy, he joined the Jupiter Mining Corporation vessel *Red Dwarf* as a lowly third technician, convinced that he could take a few exams and climb the ranks that way. Eleven attempts at Engineering and thirteen at Astro-Navigation later, he was beginning to realise that it wouldn't be that easy. Indeed, after almost fifteen years of service, he had only four things to show for his efforts: his promotion to the dizzying heights of Second Technician (the second lowest rank on the ship), his bronze and silver swimming certificates, his collection of four medals (Three Years Long Service, Six Years Long Service, Nine Years Long Service and Twelve Years Long Service) and his unfortunate death thanks, in part, to his own inefficient repair to a drive-plate.

Now, thanks to Holly, he's back, his personality reduced to an algorithm and reproduced electronically. He still makes life hell for his crew-mates, dividing his time between such pointless projects as the production of his own death video (complete with self-performed poetry readings), his attempts to assert authority over the other crew members and an impossible, ongoing quest for alien beings who might fashion him a new body. Of course, any sign of alien activity is likely to send him screaming for cover. A bold warrior in his own mind, Rimmer believes it his misfortune that he has currently been reincarnated within the body of an abject coward. He can't stand the sight of blood (unless it's Lister's), he's particularly prone to stress-related disorders even in hologram form and he's no good at anything practical, as was proven at school when it took him five terms to make a tent-peg. His contribution to the current *Starbug* mission is to enforce pernickety Space Corps Directives and to change the blue/red alert bulb every so often. And yet, despite all that, there's hope for him yet.

Even Rimmer can know true love, as his dalliance with Nirvanah Crane showed. When he sacrificed his ideal life aboard the holo-ship *Enlightenment* for her sake, we saw a side of Rimmer that even he had never dreamed existed. And when faced with evil future versions of the *Starbug* crew, and only two choices – to surrender or to fight a suicidal battle against them – even Arnold J discovered an untapped seam of courage within him, announcing that he was 'Better dead than smeg!' If the worse comes to the worse, that at least makes a somewhat better eulogy than his previous final words: 'Gazpacho soup.'

CAST NOTES: Rimmer is played primarily by Chris Barrie. However, the role has also been taken by Craig Charles and Danny John-Jules in 'Body Swap', by C. P. Grogan in 'Balance of Power' (strictly speaking, anyway) and by Simon Gaffney, who played the young Rimmer in 'Polymorph', 'Timeslides' and 'Dimension Jump'. Suzanne Bertish played Arnold's female equivalent, Arlene, in 'Parallel Universe' and Julian Lyon played his fictional replacement in 'Back to Reality'. Finally, Tim Yeates doubled for Chris Barrie (as well as for Robert Llewellyn) in the episode 'Demons and Angels'.

CAT

Full name: Cat (though if he had any need for a middle name he's sure it would be 'superficial').

He's vain, he's narcissistic, he's also selfish, self-centred and shallow, and we mustn't forget egotistical. But he's a cat, a creature of instinct, and those are some of his best qualities.

Anyway, he has proved himself consistently useful to the *Red Dwarf* crew's mission: on at least two occasions in his lifetime, he has had plans taken up by the others, and his quivering nostril hairs can detect danger even through the void of space. He's an excellent pilot, and when something needs doing, you don't have to tell him twice. Well okay then, maybe you do.

If the Cat had any understanding of the concept of gratitude – which he most certainly doesn't – then he'd have Dave Lister to thank for his very existence. The race of Cat people to which he belongs evolved over the course of three million years in the cargo hold of *Red Dwarf* because Lister hid his unquarantined pregnant pet cat Frankenstein there, safely away from the Cadmium 2 radiation that killed the rest of the crew. As a species Felis Sapiens is virtually indistinguishable from Homo Sapiens – only the tell-tale fangs and six nipples give them away – though it's highly unlikely that the Cat would ever want to be mistaken for a human, or a 'monkey' as he sees them. Sadly it is more than likely that the Cat is the last survivor of his race. Religion proved to be the downfall of felinekind – they made the fatal mistake of worshipping Dave Lister, or Cloister the Stupid as they knew their God. The story of Cloister is revealed in the Cats' Holy Book, which tells of how Cloister was frozen in time, but would one day return to take his people to the promised land of Fuchal, and of The Holy Mother Frankenstein whose miraculous virgin birth spawned the Cat race. Like many myths it had a basis in truth, but the concept of heaven as a hot dog and doughnut diner sparked off a holy war that would last for thousands of years. One faction vehemently believed that red cardboard hats should be worn, the other thought they should be blue (ironically, the hats were in fact meant to be green). Eventually, after countless casualties on both sides, two arks were constructed to take the Cats to Fuchal. Believing that a laundry list used to line Frankenstein's basket was actually a star chart, the Cats in one ark were killed when their vessel collided with an asteroid. The other ark flew out into infinity never to be seen or heard from again. Only the sick and the lame remained on *Red Dwarf*, left there to die. In time Cat was born, to a cripple and an idiot. Cat had never suspected that his father was a jelly-brain, but when he later found out it at least explained why he'd eaten his own feet.

Some of Cat's time as a youngster was spent at Kitty School learning to read the language of scents and to ignore at least one of the Cat People's Sacred Laws – the one which stated 'It is a sin to be cool'. The Cat never did have much time for a religion which, in deference to Cloister, rejected coolness in favour of slobbiness. Indeed when he did finally meet up with his 'God', Cat was decidedly unimpressed. After all, what kind of God would choose *that* face? And surely any deity worth his salt would be able to perform such a simple miracle as turning a bowl of Krispies into a woman.

In the days before Lister was brought out of stasis the Cat had the companionship of an old blind priest, but he much preferred to hang out with his own shadow which at least looked nice – he thought they made a good team. The Cat devoted all of his time to doing his favourite things – eating, sleeping, looking good, investigating things and making some of them his own with the aid of a scented spray (you can imagine what a cat would use to mark his territory with, but at least this cat bottled it first), and searching for sex. He never found any of course, there being no women on *Red Dwarf*, but nevertheless he diligently slinked around the mining ship, armed with a megaphone and a bouquet of flowers, in an endless search for lady cats. If he'd believed for one minute that his quest was in vain he's sure he'd have gone crazy.

Life for the Cat changed considerably when Dave Lister was released from the stasis booth and Arnold Rimmer was resurrected as a hologram. In Lister he found a friend with whom he was able to waste time in a multitude of pointless pursuits like 'Durex Volleyball', 'Junior Angler' and 'Unicycle Polo'. Yet despite their friendship the Cat's nature prevented him from actually caring very much about his new buddy. On one occasion when Lister contracted a virulent form of flu, and as a result collapsed, the Cat left him lying in the corridor – though he obviously thought enough of the human not to steal his shoes. Rimmer, on the other hand, he took an almost instant dislike to and time has done little to change his opinion. However, the hologram did prove useful once, when the Cat discovered his all time best ever find in the whole of that particular day, and the find in question turned out to be the cigarette supply that Rimmer had thought safely hidden from his bunk mate. In return for keeping the location secret, Cat was given instructions on the working of the food dispenser. However, his initial – greed motivated – fish binge resulted in a severe bout of food escape, but he did have the last laugh when he revealed to Lister where the cigarettes were anyway.

The Cat may not be all that bright – Commander Binks from the Holoship Enlightenment suggested that, as a race, Felis Sapiens were about half as smart as the domestic cats they evolved from – but he certainly hates to be corrected, it really gets his feckles up. Despite his lack of brain power Cat does try now and again to come up with ideas for extracting himself and the others from tricky situations – everything from laser cannons to jet powered rocket pants – all highly inventive and all equally non-existent. That doesn't worry Cat though, being a useful and productive member of the crew is probably the last thing on his mind. He certainly doesn't do the 'w' word and when he's not taking one of the nine or ten daily naps, essential to provide enough energy for his main snooze, the Cat still spends most of his waking hours eating (either fish or chicken and maybe the occasional mouse that he happens to catch and indeed absolutely anything else, unless of course Lister has prepared it), preening and, of course, attempting to fulfil his ambition of getting his end away. Naturally the Cat doesn't lack confidence, only women; he knows there can't be any female in the universe who wouldn't go for him or he'd have read about her in 'Ripley's believe it or not'. His body, he contends, is the sort that would make men wet and so, rather than leave it to medical science, he intends that it should go to the Louvre. Though it might sound as if the Cat is the unreliable type as far as women are concerned, that isn't strictly true and as soon as he finds the seven or eight that are right for him he'll be only too willing to settle down. In the meantime, he'll have to make do with a large amount of optimism and an equal number of fantasies and, judging by some of those, included in his harem would be Marilyn Monroe, a mermaid – top half fish, bottom half woman, naturally – and Wilma Flintstone. As for the rest, well, scanty-armour-clad Valkyries with cleavages you could ski down are a distinct possibility. Unfortunately the first time Cat actually did meet a real woman things didn't progress in the manner he'd anticipated. Although he knew he really wanted to do something to her, he just didn't know quite what it was.

Apart from female pussies (and himself) the great love of Cat's life is his collection of suits; he makes them all himself and even uses his tongue to launder them. If it were possible he'd like to have a wardrobe so massive that it crossed an international time zone, then he could easily make the thirty-six changes of clothes necessary in any given day, without fear of repetition. To say that being fashionable is vital to the Cat is the understatement of the millennium; without style his life would have no meaning. He was shocked when he met his sandal wearing higher self; when the aesthete explained that he found clothes to be a distraction from the pursuit of spiritual and intellectual fulfilment, Cat responded with his own personal philosophy affirming that spiritual and intellectual fulfilment were a distraction from the pursuit of clothes. A prime example of the importance placed in remaining dapper at all times occurred when he badly injured his leg and was more worried about the red blood clashing with his apricot trousers than he was about his damaged limb; indeed when he learnt that there was a danger of gangrene setting in, he brightened – green with apricot, he could probably pull that off. One of the worst experiences of the Cat's life occurred when his body was 'borrowed' by Rimmer. If it wasn't bad enough seeing his prized possession being abused he also had to spend time trapped in 'Trans-am wheel arch nostril's' own comparatively unlovely holographic form. But it was an encounter with the Despair Squid and its hallucinogenic ink that proved to be a near fatal ordeal for the normally unshakable Cat. When it led him to believe that he wasn't the universe's coolest feline with a terminal case of sexual magnetism, but was actually the singularly uncool and unattractive Duane Dibbley with a penchant for white socks, bri-nylon shirts, cardigans and anoraks, the belief drove him to the point of suicide. Luckily the whole nightmarish incident was nothing more than a hallucination and the Cat too shallow to have sustained any lasting psychological harm. And once this minor fashion predicament was behind him Cat was easily able to resume his self-appointed *Red Dwarf* post as most handsome guy on the ship.

CAST NOTES: Danny John-Jules has played Cat from episode one, with only a brief hand-over to Chris Barrie during the episode 'Body Swap', and an even briefer appearance by David Lemkin as his imaginary replacement in 'Back to Reality'. Johnny Orlando doubled for Danny in certain scenes of 'Demons and Angels', and Matthew Devitt played the Dog who was Cat's counterpart in 'Parallel Universe' – though that doesn't really count, does it?

HOLLY

Full name: Holly.

Red Dwarf, a spaceship the size of a town, takes some running and that's where Holly, a tenth-generation AI hologrammic computer with an IQ of 6000 comes in, or at least he did once. Not even a computer as complex and sophisticated as Holly undoubtedly was when first constructed is impervious to the eroding ravages of time. Even before *Red Dwarf*'s three million year jaunt into endless space began, Holly was not new; already the Jupiter mining corporation had started fitting their vessels with eleventh-generation computers with IQs in the region of 8000. One such machine was Gordon, of the Scott Fitzgerald whose vast intellect made Holly seem like a mere abacus. Nevertheless, *Red Dwarf*'s dauntless computer was prepared to take on his brighter digital kinsman in a game of postal chess. Not surprisingly, Gordon fared better in the contest, but as only one move was ever actually made Holly did not disgrace himself with his own performance.

With *Red Dwarf* lethally contaminated with Cadmium 2 radiation, Holly had little option but to take the mining ship out of the solar system and away from where it could do any harm to humans. Since its sole surviving crew member was safely sealed in stasis Holly was entirely alone. For an ordinary computer, programmed simply to carry out the functions needed to keep the ship operational and not give it a lot of thought, several million years of solitary space travel might not have caused too many problems. But for Holly – not only in possession of Artificial Intelligence, but with an almost human personality too – the loneliness and boredom proved a little too much to bear. Indeed if it weren't for the amusement provided by his collection of singing potatoes the computer believes that he might well have gone insane. To pass the time he read everything that was ever written. This comprehensive knowledge enabled him to state with complete authority that the worst book ever written was *Football – it's a funny old game* by Kevin Keegan. The novels of Agatha Christie, however, did provide a certain amount of pleasure. Such was their appeal that later on Holly decided to have them erased from his memory banks so that he could read them all again, though once they had been deleted he wasn't sure why he'd actually made the request – he'd never heard of Agatha Christie.

By the time the radiation levels had dropped sufficiently to release Dave Lister from stasis, Holly had gone decidedly peculiar. But even in this inferior state the new-found companionship of Lister and subsequently Rimmer and the Cat was not capable of providing anything approaching either intelligent or stimulating conversation. And so Holly busied himself with further tedium relieving projects such as 'Hol Rock', his innovative decimalised music, and compiling his comprehensive A-Z of the Universe. Unfortunately his plan to build a perfect replica of a woman capable of abstract thought had to be abandoned when even the nose proved to be too much of a challenge.

Despite his lack of brain power Holly was quite hurt by the fact that *Red Dwarf*'s small crew considered him a senile gibbering wreck only useful for telling the time. He decided to teach them a lesson for not appreciating him more. He devised Queeg 500, the mining ship's imaginary back-up computer. At first the efficient Queeg seemed an ideal replacement for Holly – who Rimmer considered ought to be put out of his misery and blown away like a blind old incontinent sheep dog. However, the harsh regime imposed by the 'back up' soon became unpopular and Holly was eagerly welcomed back into the fold, greatly pleased with the success of his massive 'jape'.

Back in favour once more, Holly was able to devote more time to getting everyone back to Earth. Travelling at the speed of light was not one of his favourite things and so, to avoid the navigational chaos that generally ensued, he developed the

'Holly Hop Drive', a device theoretically capable of instantaneous travel to anywhere in the universe. When the drive was put into operation, the others were convinced that the ship hadn't actually moved 'a smegging inch' but in fact it had traversed the fifth dimension into a parallel universe, a universe dominated by women. The experience of meeting his female counterpart, Hilly, proved a little too much for the crazed computer and he fell – appropriately enough – madly in love. Before this only a Sinclair ZX81 had put a spark in his circuits, but Hilly was the real thing and upon returning to his rightful universe Holly found he was unable to cope without her. His original countenance had been personally selected from the billions available because it resembled that of the greatest and most prolific lover who ever lived – although the bald pated middle-aged features prompted Rimmer to opine that he must have worked in the dark a lot – but Holly now decided to forego the face that had served him well for three million years and perform a head sex change on himself so that he might resemble his lost love, Hilly.

The operation was successful and he became a she, but although baldness was no longer a problem, computer senility certainly was. Her competence to run the mining ship properly was severely doubted in some quarters and not without some justification. There was the little incident with the auto-destruct sequence and the bomb and then there were the five black holes which turned out to be specks of grit on the scanner scope. It might also be worth mentioning the little problem with the DNA modifier but, as Holly herself pointed out, that was a mistake any deranged half-witted computer could make.

Things came to a head (no pun intended) when an ion storm had rather an extreme effect on Holly's circuitry. As a consequence she could no longer even count without banging her head against the screen. Drastic measures needed to be taken and the thoughtful Kryten decided that an intelligence compression process was the desirable alternative. Unfortunately the operation, designed to restore the computer's IQ to its original 6000 at the cost of a reduction in operational run time, was a little too successful and it didn't take much of Holly's new IQ of 12,000 to work out that, with a remaining life span of just over three minutes, she'd better switch herself off. It was just lucky that as a consequence of sealing up a time spewing white hole the whole procedure never actually took place. The effects of the ion storm were negated too, so although Holly was no longer a genius who knew absolutely everything – from the meaning of life to the winners of the double in 1994 – her counting abilities were back to normal, including her longstanding blind spot with 7s and 2s.

CAST NOTES: Originally played by Norman Lovett, Holly performed a head sex-change operation on himself between seasons two and three. The female version was played by Hattie Hayridge, who also appeared as Hilly, Holly's counterpart in 'Parallel Universe'. Strictly speaking, Charles Augins has also played Holly, as he was the computer's fictional alter-ego, Queeg, in the episode of the same name.

KRYTEN

Full name: Kryten 2X4B 523P.

Constructed in the 24th century (c 2340) by one Professor Mamet for Diva-Droid International, the series 4000 mechanoid Kryten was originally supplied to the *Nova 5*, an Earth ship engaged in a stellar mapping mission. From the outset the 'noid took his position as ship's service mechanoid very seriously. Like all androids Kryten was programmed to believe in 'Silicon Heaven', the electronic afterlife where he would someday find reward for his faithful and diligent servitude to mankind, but the real reason he performed his menial tasks with such enthusiasm was simply because he took such great pleasure in them.

Kryten's presence proved to be a godsend when the Nova 5 crash-landed on an inhospitable rock light years from anywhere. The three slightly injured survivors, Jane Air, Anne Gill and Tracey Johns, would have found it increasingly difficult to cope without his attentive ministrations. Sadly, despite the perpetual signal of the ship's distress beacon, rescue never came and eventually the remaining crew members died. Rather than be denied a purpose for his existence, Kryten refused to accept the deaths and continued to conscientiously carry out his duties in the normal manner as if nothing had happened.

With only countless reruns of the soap opera *Androids* providing any respite, the mechanoid remained in a state of self-induced enslavement for countless millennia, until finally the distress call was heeded – by the crew of *Red Dwarf*. Despite the fact that none of his rescuers were actually doctors, Kryten was eventually persuaded that his decomposed mistresses were indeed dead. He was devastated, his artificial life no longer had any meaning; without masters the android philosophy 'I serve therefore I am' was no longer germane, the only option he could see was to activate his shut-down disc.

Kryten needn't have worried, however. Rimmer was only too glad to have someone other than the rebellious Skutters dance attendance to his every whim. The horrible hologram was more than willing to provide a duty list that would have taken even the most dynamic series 5000 a couple of centuries to complete, let alone a clapped-out antique like Kryten. The situation would have endured were it not for Lister's violent opposition to the concept of 'masters and servants'; he was determined that Kryten should become his own android, and so began the foundation course in advanced rebellion. It was a slow and difficult process but with the help of films such as *The Wild One*, *Rebel Without a Cause* and *Easy Rider*, Kryten was able to break his programming and simulate some of the qualities he so admired in humans by becoming deceitful, unpleasant and offensive.

Apart from the escape he found in watching *Androids*, Kryten took delight in his down-time dreams – especially the one in which he had a garden of his own to nurture and watch grow. Now that he finally had his freedom there was nothing to stop him from making his desires become reality. On a space bike, borrowed from Lister, he set off in search of an S3 planet on which he could cultivate both his plants and his ambitions.

In the fields of hoovering and washing up Kryten was without equal, but the art of space bike riding was to prove a little too tricky for the novice droid cyclist. The bike collided with an asteroid and this time there was to be no lucky escape; Kryten's metal and plastic body was extensively damaged. Fortunately, after some time spent lying around in bits and pieces, the 'noid was once again salvaged by the *Red Dwarf* crew. Although Lister wasn't a fully qualified engineer and his attempts at repair would invalidate Kryten's guarantee, he did his utmost to restore the parts into a fully functional whole. The head was irreparable, but as the series 4000 is supplied complete with spares Lister simply fitted a replacement. Although managing to get the android into a state of working order, Lister's technical inexperience coupled with the severity of the crash made it impossible to re-create Kryten's original personality. His new traits were not too far removed from those of his old self, indeed if not for the freshly developed Canadian accent it's possible that no one would ever have noticed the difference.

One unfortunate side effect of the accident and subsequent repair was the undoing of many of Lister's instructions in dissent. He was forced to resume the lessons in lying and insubordination. Kryten found lying in particular difficult to come to terms with. In Lister's company he could manage it easily, but any attempt in the presence of others was futile until the act of being dishonest was required in order to save his own life. Despite the fact that their series 4000s had received the award for 'Android of the year' five times on the trot, Diva-

Droid International were in business to make a profit. Sometime in the dim and distant past, Kryten had reached his expiry date and a replacement had been promptly dispatched from Earth. The model selected to take the place of the 'slow, stupid and ugly' Kryten was a Hudzen 10 – a highly advanced super android, programmed to become violent should his predecessor-to-be put up any resistance.

Kryten had no intention of presenting any opposition. When he learned of Hudzen's imminent arrival, he was quite prepared to activate his shut-down disc, for he had served his human masters well and now had a lasting and peaceful existence in 'Silicon Heaven' – the afterlife machines were programmed to believe in – to look forward to. But at a surprise party thrown by the others, he discovered for the first time that the employment of time in a profitless and non-practical way really could be fun and he decided that he wanted to experience more of it. Although waking up with a 45 per cent dehydration level, a 2 per cent recall of the previous evening and a 91 per cent embarrassment factor – in other words a raging hangover – the mechanoid was determined not to be dismantled by his would-be replacement. And fortunately, the now quite deranged Hudzen was easily induced to crash and consequently shut down after hearing Kryten's 'untruthful' revelation that 'Silicon Heaven' was actually a myth.

However, Kryten needed to fall in love to discover that, in certain circumstances, lying could actually be a noble thing. When he first met Camille he believed that, like him, she was a series 4000 mechanoid – albeit the more upmarket GTi model with slide back sun roof head and realistic toes. They hit it off immediately, he loved the perfumed aroma of the WD40 on her neck hinges and she thought he made the most romantic calculations. The old cliché that 'love is blind' was certainly applicable in this instance for even after learning that Camille was actually a tentacled green blob, Kryten still thought she was cute. Of course he was no oil painting himself, resembling at best a huge, half-chewed, rubber-tipped pencil and at worst a novelty condom for the enormously endowed. Sadly, despite overcoming the problems inherent in mixed relationships, the affair was doomed to failure; the arrival of Camille's husband Hector was enough to terminate Kryten's short-lived stint in happiness mode. She was quite prepared to leave her amorphous spouse and remain on *Red Dwarf* with her android admirer, but Kryten knew it wasn't for the best. Without his wife at his side Hector would not have the resolve to complete his research into a cure for their condition, so Kryten lied once again in order that his love would leave him.

After learning both to enjoy life and to experience the emotion of love, Kryten had but one wish – to become human. Though he believed it to be an impossible goal, the discovery of a DNA modifier actually allowed him to realise his dream. Using the organic part of Kryten's brain as a blueprint, the highly advanced technological device was able to transform the android into a fully functional flesh and blood human. Ironically, Kryten's new features resembled those of Jim Reaper, the Diva-Droid employee who had once described him as ugly.

Despite relishing his new-found humanity, Kryten was disappointed with the accompanying body. Particularly unsatisfactory were the eyes. He'd always been extremely fond of his old 579s with the automatic 15F stop corneas and the new ones not only didn't have a zoom function but couldn't even manage quantel. But it was the overlarge and ugly appendage that suddenly appeared in the vicinity of his old groinal socket that really disgusted him, especially as it refused to behave itself when he was reading an electrical appliance catalogue. Kryten had a problem: although he looked human, his thought processes were still those of a mechanoid. Making the most important decision of his life he elected to return to his mechanical form.

It was a more confident Kryten that emerged from the operation. Thanks to Lister's influence he was no longer the guilt-ridden slave that he had been assembled to be. He had broken his programming to such an extent that he was able to take his place with the others of the *Red Dwarf* crew as an equal, although admittedly a significantly more intelligent, resourceful and capable equal. In time he would even overcome his deep-rooted belief in the falsehood of 'Silicon Heaven'.

One incident did shake his belief system though, when his master Dave Lister turned out to be an earlier model android and technically inferior to him. After years of scrubbing out gussets and offering to pointlessly sacrifice his own life for the crew's sake, the revelation was almost too much to bear, and Kryten took out his bitterness by turning his one-time icon into a downtrodden slave. When he discovered that the whole thing was an illusion caused by *Starbug* passing through a pocket of unreality, he had a lot of apologising to do.

CAST NOTES: The first person to play Kryten (and later, the second to play Talkie Toaster) was David Ross, who made a single appearance in the episode 'Kryten'. When it was decided to bring the mechanoid back as a regular character for the third season, it was Robert Llewellyn who took on the now familiar mask and re-defined the android for his new role. The only actors to have appeared in the role since then are Tim Yeates and Scott Charles-Bennett, who played more 'worthwhile' versions of Kryten in 'The Inquisitor' and 'Back to Reality' respectively. Tim Yeates also doubled for Robert Llewellyn (as well as for Chris Barrie, as mentioned above) in 'Demons and Angels'.

SECTION THREE:

THE PROGRAMMES

SEASON ONE

Regulars: Rimmer – Chris Barrie. Lister – Craig Charles. Cat – Danny John-Jules. Holly – Norman Lovett. Written by Rob Grant and Doug Naylor. Produced and directed by Ed Bye. Developed for television by Paul Jackson Productions.

1: THE END

Broadcast date: 15 February 1988.

Guest cast: Robert Bathurst (Todhunter), Paul Bradley (Chen), David Gillespie (Selby), Mac McDonald (Captain Hollister), Robert McCulley (McIntyre), Mark Williams (Peterson – spelling later changed), C. P. Grogan (Kochanski).

Introducing Dave Lister and Arnold Rimmer – work-mates and room-mates on the mining ship *Red Dwarf*, with the only drawback being that they can't stand each other. Lister just wants to slob around and enjoy George McIntyre's funeral – and his subsequent welcome back party as the ship's computer, Holly, resurrects his mind in a hologramatic body. Rimmer on the other hand is cramming for an important exam – yet another attempt at passing Engineering. Sadly, neither of their plans are to come to fruition. Even as Rimmer is being carried out of the examination room on a stretcher after a nervous breakdown, Lister is summoned to see Captain Hollister. Holly has discovered the unquarantined cat that he has smuggled on board. Lister is given a choice: hand over Frankenstein, or spend the remaining eighteen months of the voyage in stasis. To him, it is no choice at all – the cat remains at liberty and Lister is frozen in time. However, Lister's incarceration has unexpected consequences. Unaccompanied on his maintenance rounds, Rimmer makes a mistake which ultimately causes a massive leak of Cadmium 2 radiation. The entire crew of the ship is killed with only one exception. Shielded from the radiation in stasis, Lister survives and is awakened by Holly when the danger is over. Unfortunately, this is some three million years later, during which time *Red Dwarf* has been heading directly away from Earth. If he is to survive the voyage home, Lister needs somebody to keep him sane. Holly is capable of sustaining only one hologram at a time, and for reasons best known to himself, he chooses to resurrect Arnold Rimmer. Lister's sanity is perhaps more truly saved, however, by the presence of a third person on the ship. Safely sealed in the hold, Frankenstein has given birth to a litter – and over the last three million years, the species has evolved. What confronts Lister and Rimmer now is an example of Felis Sapiens: a humanoid Cat, from a race which worships Lister – or rather, Cloister the Stupid – as its God. Lister's destiny is clear. He may have been deprived of the love of Kristine Kochanski and of his dream of a farm on Fiji, but he still has his cat, and now he's the deity of an entire race. So the Earth can look out . . . Lister's on his way home!

2: FUTURE ECHOES

Broadcast date: 22 February 1988.

Guest cast: John Lenahan (Toaster), Tony Hawks (Dispensing Machine).

As Holly turns *Red Dwarf* around and heads back towards Earth, strange things begin to happen. The mirror reveals images of events that haven't yet occurred and a photograph inexplicably shows Lister with twin sons. The explanation for what is happening is simple – or at least, according to Holly it is. The ship has broken the light barrier and as a consequence, the crew are seeing random future echoes – images of things that are yet to come. Things take an ominous turn when, in one such vision, Rimmer sees Lister die horribly in an accident in the drive room. He is actually quite amused by this turn of events, and he takes pleasure in assuring his companion that the future cannot be changed. Of course, Lister has to try. Having seen the Cat break a tooth in one of the echoes, he sets his mind to preventing the injury, thus changing the course of the future. Too late, he realises the accident's cause. He tackles the Cat in an effort to prevent him from sinking his teeth into one of his robot goldfish and the ensuing fall actually causes the mishap he had hoped to prevent. The future seems inevitable – and never more so than when Holly announces that there is an emergency in the drive room. Come in number 169, your time is up. But Lister is determined to meet his fate kicking and screaming. Nobody then is more surprised than he when the emergency is diverted without the fatal consequences that were predicted. A version of Lister from the far future sheds some light on the situation. The man who Rimmer saw die in the drive-room was actually Bexley, one of Lister's sons – and Lister himself certainly has plenty more years left in him. As for Rimmer's future, well, he isn't letting on about that. So that just leaves one more conundrum. How, with no women on board the ship, does Lister get twin sons? He doesn't know, but he's certainly looking forward to finding out.

3: BALANCE OF POWER

Broadcast date: 29 February 1988.

Guest cast: Rupert Bates (Trout á la Crème and Chef), Paul Bradley (Chen), David Gillespie (Selby), Mark Williams (Peterson), C. P. Grogan (Kochanski).

Rimmer is relishing his new-found position as the senior officer on board *Red Dwarf*, despite the fact that Lister is determined not to actually obey him. Rimmer's solution is to take hostage every cigarette on the ship, promising to return one for every day that his subordinate follows orders. However, that is certainly not the only bone of contention between the two. Lister is unhappy with Rimmer's presence altogether, and wonders why Holly couldn't have re-created somebody he actually liked. Kristine Kochanski would have been ideal, he decides, but in this too, Rimmer blocks his desires. After all, Holly can only sustain one hologram at a time, and there's certainly no way he's allowing Lister to turn him off and bring Kochanski back. Apart from anything else, he fears he would never be turned back on again – and he's probably right. So the hologram discs, like the cigarettes, have been removed to a safe place. Eventually, Lister hits upon the answer. All he has to do to get his own way is to become Rimmer's superior. Unlike himself, Rimmer has a moral code that will force him to obey the every wish of an officer, even if that officer be Dave Lister. Rimmer of course is hardly worried. After all, if he couldn't pass his Engineering exams and become a Space Corps officer, what hope could Lister have? Every hope, as it turns out – for Lister has no intention of passing the Engineering exams at all. He is studying to become a chef – the easiest exam available, but one which will result nevertheless in automatic promotion. Holly duly sets the exam and Rimmer can only watch as the balance of power looks set to alter. Finally, it is all too much for Rimmer. Even as the exam commences, Lister's heart's desire arrives in the teaching room. It is Kristine Kochanski, in hologram form at least. Rimmer has given in. Or has he? Lister becomes suspicious when 'Kochanski' tells him that she doesn't really like him at all and that she would never dream of going out with him. It doesn't take him too long to work out that, although this is Kochanski's body in front of him, Rimmer has tampered with the hologram disc so that his own mind is in there. Lister continues with the exam, the attempt at distraction having failed, and Rimmer looks on worriedly as the computer delivers the results. With an ecstatic yell, Lister reveals that he has passed.

4: WAITING FOR GOD

Broadcast date: 7 March 1988.

Guest cast: Noel Coleman (Cat Priest), John Lenahan (Toaster).

Okay, so Lister was lying about passing the chef's exam, but any notions of a resit have now been driven from his mind. The Cat has been teaching him how to read the books of his people, their language being made up of a system of differing scents. Now, Lister is ready for the big challenge – the Cat Bible, which tells the full story of the Cat Race. Lister is able to confirm what Cat originally told him. He is Cloister the Stupid, the Cat People's God – and he is appalled when he learns of the killing that has been done in his name. He discovers that thousands of Cats were slain during millennia of Holy Wars, simply over the colour of the cardboard hats in his proposed Hot Dog and Doughnut Diners on Fuchal. And what saddens Lister most of all is that both sides were wrong. Rimmer, meanwhile, is somewhat less than interested in Lister's problems. Holly has picked up an Unidentified Object, and Rimmer is convinced that it is the product of alien science. The Quagaars, as he calls his imaginary alien race, will doubtless extend the hand of friendship – and they'll probably give him a new body too. In reality, the pod is something quite different, as Lister has already surmised. Dismissing it from his thoughts, he delves more deeply into the history of the Cats, discovering that his every word to his pet cat Frankenstein has been corrupted through generations of the Cat Race. He is particularly saddened when he learns of the deaths of half the Cat People, who left *Red Dwarf* to look for Fuchal, using one of his old laundry lists as a star chart. If only he owned more than one pair of underpants, a tragedy might have been diverted. The rest of the Cats, apparently, have now also left the ship, leaving behind only the sick and the lame. The Cat that Lister is already familiar with is the son of two of these people, and as such is the last of his race to live on the ship. Well, almost. In fact, there is one other Cat on board – a blind old Priest, dedicated to the service of Cloister, and now on his death-bed. Taking pity on him, Lister ensures that his lifetime of belief is finally rewarded. He enacts Cloister's 'second coming', even as the Priest finally dies. With that drama over, Lister is able to turn his attention to the Unidentified Object – and just in time. He has the pleasure of being present as Rimmer finally realises that the object is, in fact, nothing more than one of *Red Dwarf*'s own garbage pods.

5: CONFIDENCE AND PARANOIA

Broadcast date: 14 March 1988.

Guest cast: Lee Cornes (Paranoia), Craig Ferguson (Confidence).

Since coming out of stasis, Lister has been longing for the day when he could finally visit Kochanski's sleeping quarters. In particular, he wishes to view her dream recorder, just to check if she ever dreamed about him. Now, finally, that day has come. The radiation has been cleared from the officers' block and his journey of discovery may commence – or so he believes. In fact, Rimmer is a little behind schedule in that department, and by entering the still contaminated zone, Lister has subjected himself to forces unknown. Soon, for no apparent reason, it is raining herrings in the bunk room – something which delights the Cat no end – and when the mayor of Warsaw spontaneously combusts in the corridor, Rimmer theorises that something must be wrong. Medical tests show that Lister has contracted a mutated strain of the pneumonia virus. The effect of this is that he is having hallucinations, which are being made startlingly real. And there is worse to come. Lister and his old friend Chen had always theorised that a person's mind is made up of two opposing forces – his Confidence, which urges him forward to achieve things, and his Paranoia, which holds him back and points out what could go wrong. The virus latches on to those images and makes them solid, manifesting Lister's Confidence and his Paranoia in human form. Quite naturally, Confidence immediately wins Lister over with his incessant compliments, making him believe he can do anything he wants to. Meanwhile, Paranoia seems to have found an ally in Rimmer – after all, their opinions of Lister are very much the same. But Rimmer has seen both men for what they really are – germs created by the infection. He tries to persuade his companion to help him dispose of them but, spurred on by his Confidence, Lister refuses to listen to reason.

Rimmer's problems intensify when Confidence's support actually begins to have a positive effect upon Lister's mental processes. Not only is he able to work out how Holly can temporarily generate two holograms at once, he is also able to locate the personality discs hidden by Rimmer. At last, he will be able to bring back his lost love, Kristine Kochanski. Things take a nasty turn however, when Confidence murders Paranoia and is on the verge of persuading Lister that he can breathe in space without an oxygen mask. Coming to his senses, Lister refuses to give in without a struggle, and eventually it is Confidence himself who suffers the fate in store for anybody attempting such an action. Lister has to admit that Rimmer was right. But still, the episode has had its advantages. Lister attempts to restore Kochanski to hologramatic life – but Rimmer still has one more trick up his sleeve. He has shuffled the discs about in their boxes, so that when the second hologram forms, it is not Kochanski at all – but a second Arnold Rimmer!

6: ME²

Broadcast date: 21 March 1988.

Guest cast: Mac McDonald (The Captain).

There are two Rimmers on board – and life is now doubly hell for poor Lister. There are some advantages, though. He certainly doesn't complain when Rimmer leaves their shared bunk room to move in with his counterpart. Indeed, the move has its definite pluses, particularly when it unearths a certain video tape that Rimmer has been keeping hidden. A tribute to Arnold Rimmer, the video features Holly's recording of his death, preceded by an over-long eulogy (including poetry readings) narrated by the man himself. Lister's curiosity is aroused when he learns that Rimmer's dying words were 'Gazpacho Soup!' but the man's personal diary fails to shed any light on the subject. November 25 is marked as 'Gazpacho Soup Day', but no explanation is provided. Lister's curiosity has to be put to one side when Holly announces the arrival of a fighter ship belonging to the Norweb Federation. Apparently, Lister left a light on in his bathroom when he left Earth over three million years ago – and they want payment. In fact, the whole thing is a joke on Holly's part, but in the meantime, Rimmer's problems have become only too real. It seems that he is incapable of getting on even with himself, and the arguments between the two Arnolds soon reach ridiculous proportions. Lister decrees that one of them has to go, and both Rimmers agree. What they don't agree on is which it is to be. Lister makes a random selection – and it is the original Rimmer who loses out. With nothing to lose, and drunk from his final round of computer generated drinks, Rimmer is easily persuaded to tell Lister all about Gazpacho Soup Day. That day, he says, should have been the happiest of his life. He had been invited to dine at the Captain's table and, hoping to impress the officers, had sent back his first course – Gazpacho Soup – because it was cold. He had later discovered that it should have been served cold, and that the officers' laughter he had thought directed at the chef had in fact been targeted at him. He has never lived down the humiliation of that moment, and blames his subsequent lack of success upon it. For his part, Lister is almost sympathetic but the emotion doesn't last. He gleefully reveals that he has in fact already switched off Rimmer's double, and that the whole charade has just been a ruse to prise the secret of the soup from him. Still, Lister swears not to say a word on the subject again – but very soon discovers that the temptation to break that promise is just far too great.

SEASON TWO

Regulars: Rimmer – Chris Barrie. Lister – Craig Charles. Cat – Danny John-Jules. Holly – Norman Lovett. Written by Rob Grant and Doug Naylor. Produced and directed by Ed Bye. Developed for television by Paul Jackson Productions.

1: KRYTEN

Broadcast date: 6 September 1988.

Guest cast: David Ross (Kryten), Johanna Hargreaves (The Esperanto Woman), Tony Slattery (Android Actor).

Red Dwarf receives a distress call from Kryten, the service android upon the *Nova 5*. His ship has crashed, and its three crew members need help. For Lister, Rimmer and Cat, this is the moment they have been waiting for. Not only is it their first contact with life in three million years, but that life also comprises three very eligible female humans. When Kryten beams them ship's records – and photographs – of his charges, it is confirmed that Jane, Tracey and Ann are just what everybody has been waiting for. As *Red Dwarf* rushes to the rescue, its crew have their minds on first impressions and what they might lead to later. Lister is wearing his least smeggy clothes (including the T-shirt with only two curry stains) and Rimmer, resplendent in his Admiral's uniform, implores the others to refer to him as Ace. This was apparently his childhood nickname, although he bemoans the fact that no matter how much he let them beat him up, the rest of his school would never use it, preferring instead to refer to him as Bonehead. Even Holly fits his computer image with a toupee as the rendezvous draws closer, and the Cat, even more magnificent in his appearance than normal, has severe problems of self-control whenever he encounters a mirror. Unfortunately, the effort has been in vain. Upon arrival on *Nova 5*, it swiftly becomes obvious to everybody that the girls are all dead. In fact, it seems that they must have been dead for centuries, as they now have less meat on them than a Chicken McNugget. Programmed only to serve mankind, Kryten has been unable to accept this fact, and has continued to wait on the skeletons of his former owners. It doesn't prove easy persuading Kryten that he no longer has a purpose in life, but Rimmer eventually manages it, turning the situation to his own advantage at the same time.

Kryten returns to *Red Dwarf* with its crew and, within moments of his arrival, Rimmer has put him to work on a hundred and one menial tasks. For Lister, the mechanoid's constant desire to serve is nothing more than an irritation. All of a sudden, he can bend his boxer shorts, and, to make matters worse, Kryten has destroyed Albert, his pet mould, which he was growing specifically to annoy Rimmer. Things have to change, he decides, but how can he alter the attitudes of a mechanoid whose only joy in life is watching the soap opera *Androids*? Still, Lister perseveres in his chosen task and, using the film *The Wild One* for inspiration, he begins to programme a few new ideas into Kryten's head. It isn't long before his tuition pays off. Inspecting a painting of himself that he has ordered Kryten to create, Rimmer is furious to discover a major deviation from the specification. He confronts the android about his disobedience, and Kryten announces that he is rebelling. He tells Rimmer to 'swivel on it' and, borrowing Lister's space bike, heads off into space, leaving *Red Dwarf* behind forever – or at least until the next series.

2: BETTER THAN LIFE

Broadcast date: 13 September 1988.

Guest cast: John Abineri (Rimmer's Dad), Debbie Ash (Marilyn Monroe), Jeremy Austin (Rathbone), Nigel Carrivick (The Captain), Tony Hawks (The Guide), Judy Hawkins (McGruder), Tina Jenkins (The Newsreader), Ron Pember (The Taxman), Gordon Salkilld (Gordon).

For the last three million years, a post pod has been following *Red Dwarf* as it headed away from Earth, and now that the ship has turned around, it has finally been able to reach it. Naturally, most of the post is made up of bills and junk mail, although the Skutters are pleased to receive their latest package from the John Wayne Fan Club. Rimmer is less happy when a letter from his mother (addressed to 'Dear Rimmer') informs him that his father is dead. Well, he knew that of course, but seeing it in black and white like that upsets him. He confides in Lister, telling him some of the details of his unhappy childhood and of his memories of a father that he spent his whole life failing to impress. Obviously Rimmer needs a diversion, and thanks to another item in the post pod, Lister is able to provide one. Together with the Cat, the two of them plug their minds into Better Than Life – the total immersion video game in which everybody's dreams come true. As they wander around a mental landscape made from their dreams, Lister becomes incredibly rich and successful, whilst Cat two-times Marilyn Monroe for a beautiful mermaid with the top half of a fish and the bottom half of a woman. Well, the other way round would be stupid, wouldn't it? For Rimmer, a swift promotion to Admiral and the undying admiration of his father prove to be short-lived fantasies, as Cat's desires intrude upon his own. His worst enemy, however, turns out to be himself – and before long he finds himself married to a pregnant Yvonne McGruder, with seven children, a mortgage, and the taxman in pursuit. Deep down, it seems that Rimmer really hates himself – and when his self-loathing gets out of hand, everybody else is caught up in the consequences. When all three players find themselves buried in sand and about to be eaten alive by an army of ants, their combined wills end the game, returning them to *Red Dwarf*. Rimmer is more unhappy than ever, but a previously unnoticed letter looks like it could solve his problems once and for all. His last exam result was wrongly computed, it says. He really did pass, and is now a fully-fledged officer. Rimmer's jubilation is cut short, however, by the sudden arrival of the taxman and the jarring realisation that he is actually still playing Better Than Life. Even as his fingers fall victim to the taxman's hammer, the game finally ends for real.

3: THANKS FOR THE MEMORY

Broadcast date: 20 September 1988.

Guest cast: Sabra Williams (Lise Yates).

It's Rimmer's deathday, and Lister, Cat and Holly get together to organise a party for him on a nearby planet. The festivities continue into the small hours of the morning and Rimmer finds himself becoming more than a little intoxicated. Back on *Red Dwarf*, a fit of drunken melancholy prompts him to reveal the details of his sex life to Lister. Lister tries in vain to convince him that he will regret any such disclosures the following morning, and is dismayed when even so, Rimmer admits to only ever having had sex once in his entire life. That, he reveals, was with Yvonne McGruder, the ship's female boxing champion. It took place on 16 March, and lasted from 7:31 until 7:43. And that included the time it took to eat the pizza. Rimmer's despair at never having shared a real relationship with anybody arouses sympathy within Lister, who determines to do something about it. The following morning, however, the crew find a number of other things to worry about. *Red Dwarf* has been visited by aliens – or so Rimmer theorises. Four days have apparently gone missing, none of which are present either in Holly's data banks or in Lister's diary. Coupled with that is the mystery of why Lister and Cat suddenly have a broken foot each; but most amazing of all is the fact that Lister's jigsaw puzzle has somehow been completed.

In an effort to learn what happened during the missing days, Holly manages to track down the ship's black box recorder, which has been buried in a grave marked 'To the Memory of the Memory of Lise Yates'. This confuses Lister even more, as Lise was one of his old girlfriends. Still, the recording should shed some light on what has happened – except that it begins with a warning from Holly that, should it ever be discovered, Lister and Rimmer should not under any circumstances view it. Of course, they ignore the warning and watch on. To Rimmer's embarrassment, they see once again his admissions of sexual inadequacy, but this time, they see what happens next. Lister heads for the Hologram Projection Suite, where he is determined to give Rimmer the best present he has ever had. He lifts the memories of an old girlfriend from his own mind and copies them into Rimmer's, giving him the illusion that he has had an affair with

Lise Yates. The transference has its problems, of course. Rimmer is confused about his total change of life-style during the affair, but puts it down to the love with which he was besotted. He is more concerned about the fact that he seems to have had his appendix out twice. But after all, he now cherishes the memory of a girlfriend that he never really had, and he is far happier for it. Things turn sour though, when Rimmer discovers the letters that Lise sent to Lister. She refers to having sex with Lister six times in one night – the same night that she had sex six times with Rimmer as well. Convinced that his only true love was a two-timing nymphomaniac, Rimmer becomes more unhappy than ever, and Lister is forced to admit the truth. Brutally disappointed, Rimmer insists that the memories of Lise Yates are purged from his mind. Moreover, he wants all records of the whole unhappy event to be destroyed. Lister and Cat bury the black box recorder, breaking their feet as they drop the gravestone they are carrying to mark its resting place. Lister removes the pages from his diary, and all concerned – including Holly – voluntarily undergo a memory wipe. As Lister climbs into bed, he slots the last piece into his jigsaw puzzle.

4: STASIS LEAK

Broadcast date: 27 September 1988.

Guest cast: Morwenna Banks (The Lift Hostess), Sophie Doherty (Kochanski's Room Mate), C. P. Grogan (Kochanski), Richard Hainsworth (The Medical Orderly), Tony Hawks (The Suitcase), Mac McDonald (Captain Hollister), Mark Williams (Petersen).

Whilst going through Kristine Kochanski's personal possessions, Lister discovers a photograph which clearly shows the two of them getting married. Startled but ecstatic, he realises that the only explanation is a future excursion back through time. His quest for the source of the journey leads him to Rimmer's diary, in which he intends to investigate the truth about a certain event of three million years before. Bingo! Rimmer reports seeing a ghost of himself in his bunk room: one which attributed its sudden appearance to 'a stasis leak on Level 16'. At the time, he put the experience down to an overdose of Titan Mushrooms – or Freaky Fungus – accidentally fed to him by Lister, but now, of course, both know better. A harrowing lift journey takes Lister, Rimmer and Cat to Level 16, where they do indeed discover a stasis leak – that is, a 'magic door' to the past, as Cat puts it. Emerging rather embarrassingly in the shower room, they find themselves on the *Red Dwarf* of three million years before. Although anything they try to take back with them crumbles to dust, Lister realises that by persuading Kochanski to step into the spare stasis booth, he can ensure her survival right up to the present day. Rimmer, however, has other ideas. After all, there's only one spare booth – and it's got his name on it.

While Lister tracks Kochanski down to the Ganymede Holiday Inn and Cat leaps into ferocious battle against a deadly fox fur, Rimmer reaches his living self and tries to reason with him. But things happen exactly as he remembers, and the Rimmer of the past doesn't believe a word he says. When Captain Hollister arrives, dressed in a chicken suit for the evening's fancy dress party, the younger Rimmer is absolutely convinced that he is hallucinating and manages to talk himself into rather a lot of trouble. Meanwhile, Lister is deeply upset when he finally locates Kochanski – in the honeymoon suite. Another look at his photograph convinces him that he is, in fact, not the groom, but rather an onlooker. However, he is wrong. Kochanski appears at the door and introduces him to her husband . . . himself. Apparently, in five years' time, he will find another way to travel back in time, and it is then that the two will marry. In the meantime, he has to content himself with the bottle of champagne he manages to steal from her room. Meanwhile, things are going from bad to worse for Rimmer, and the appearance of his older self – the one who is destined to travel back in time with the Lister of five years hence – doesn't help matters. When all three Listers and all three Rimmers congregate in one room, along with Kochanski and Cat, the contemporary Rimmer's sanity reaches breaking point.

5: QUEEG

Broadcast date: 4 October 1988.

Guest cast: Charles Augins (Queeg).

A meteor crashes into *Red Dwarf*, damaging the Hologram Projection Suite. Rimmer goes to pieces, literally, as the bottom half of his body becomes independent of its top half, and his personality is upstaged by that of Brannigan, the ship's psychiatrist. It is left to Lister to repair the damage, with some help from Holly, whose less than sound advice almost leads to his untimely death. The incident, only the latest in a long series of foul-ups by the senile computer, precipitates the unexpected arrival of his replacement, Queeg 500. *Red Dwarf*'s back-up computer is scornful of Holly, claiming that he gets all of his information from the Junior Colour Encyclopedia of Space. He accuses Holly of gross negligence leading to the endangerment of personnel, and in accordance with Article 5, he immediately replaces him. Lister, Rimmer and Cat put up little objection, expecting that Queeg will perform better than Holly ever did, but they are in for a shock. A fierce enforcer of Space Corps policy, Queeg soon makes life hell for all aboard. Lister and Cat are forced to work for their food, whilst Rimmer's hologramatic body is put through the regulation 500 jerks and a gruelling three mile run every day – whether he is conscious or not. In their misery the crew turn to Holly, now the ship's night watchman, for support. Forgiving their earlier lack of support, he challenges Queeg to a game to decide who will run *Red Dwarf* in future. For the loser: erasure.

Queeg accepts, but despite Holly's numerous other suggestions, chooses chess as the deciding game. Needless to say, Holly loses and the others watch sadly as he says his last goodbyes and is erased forever. Queeg is now in control of the ship – or so it seems. In fact, Queeg never existed at all – the whole thing has simply been a joke on Holly's part. The moral of the story? 'Appreciate what you've got – because basically, I'm fantastic!'

6: PARALLEL UNIVERSE

Broadcast date: 11 October 1988.

Guest cast: Suzanne Bertish (Ms Rimmer), Angela Bruce (Ms Lister), Matthew Devitt (The Dog), Hattie Hayridge (Hilly).

For once, Holly has good news. He has perfected the Holly Hop Drive, a device capable of taking *Red Dwarf* instantaneously back to Earth. The crew are sceptical when they see his innovation as, basically, it is a large box with stop and start buttons. Nevertheless, they take the plunge and try the machine out. However, instead of taking them home, the Drive transports them into a parallel universe; one where history has run parallel to our own, but in which the positions of the sexes have been reversed. Dave and Arnold meet Deb and Arlene, their own equivalents in this dimension, and both are disgusted. Arnold feels insulted by Arlene's attempts to pick him up by hypnosis, even though she is acting towards him only in the same way that he has always acted towards women. Likewise, Dave is appalled by Deb's party piece of belching 'Yankee Doodle Dandy', despite the fact that it is his party piece too. However, it is Cat who is the most disappointed by his counterpart – as rather than being female, it turns out to be a humanoid Dog. The machines, conversely, fare very well, with one of the Skutters actually managing to mate with its female equivalent and producing a stream of baby

Skutters. Holly too gets on exceedingly well with his female equivalent, Hilly, which rather delays the repair process on the Holly Hop Drive. Work continues into the night and, despite his reservations, a drunken Dave Lister finds himself sleeping with Deb. Arlene Rimmer is scornful, hoping the 'little slut' will become pregnant – and she's not talking about Deb. Dave is appalled to learn that in this universe, it is the men who have babies, and when *Red Dwarf* finally returns to its own dimension, he immediately undergoes a pregnancy test. It is positive.

RED DWARF III

Regulars: Rimmer – Chris Barrie. Lister – Craig Charles. Cat – Danny John-Jules. Holly – Hattie Hayridge. Kryten – Robert Llewellyn. Written by Rob Grant and Doug Naylor. Production by Ed Bye, Rob Grant and Doug Naylor. A Paul Jackson Production for BBC North West.

NOTE: Things have changed aboard *Red Dwarf*. As a speedy pre-titles caption informs us, Lister is no longer pregnant, having had his twin sons sent to the Parallel Universe to live with their 'father'. The increasingly eccentric Holly has had a head sex change operation and is now a woman, and the crew have met up once again with the android Kryten who, having been rebuilt by Lister after an almost fatal accident, now has a slightly different personality. The Saga Continuums . . .

1: BACKWARDS

Broadcast date: 14 November 1989.

Guest cast: Maria Friedman (Waitress), Tony Hawks (Compere), Anna Palmer (Customer in Cafe), Arthur Smith (Pub Manager).

Whilst Lister and Cat are busy admiring the delectable form of Wilma Flintstone, Rimmer escorts Kryten on his driving test in *Starbug* 1. Kryten however is far from expert with the craft's controls, and manages to send them both spinning through a time hole. They emerge on what seems to be the planet Earth, although a few anomalies are immediately apparent. There is a theory that states that, once the universe has stopped expanding, it will contract, causing time itself to run backwards – and that is exactly what is happening here. Indeed, time has already retreated past Rimmer's era, reaching the latter end of the twentieth century. With *Starbug* destroyed, Rimmer and Kryten resign themselves to the fact that they could be stuck in the year 3991 for quite some time. They will obviously need some way of supporting themselves, but Rimmer bemoans the fact that there is nothing they can do. He can't even decipher the backwards speech of this world's inhabitants without Kryten's translation unit to help him. Kryten is quick to remind him, however, that on this world, everything they do is special.

Meanwhile, Holly has located the crashed *Starbug*, and Lister and Cat take one of the other vessels through the time hole after their crewmates. Lister is overjoyed to find that the trail leads back to Earth and, seeing a signpost for Nodnol, he is convinced that they have landed somewhere in Bulgaria. It isn't long before the whereabouts of Rimmer and Kryten becomes apparent. Their presence is advertised everywhere as a great new novelty act, The Sensational Reverse Brothers – or rather, Srehtorb Esrever Lanoitasnes Eht. Indeed, they are doing so well that Rimmer feels he has finally found his niche in life, and doesn't wish to leave. Unfortunately, he has little choice in the matter. He and Kryten are unexpectedly fired from their job for a fight that is about to happen. The skirmish, of course, is caused by Lister, and he delights in the sudden disappearance of the bruises he has had since landing on this strange planet. As the bar-room 'tidy' is concluded, the crew leave for *Starbug* and, eventually, *Red Dwarf*. Only the Cat lingers, first to take some money from the charity box, as is the custom, and secondly to make use of a nearby bush – something which turns out to be a big mistake.

2: MAROONED

Broadcast date: 21 November 1989.

Guest cast: None.

Holly is shocked to discover that *Red Dwarf* is suddenly heading towards no less than five black holes. Time to abandon ship. Holly will do her best to navigate around the dangers and pick the crew up again afterwards. Unfortunately, Lister and Rimmer may not be around to be picked up. Colliding with an asteroid, *Starbug* crashes on to an arctic planet, where the two find themselves marooned. There is precious little food although fortunately, the presence of a tin of dog food prevents Lister from having to eat a Pot Noodle. Worse still, there is no source of heat. Rimmer doesn't need either, but it seems that Lister's days are numbered. As they try to lift each other's spirits, it seems that the pair are finally becoming closer. Lister tells of his loss of virginity on the Bootle Municipal Golf Course, and Rimmer is horrified at his admission that he never paid any green fees. Rimmer in turn makes a disclosure of his own, waxing lyrical on his past life as Alexander the Great's Chief Eunuch. To this day, he can't look at a pair of nut-crackers without wincing. However, the conversation is curtailed as heating problems become paramount. Rimmer's money has already been burnt, as have all his books. That only leaves his nineteenth-century figures of Napoleon's Armies Du Nord and the priceless camphor-wood chest which is the only thing his disapproving father ever gave to him. Not surprisingly, Rimmer is less than happy with the situation, but he soon finds a solution. Why should any of his things be destroyed when Lister's guitar would make such good firewood? Lister agrees – or so it seems – and Rimmer is deeply impressed by his selfless sacrifice of his most prized possession. He consigns his own soldiers to the flames, seeking to prove himself as much a man of honour as his companion.

Finally, the ordeal ends. Cat and Kryten track down the crashed shuttle-craft, and Lister's life is saved. Rather ashamedly, Holly admits that the five black holes didn't actually exist at all – they were simply five specks of grit on the scanner scope. Well, they were black, weren't they? However, the trouble isn't over yet. The reappearance of Lister's guitar and the discovery of a guitar-shaped hole in his priceless trunk causes Rimmer to cry out for the hacksaw. He's going to do to Lister what Alexander the Great once did to him!

3: POLYMORPH

Broadcast date: 28 November 1989.

Guest cast: Frances Barber (Genny), Simon Gaffney (Young Rimmer), Kalli Greenwood (Mrs Rimmer).

Holly detects a non-human life-form aboard the ship, but Rimmer is sceptical. After all, the last one she alerted them to was simply one of Lister's socks. This time though, Holly is frighteningly correct. The ship has been invaded by a genetic mutant gone wrong – a Polymorph, which can alter its shape into that of anything, whether animal, vegetable or mineral. Arriving on *Red Dwarf* as a beachball, the creature focuses its first attack upon Lister. Its initial masquerades as a shami kebab and a pair of boxer shorts cause him enough problems, but the real trouble starts when it metamorphoses into an armour-plated killing machine and launches a vicious attack. Not surprisingly, Lister is frightened – and the true purpose of the Polymorph suddenly becomes obvious. It feeds off negative emotions, removing them from their originators for its own nourishment. Now it has taken Lister's fear away from him, he is determined to stage a suicidal re-match, and has to be sedated by the others. There's no point fighting it, they decide, so all are happy to follow Rimmer's suggestion that they run away instead. Unfortunately, the Polymorph is lurking in the cargo decks, ready to interrupt their packing. In the form of a beautiful woman, it arouses the Cat's vanity before stealing that emotion from him. Posing as Rimmer himself, it steals Kryten's guilt, and the sight of his mother in bed with Dave Lister causes Rimmer enough anger to feed it further. Emotionally crippled, the *Red Dwarf* crew disagree over their next move. Rimmer wants to hit the creature with a major leaflet campaign – 'Chameleonic Life Forms, No Thanks' – whereas Kryten imagines that he can buy his own freedom by handing over the others. Cat feels he is too unimportant to have an opinion, but Lister wants to 'nut the smegger into oblivion', and eventually all agree that that is the best option. In the end, it is a complete accident that causes the Polymorph to die under heat-seeking bazookoid fire. Still, there's always time for a re-match. Apparently, they travel in pairs . . .

4: BODY SWAP

Broadcast date: 5 December 1989.

Guest cast: None.

A malfunctioning Skutter has run amok on *Red Dwarf*, causing over two thousand wiring faults and turning the whole ship into an enormous booby-trap. Whilst Rimmer and Kryten try to repair the damage, Lister operates the food machine and is more than mildly surprised to find that he has accidentally activated the self-destruct system instead. The problem is further compounded by Holly's admission that only the Captain and the senior officers can avert the coming catastrophe. They're all dead of course, but she never quite got round to updating the system. As the count-down nears its conclusion, it is Kryten, as always, who has the solution. During his time on the *Nova 5*, he had been involved in a mind swap experiment. It had been a total failure, but at least he thinks he knows what went wrong. Lister is uncertain but, as Rimmer says, the worst that can happen to him is that he will have to spend the rest of his life as a mindless gibbering vegetable – and how long will that be? Thus, Lister's body is given the mind and voice of Executive Officer Carole Brown. She orders the cessa-tion of the destruct sequence, but nothing happens. The count-down continues, and finally reaches zero . . . at which point Lister's meal arrives as ordered.

The excitement is over, but the mind swap has given Rimmer an idea. Now that Kryten has perfected this new science, why doesn't he swap bodies with Lister? He can enjoy the benefits of a living body for a fortnight in return for getting his companion fit again. Lister reluctantly agrees – but instantly regrets that decision. Rimmer has been denied the pleasures of the flesh for too long, and the sensual experience causes him to go overboard on eating, drinking and smoking. Lister demands his body back upset at its growth of breasts and at the sudden addition of two stone to its already ample frame. But Rimmer hasn't had enough. Pressing Kryten into service, Rimmer anaesthetises Lister as he sleeps, and steals his body. He flees *Red Dwarf* in *Starbug*, and Lister's pursuit leads to disaster as the shuttle-craft crashes. Rimmer has lost one of Lister's arms for him – or so he claims. But Lister is not amused by his little joke. All he wants is his own body back – now! Rimmer has to concede, but he's not beaten yet. Once again, Kryten and his chloroform pad are pressed into service – and the Cat's in for a big surprise.

5: TIMESLIDES

Broadcast date: 12 December 1989.

Guest cast: Robert Addie (Gilbert), Rupert Bates and Richard Hainsworth (Bodyguards), Emile Charles (Young Lister), Simon Gaffney (Young Rimmer), Stephen McKintosh (Thicky Holden), Louisa Ruthven (Ski Woman), Koo Stark (Lady Sabrina Mulholland-Jjones), Mark Steel (Ski Man), Ruby Wax (American Presenter). With special guest star Adolf Hitler as Himself.

Kryten accidentally makes a miraculous discovery. A batch of developing fluid, strangely mutated over three million years' storage, is suddenly capable of bringing photographs to life. Better still, when the same fluid is used to create slides, it becomes possible for the *Red Dwarf* crew to step into the action. After trying out the effect with photos of Rimmer's brother's wedding and of Adolf Hitler, only one drawback is found – it is impossible to move out of the confines of the original photographs. Still for Lister's purposes he doesn't need to. Lister is bored with his existence on *Red Dwarf*. He longs to change the course of his life and to that end, he is determined to go back in time and ensure that his younger self never joins the Space Corps as he did. Thanks to a photograph of his teenage band, 'Smeg and the Heads', he is able to do so. Moreover, he gives to himself the secret of the Tension Sheet, an amazingly simple device based on bubbled packing sheets which was actually invented by Arnold Rimmer's boarding school room mate, Fred 'Thicky' Holden. The experiment is a total success. The timelines alter, and Lister vanishes from *Red Dwarf*. So do Cat and Kryten as, without Lister's influence, they never would have existed. Rimmer is left alone, and he considers it his duty as a complete and total bastard to restore things to the way they were. Delving into her newly altered memory banks, Holly is able to provide a picture reference of Lister's new life. A quick application of the fluid allows Rimmer to step into it, and he is alarmed to find his one-time companion a multi-millionaire, married to sex symbol Sabrina Mulholland-Jjones. Rimmer tries to talk Lister into going back to his past life but of course, in this timeline, Lister's never heard of him. So Rimmer decides to beat Lister at his own game. He uses a slide of himself in the school dormitory to go even further back in time and give the secret of the Tension Sheet to himself. As he does so, however, he fails to realise that 'Thicky' Holden is listening from the next bed, and it is he who beats Young Rimmer to the patent office. Credit for the Tension Sheet reverts to him, and the timelines are returned more or less to normal. Lister, Cat and Kryten are returned to *Red Dwarf* with no memory of what has happened, but still, Rimmer is miserable. He has lost his chance to become a millionaire and to endure constant sex with Sabrina. Why is it, he complains, that whenever anything good happens to him, it always goes wrong? His spirits are suddenly lifted as Holly announces that, for reasons she can't quite fathom, the alterations to the timelines have meant that he is now alive. But Rimmer's earlier pessimism seems to be proved correct when, in his enthusiasm, he sets off an explosion which kills him once again.

6: THE LAST DAY

Broadcast date: 19 December 1989.

Guest cast: Julie Higginson (Girl Android), Gordon Kennedy (Hudzen).

A message pod from Diva-Droid International finally locates Kryten, and delivers its message to his 'owners'. A video of sales executive Jim Reaper announces to a stunned Lister that Kryten's service contract has expired. It's shut-off time. Kryten has twenty-four hours in which to prepare himself for his death, a fate which he accepts with disturbing equanimity. Well, after all, this isn't really the end for him – it's merely the beginning of a new life in Silicon Heaven. Lister is appalled. Silicon Heaven is obviously a fictional concept programmed into all androids by their makers. It is only their belief in it that ensures their loyalty to humankind. As Kryten says, why would mechanoids spend their entire lives in service, if they didn't know they were going to get their rewards in the afterlife? Okay, so Lister can't stop Kryten's shut-off disc from activating, but he can certainly make the mechanoid's last day one to remember. Kryten is invited to a party in the Officers' Club, and treated to a special mechanoid menu devised by Holly. He is also the grateful recipient of a number of farewell gifts, including an ear-ring which Cat always hated anyway, and a robotic Marilyn Monroe which, despite its obviously shoddy construction, he finds quite enchanting.

The following day though, Kryten finds himself faced with a dilemma. For the first time in his life, he has actually experienced 'fun' – and it wasn't enough. He wants some more. Overriding the shut-down disc is no real problem. What is a problem though, is the impending arrival of Kryten's replacement, Hudzen. If Kryten doesn't terminate himself, Hudzen has orders to help him do so. Lister isn't worried. All they have to do is meet the replacement on the landing gantry and tell him he's not wanted.

Simple enough, yes? No. Having tracked Kryten for thousands of years, Hudzen has gone completely mad. Not only that, but he's a good deal stronger than any of them. Of course, androids aren't allowed to harm humans ... but the only person who truly fits that description is Lister and what the hell?! The ensuing battle is very much a one-sided affair. Kryten is to be the first to die, and Hudzen grips him by the throat, ready to administer the killing stroke. Time to visit Silicon Heaven – except that Kryten knows it doesn't really exist. Holly sides with him in persuading Hudzen of that truth, and the newcomer is stricken by a metaphysical dichotomy and forced to shut down. Lister is confused. If Hudzen's android mind couldn't handle the concept of there being no Silicon Heaven, how could Kryten's? The answer, says Kryten, is simple. He knew something that Hudzen didn't. He knew he was lying.

RED DWARF IV

Regulars: Rimmer – Chris Barrie. Lister – Craig Charles. Cat – Danny John-Jules. Holly – Hattie Hayridge. Kryten – Robert Llewellyn. Written and produced by Rob Grant and Doug Naylor. Produced and directed by Ed Bye. A Grant Naylor Production for BBC North West.

1: CAMILLE

Broadcast date: 14 February 1991.

Guest cast: Judy Pascoe (Mechanoid Camille), Francesca Folan (Hologram Camille), Suzanne Rhatigan (Kochanski Camille), Rupert Bates (Hector Blob).

Lister becomes frustrated with Kryten's inability to lie and to disobey orders, particularly as Rimmer so often uses that to his own advantage. Using a series of simple exercises, he is determined to force the android to deviate from his programming – but even as Kryten believes he is getting the hang of things, he finds he just can't lie in front of an audience. The lessons do seem to have some effect, however. Whilst out in *Starbug*, Kryten and Rimmer pick up a distress signal from another android, who is trapped on a planet about to explode. Against Rimmer's express orders, Kryten guides the craft into terrible danger and succeeds in rescuing Camille. For both mechanoids, it is advanced mutual compatibility on the basis of a primary initial ident – but as always, things aren't what they seem. When Kryten returns Camille to *Starbug*, he is baffled by Rimmer's references to her as a beautiful woman. In fact, to Rimmer, she looks like a hologramatic bombshell and as holograms can touch each other, he suddenly finds himself very glad that Kryten did see fit to disobey him. Lister sees Camille as a female cross between himself and his lost love, Kristine Kochanski. Time to start recreating the human race, he thinks. But even before he can get his Spider Man suit out of storage, he realises that something is wrong. When he compares notes with his shipmates, his suspicions are painfully confirmed. Eventually, Camille admits the truth. She is a Pleasure GELF – a Genetically Engineered Life Form, who is seen by everybody as the object of their own desire. Whilst coming as a disappointment to Lister, Rimmer and Kryten, the news causes only excitement for the Cat, who rushes to see what form Camille will take for him. Perhaps not surprisingly, the object of his own desire turns out to be . . . himself. Ashamed, Camille finally reveals her true form, and Lister, Rimmer and Cat are repulsed by her appearance. But Kryten, already infatuated with the GELF, doesn't seem to care. He feels sure that their romance can continue, despite the obstacles in their path, and despite the fact that he is an android and she is a huge, green blob with tentacles. At last, both seem to have found true happiness. But it is not to last. Their blissful relationship is all too soon shattered by the arrival of Hector, the blob who has the honour of being Camille's husband. Camille doesn't want to hurt Kryten by leaving, but it seems that the mechanoid has finally become versed in the use of lies and, borrowing his inspiration from Casablanca, he persuades Camille to accompany Hector, leaving his life forever.

2: DNA

Broadcast date: 21 February 1991.

Guest cast: Richard Ridings (DNA Computer Voice).

Red Dwarf encounters a spacecraft of unknown origin and Rimmer is convinced that they have discovered aliens. A three-headed skeleton seems to confirm this – but then, why does it have a video club card in its wallet? In fact, the ship is from Earth, where technology has obviously advanced since the twenty-third century. The skeleton is the product of a DNA modifier, a machine that can change any living thing into any other living thing by rearranging its molecular structure. When Cat accidentally triggers the machine, Lister is turned into a chicken, and Kryten, whose brain is part organic, achieves his fondest desire – to become a human. It is no surprise then that, even once a way of reversing the transformations is discovered, Kryten wishes to stay as he is. His new form does have a few problems, however, The eyes don't seem to have a zoom facility and his nipples no longer pick up Jazz FM. Worst of all, he is worried about the unfamiliar and very ugly thing which hangs between his legs – and the effect which the sight of a super-deluxe vacuum cleaner has upon it. Lister is worried too. It is obvious that Kryten still has the mind of a mechanoid, and Lister feels that his transformation may not have been for the best. Eventually, after an uncomfortable confrontation with his spare heads, Kryten agrees. However, before Kryten's transformation can be properly reversed, it is necessary for Holly to master the controls of the Modifier and in doing so, she makes a mistake so simple that any deranged, half-witted computer could have made it. The result is that Lister's mutton vindaloo suddenly becomes a rampaging beast, half man, half curry. It shrugs off bazookoid fire undamaged, and it seems that there is no way to stop it – unless Holly can get things right this time and use the Modifier to turn Lister into a super-human. She gives it a try, but the results aren't all they could have been, and a minuscule Lister is left at the mercy of the rampaging creature. Quite by accident, he hits upon the answer. Lager – the only thing that can kill a vindaloo.

3: JUSTICE

Broadcast date: 28 February 1991.

Guest cast: Nicholas Ball (Simulant), James Smillie (Justice Computer Voice).

Even a bout of space mumps isn't enough to keep Lister in the medical unit when he learns that there might be a woman on board. Rushing to the scene, he discovers that *Red Dwarf* has picked up an escape pod from a prison ship which was transporting a bunch of psychopathic simulants to Justice World. The ship's black box tells of a mutiny that resulted in the deaths of everybody on board. Everyone, that is, except for prison officer Barbra Bellini and one of the simulant prisoners. Obviously, one of them is cryogenically frozen in the pod – but which one? There is little time for debate, as Cat has already started the thawing process. In twenty-four hours, it's either death or a date. For once, Holly finds a solution. She suggests that they travel to the fully automated Justice World themselves and beg the use of its facilities. These should be adequate to handle the occupant of the pod, should it prove not to be Babs. The others take her advice, and Lister is relieved when he makes a sudden recovery from his disease during the journey. The Cat is less pleased; the main symptom of the recovery was the bursting of a large, pus-filled swelling on Lister's head – and guess who was in the vicinity? Soon enough though, all are presented with slightly more to worry about than the colour co-ordination of Cat's clothing. Although the Justice Computer grants them permission to land on Justice World, it fails to warn them of its foolproof security system. The Computer needs to ascertain whether or not its visitors are suitable to enter or whether they should be locked away for good, and they are frozen into position as their minds are probed for any evidence of past misdemeanours. Lister in particular is worried. He is sure that his teenage record of petty crimes will earn him a stay in prison. He is therefore extremely relieved when clearance is granted. Rimmer, however, fares rather less well. He is found guilty of 1,167 counts of second degree murder – the deaths of everybody on board *Red Dwarf*. He is sentenced to eight years for each of his crimes, and given his hologramatic status, these sentences are to be served consecutively. He is to go to prison for over nine thousand years. Rimmer is sent to Justice World's containment area, known as the Justice Zone. At first, he is surprised to see that there are no bars or doors to keep him in position, but he soon learns why. The entire zone is surrounded by an amazing development known as the Justice Field, which acts to ensure that no crime can be committed within its confines. Anybody attempting to do anything illegal will immediately have the consequences of the act turned back upon himself – as Lister discovers, when Rimmer encourages him to try a spot of arson.

Meanwhile, Kryten lodges an appeal, building up a case around the fact that his client is a complete dork. Somebody like Rimmer, he contends, could never have been given enough responsibility to cause the leak of radiation that killed the *Red Dwarf* crew. Kryten theorises that what the mind probe has detected is the guilt which Rimmer himself feels about the incident, and that his actual culpability is nil. Despite Rimmer's constant objections to the insulting words of his own counsel, the Justice Computer accepts the plea, and he is set free. That still leaves one problem, however. The escape pod has opened – and it wasn't Barbra Bellini on board. Everybody flees into the Justice Zone, but the simulant tricks Lister into confronting him, to 'talk'. Although Lister has broken his promise and brought along a weapon, the simulant has done likewise and brought two. But in the ensuing battle, Lister is the first to realise that the Justice Field is turning each participant's blows against their perpetrator. Encouraging his attacker to assault him in the most vicious ways possible, he is amused to see the simulant defeat itself. Lister is left to realise that, no matter how much technology humans build to create true justice, life will always be basically unfair and, bored by his moralising, the rest of the crew are pleased to see the point proven by a mis-step into a gaping hole.

4: WHITE HOLE

Broadcast date: 7 March 1991.

Guest cast: David Ross (Talkie Toaster).

Lister is horrified to discover that Kryten has repaired Talkie Toaster. Horrified because it was he himself who was responsible for smashing it to bits. He insists that it is nothing more than a one-dimensional, bread-obsessed electrical appliance and, once fixed, Talkie proves him right with his non-stop offers of bread-related products. However, Kryten has good reason for his actions. He has pioneered a process which can restore the mechanical intelligence of a device at the cost of reducing its operational life-span, and Talkie is his guinea pig. When the experiment is proved to be a complete success, Kryten reasons that the process should also work on Holly, curing her advanced case of computer senility and restoring her IQ to six thousand. In fact, the operation seems more than successful. Her intelligence raised to double its original level, Holly's only problem is that she can't get an intelligent, non-toast-related conversation out of Talkie. Then, making a quick check of her systems, she discovers the worst – the experiment has had a disastrous side-effect. Although Holly's intelligence has increased to twice the desired level, there has been an exponential reduction in her life-span. She only has 3.45 minutes of run-time left. Taking the only logical choice available, Holly shuts herself down and as a consequence, all of the ship's power systems do the same. Left to fend for themselves, the crew are in danger of either freezing to death or starving. Rimmer refuses to conserve emergency power by switching himself off, and Kryten advises that the life support systems will cease to function in all too short a time. As if that weren't bad enough, there is another problem – without Holly to guide it, *Red Dwarf* has run straight into a white hole. The opposite of a black hole, this spews time and matter back into the universe, and in doing so, it creates chaos aboard the ship. Holly is switched back on for one quick computation, and Lister is amazed at the solution she comes up with. The answer, it seems, is to play planetary pool, knocking a nearby planet into the 'pocket' of the white hole and thereby sealing it up. But Holly has got the shot wrong, he is sure. If they do it her way, the planet will be off the table and straight into someone's beer. To the horror of the others, Lister decides to trust his own pool skills over Holly's computations. He takes aim – and misses! *Starbug* is trapped in the path of an oncoming planet, and all aboard are doomed – until the 'balls' ricochet and the pot is achieved. A trick shot, claims Lister, played for and got. The incident also has an unexpected side effect. Now that the white hole is gone, the time it spewed into the universe no longer exists, and as it was during this time that Holly and the Toaster were 'repaired', these events no longer occurred. As *Starbug* fades around them and the *Red Dwarf* crew are returned to their ship with no memory of what has happened, Kryten takes this golden opportunity to tell Rimmer exactly what he thinks of him.

5: DIMENSION JUMP

Broadcast date: 14 March 1991.

Guest cast: Kalli Greenwood (Mrs Rimmer), Simon Gaffney (Young Rimmer), Hetty Baynes (Cockpit Computer).

A glimpse into a parallel universe shows us the dramatic effect upon Arnold Rimmer's life of one single event in his childhood. In one dimension, he was kept down a year at school; in another, he wasn't. In our universe, this led to young Arnold's growth into the pathetic character we already know. In another, he became instead a handsome, heroic test pilot in the Space Corps, known to all as Ace. Ace Rimmer is everything that Arnold Rimmer is not, and chief amongst his outstanding attributes is his unparalleled courage. It is this that spurs him into accepting the greatest challenge of his life. He is to test-fly a prototype craft which will exceed the speed of reality and take him into another dimension. Naturally, that dimension is ours, and Ace Rimmer makes an unexpected arrival directly in front of *Starbug*, which is currently taking the *Red Dwarf* crew on a fishing trip to an ocean planet. Despite the best efforts of the others, Arnold Rimmer has accompanied them on the expedition, so when Ace rushes to the crashed vessel to offer his assistance, the two Rimmers meet. It is hate at first sight. Arnold despises Ace, who he sees as the living proof of what he could have been had he had the lucky breaks in life that his counterpart obviously had. Ace, on the other hand, takes a dislike to the cowardly and incompetent Arnold, disgusted that he himself could ever be reduced to such a state. Naturally, Lister, Cat and Kryten side with Ace on the subject, sick as they are of Arnold's endless tales of morris dancing and his recitals of Reggie Wilson Hammond Organ classics. Indeed,

Ace and Lister become firm friends, and Lister is pleased to hear that his other-dimensional counterpart, known as Spanners, is doing just as well for himself as Ace as a Space Corps engineer. However, Ace soon realises that he and Arnold simply cannot live together. One of them has to go! Despite the objections of the others, Ace prepares to leave, revealing as he does that in fact he was the one who was kept down a year at the age of seven. By Arnold's standards, it was he who got the lucky break – but in Ace's case, the humiliation had forced him to pull himself together and make a life for himself. With that, Ace leaves *Red Dwarf* forever, his departure not in the least obstructed by his counterpart's clumsy attempt at envy motivated retribution. His destiny, he decides, is to roam the dimensions, meeting other versions of himself. He can't go back, but maybe one day, he'll find a universe that approximates his own. And perhaps one day, he'll even find an Arnold Rimmer who is as sad and worthless as the one he met aboard *Red Dwarf.* His impossible quest continues . . .

6: MELTDOWN

Broadcast date: 21 March 1991.

Guest cast: Clayton Mark (Elvis), Kenneth Hadley (Hitler), Martin Friend (Einstein), Stephen Tiller (Pythagoras), Jack Klaff (Abraham Lincoln), Tony Hawks (Caligula), Michael Burrell (Pope Gregory), Forbes Masson (Stan Laurel), Roger Blake (Noel Coward), Pauline Bailey (Marilyn Monroe).

Kryten unearths a prototype matter transporter in the research labs, and Holly is pleased to report that it is capable of homing in on any atmosphere-bearing planets within 500,000 light years. When activated, it takes the *Red Dwarf* crew only a modest 200,000 light years away, to Wax-World, a Wax-Droid theme park. Unfortunately, this particular park has been left unattended for millions of years. The Wax-Droids have broken their programming, and a terrible war has begun between the exhibits in Hero World and those in Villain World. Rimmer and Kryten, arriving first to check the atmosphere, find themselves in the middle of Prehistoric World, where they are chased by a number of unconvincing dinosaurs into neighbouring Hero World. Lister and Cat, meanwhile, arrive in Villain World, falling right into the hands of a wax Adolf Hitler. Whilst Rimmer is busy assembling such luminaries as Einstein, Pythagoras and Mother Theresa to form an army, aided by Sergeant Elvis Presley, Lister and Cat witness the execution of Winnie the Pooh and find themselves being interrogated by Caligula. Lister is threatened with soapy frogs, but Cat is more worried that he might be forced into unfashionable clothing. Fortunately, neither of those dire fates comes to pass as, with the help of Abraham Lincoln, they manage to escape from their prison and flee to the camp of the good guys. There, Lister is horrified by Rimmer's behaviour. His battle strategy of a charge across a minefield under cover of daylight is an obviously suicidal one. Rimmer, it seems, is going mad – and Holly theorises that Lister is the cause. Well, perhaps he shouldn't have popped Rimmer's hologram-projecting light bee into his mouth like that. However, there is some method to Rimmer's madness. Whilst the forces of evil are occupied by their enemies' charge, Kryten and Queen Victoria stage a sneak attack from behind, and Kryten is able to ensure victory with one twist of a handy thermostat. With the heroes blown up and the villains melted down, Rimmer's tactics have succeeded in killing every single Wax-Droid on the planet. Lister is further disgusted by his companion's insistence that the sacrifice was well worth it for the 'grand victory' he has won. This time, he doesn't just put the light bee in his mouth, he swallows it whole, deciding to let Rimmer experience a complete trip through his digestive system. Does anyone fancy a curry?

RED DWARF V

Regulars: Rimmer – Chris Barrie. Lister – Craig Charles. Cat – Danny John-Jules. Holly – Hattie Hayridge. Kryten – Robert Llewellyn. Written by Rob Grant and Doug Naylor. Produced by Hilary Bevan Jones. Directed by Juliet May (all except 'Quarantine') and Grant Naylor (all except 'Holoship' and 'Terrorform'). A Grant Naylor Production for BBC TV/BBC North.

1: HOLOSHIP

Broadcast date: 20 February 1992.

Guest cast: Jane Horrocks (Nirvanah Crane), Matthew Marsh (Captain Platini), Don Warrington (Commander Binks), Lucy Briers (Harrison), Simon Day (Number Two), Jane Montgomery (Number One).

Rimmer is repelled by Lister's choice of films: he has just been forced to sit through a love story, and he isn't convinced. Why on earth, he wonders, would somebody sacrifice his career for the sake of the woman he loves, knowing that he will never see her again? It just doesn't make sense. The rest of the crew are spared Rimmer's further comments as he is suddenly teleported away from *Starbug*. The Cat is all for getting away while they've got the chance, but of course, they have to find out what's going on first. Rimmer has, in fact, been teleported to a holoship – a hologramatic spaceship, inaccessible to living people, but a godsend to the dead. On *Enlightenment*, holograms can touch, feel and taste, and even have sex – something which ship's regulations require them to do at least twice a day for their own health. Rimmer is alarmed – that's more than some people manage in a lifetime! However, after his first act of sexual congress with Nirvanah, he begins to realise that he likes this place very much indeed. Moreover, though both deny it, the experience has affected them deeply. The two are falling in love. Naturally Rimmer wants to stay, but *Enlightenment* is a pioneering vessel crewed by the hologramatic cream of the Space Corps, and he, as a Class One hologram of a 'Tosspot by Royal Appointment', doesn't come up to scratch.

Desperate now, Rimmer applies – much to the amusement of the Holoship crew – to undergo the rigorous intelligence test which, if he passes it, will allow him to replace one of their number. *Enlightenment*'s computer, Stocky, runs his data through its systems and selects the crew member against whom he has the most chance of success. Unknown to Rimmer, that turns out to be Nirvanah. Faced with a projected 96 per cent chance of failure, Rimmer decides that, as always, he will have to cheat. He persuades Kryten to give him a mind patch and, with his own rather minimal intelligence augmented by the brains of two of the most intelligent people who ever worked on *Red Dwarf*, it is a very different Rimmer who sits down at a console and gets to work. Just when he is succeeding brilliantly, however, his mind rejects the patch and he is left floundering. He returns to *Red Dwarf*, where he finds the others interviewing replacements for the post of ship's hologram, and he is mortified to learn that Kryten is unable to perform a second operation. Rimmer returns to the holoship dejectedly, seeing no alternative but to withdraw from the contest. However, touched by his misery, Nirvanah not only persuades him to carry on, but withdraws herself, ensuring his victory. Nirvanah is deactivated and Rimmer takes her place as Navigation Officer on board the ship. Finally, his dreams have all come true until he is shown to his new quarters. Recognising them as Nirvanah's old ones, he realises the dreadful truth. Hardly believing his own actions, Rimmer resigns his commission and leaving behind a note for Nirvanah, returns forever to *Red Dwarf*, throwing away everything he has ever dreamed of for the sake of the woman he loves, even though he'll never see her again. He can't quite believe he just did that!

2: THE INQUISITOR

Broadcast date: 27 February 1992.

Guest cast: John Docherty (Inquisitor), Jake Abraham (Second Lister), James Cormack (Thomas Allman).

Starbug is taken over by a being called the Inquisitor, and returned to *Red Dwarf*. The Inquisitor, it seems, is a self repairing simulant who survived to the end of time and, realising that there is no God and no afterlife, decided that the only point of life is to make something of yourself. With that in mind, he built himself a time machine, and now roams all of history, visiting every living being in turn and judging their worthiness to hold on to the gift of life. Anyone who has wasted their time alive is exterminated and retrospectively erased from history, being replaced by a version of themselves that might have been, had a different sperm reached a different egg. Now, it is the turn of the *Red Dwarf* crew to be judged and needless to say, all are somewhat worried. The four trials take place on *Red Dwarf* itself. The Inquisitor takes on the appearance and the personality of the person he is judging, ensuring that they get the fairest trial possible, as they are tried by themselves. As it turns out, Rimmer and the Cat are acquitted. They are both shallow and selfish people, the Inquisitor proclaims, but having started with nothing in life, they have certainly lived up to their own extremely low expectations. Lister and Kryten, however, are not so fortunate. Kryten manages to talk himself into an early grave, whilst Lister's refusal to answer the charges against him seals his death warrant as well. Both are eradicated from history so that only their bodies remain to be disposed of. Death looks certain – until the Kryten of a few hours hence pops into existence, taking the Inquisitor from behind. The future Kryten is killed, but not before he has ripped off the Inquisitor's time gauntlet and thrown it to an astonished Lister. Lister and Kryten make a run for it, but find that they can't get very far. The Inquisitor has altered the timelines so that they never existed, and Holly will not let them through any of the security doors. Worse, she summons the crew of *Red Dwarf* to deal with the 'intruders', and Lister and Kryten are confronted by their ex-crewmates – who no longer recognise them – and two very different versions of their own selves. They are escorted to the brig but, as they proceed, the Inquisitor attacks, his mad assault causing the deaths of the new Lister and Kryten. The original Lister appropriates the hand of his dead 'sperm-in-law' and uses it, much to Kryten's total disgust, to get him through the ship's palm-operated doors.

They retreat to the hold, where Cat and Rimmer find them. Forming an uneasy alliance, the four head towards the storage bay where, according to Kryten's future self, the final confrontation with the Inquisitor is to take place. The Inquisitor is indeed there, and Rimmer and the Cat are gunned down mercilessly. However, the simulant chooses to toy with Lister, first regressing him to youth and then aging him enormously. His mistake! Kryten provides a distraction, enabling Lister to use the time gauntlet on the Inquisitor himself. He is frozen for just under ten minutes, during which time Kryten takes the gauntlet and travels to the past to carry out the act of self sacrifice which will get them into this mess in the first place. Lister is now alone, but he has a plan in mind. When the Inquisitor awakens, he is suspended over an abyss by a rope – a rope which Lister suddenly burns through. At the last possible instant, he hauls the simulant to safety, proudly proclaiming that, since he has saved the Inquisitor's life, any attempt to eradicate him totally from history will cause the creature's own death too. Having nothing to fear now, he returns the Inquisitor's gauntlet to him. However, it seems that Lister has miscalculated. After all, if he is erased from time, he will never be around to threaten the Inquisitor's life in the first place. The Inquisitor can erase him with no problem whatsoever. Lister hadn't thought of that. Or had he? Before his untimely death, Kryten had re-rigged the time gauntlet. When the Inquisitor tries to use it, it backfires, and it is he who is himself erased from the time continuum. All of his past works are thus undone, and Rimmer, Cat and Kryten are restored to life, unharmed. An appropriate time, says Kryten, for Lister to 'give him five'. But Lister can do better than that – he can give him fifteen!

3: TERRORFORM

Broadcast date: 5 March 1992.

Guest cast: Sara Stockbridge and Francine Walker-Lee (Hand maidens).

Rimmer and Kryten have met with a rather nasty accident whilst out moon-hopping. Kryten lies crushed and broken in the wreckage of *Starbug*, and Rimmer has gone missing altogether. With only sixty-seven minutes to live, Kryten is able to disconnect his own hand and send it back to *Red Dwarf* to fetch help. At first, the already arachnophobic Lister is alarmed by Holly's description of a tarantula-like intruder on the ship – and his fear grows when he finds it crawling up his leg. Eventually though, a VDU keyboard gives the hand the medium it needs to communicate its message, and Lister and Cat rush to the rescue of their crewmates. Repairing Kryten is a simple enough task, thanks to Lister's DIY skills, although as always, there are a few bits left over. Rimmer, however, is still missing, and it seems that he could be in deadly danger. The moon on which he and Kryten crashed is apparently a Psy-Moon, one of those rare planetoids that terra-form themselves in the pattern of the psyche of anybody landing upon them. That means that the whole moon has now grown into the shape of Rimmer's subconscious mind – and that's not a very nice place to be. As the others search for him, their journey takes them through the Swamp of Despair (where the frogs cry out 'Useless!' and huge, blood-sucking leeches bear the face of Rimmer's mother) and past the numerous gravestones of those qualities in Rimmer which have been long dead – amongst them Honour and Generosity, and a minute stone which marks the resting place of his Charm. A freshly-dug pit looms open, awaiting the arrival of his Hope, and Kryten realises that Rimmer is in very grave danger indeed. In fact, the entire landscape is dominated by Rimmer's strongest emotion, as he is about to discover. His cries for a solicitor ignored, he has been captured and tied to a stake, the British Embassy nowhere in sight. The brief appearance of two skimpily-clad, oil-bearing handmaidens gives him cause for hope, but it seems that their job is only to anoint him in preparation for the main event. Much to his dismay, it seems that this is to be his torture and sacrifice, at the hands of a hideous creature formed by his own Self-Loathing.

The rest of the crew arrive just in time to put their bazookoids to good use, but all watch on in horror as the weapons seem to have no effect. Rimmer, however, is touched by the very fact that they have risked their lives for him, and the momentary rekindling of his Self-Respect weakens the creature and forces it to retreat, at least long enough for him and the others to make a run for it. Rimmer's Self-Loathing isn't dormant for long though, and even as Holly tries to lift *Starbug* off the Psy Moon's surface, she finds it dragged back down again. The creature demands that Rimmer be handed over, otherwise it will never let the shuttle-craft leave. Things look bleak – until Kryten has an idea. In order to defeat the Self-Loathing creature, the others have to eliminate that emotion in Rimmer himself, by making him feel that he is loved. The words come harder to some than to others, and the Cat in particular has great difficulty, but the plan seems to work. On the surface of the moon, the change in Rimmer's psyche is mirrored in physical terms by the resurrection of his Self-Confidence and Self-Respect, which leap into battle against his Self-Loathing. The creature is weakened just enough for *Starbug* to break free, and Holly guides the craft back towards *Red Dwarf*. By now, of course, Rimmer has realised that there was only one reason for the words of friendship he has been hearing, and now that freedom has been achieved, the others decide that there is no need to keep up the pretence any longer.

4: QUARANTINE

Broadcast date: 12 March 1992.

Guest cast: Maggie Steed (Dr Hildegarde Lanstrom).

Answering a distress call from a hologramatic doctor, the *Red Dwarf* crew realise that they will have to commandeer Rimmer's remote projection unit to get her back to the ship. Furthermore, with Holly being capable of projecting only one hologram at a time, there are going to be problems when she gets there. Rimmer objects strenuously, but he is undone by Kryten's knowledge of Space Corps Directives. He is left to return to *Red Dwarf*, while the others go in search of Doctor Hildegarde Lanstrom.

They finally find her in a Viral Research Department, where she is preserved in a stasis pod. Their arrival triggers her release and all are alarmed to see that she is, in fact, completely mad. Worse still, Lanstrom has developed amazing powers of telepathy, telekinesis and, most worrying of all, hex vision, with which she attempts to fry her would-be rescuers. Kryten theorises that she has caught a mutated holo-virus, which has stimulated the normally unused areas of her brain, at the same time taking so much energy from her that she will shortly expire. Lister tries to contact Rimmer, who is still sulking on *Starbug*, for back-up, but Rimmer delights in the opportunity to take his revenge. While he is still pretending not to hear Lister's frantic transmission, Lanstrom seizes the communicator and screams a death threat to him. Time, thinks Rimmer, to return to *Red Dwarf* after all. Fortunately for the others, they manage to avoid Lanstrom's deadly blasts until the virus finally strikes her down. They return to *Starbug* and make the journey back to *Red Dwarf*. En route, Kryten reveals a fantastic discovery. Lanstrom, it seems, had been working on a theory that viruses can be both negative and positive. To this end, she had synthesised viruses that cause positive effects. The Cat is worried that, if sexual magnetism is a virus, then he has a terminal case, but Kryten and Lister are more interested in Lanstrom's good-luck virus, which Lister tries out to great effect. However, none of the three are lucky for very much longer. Rimmer has been using his time alone to study the Space Corps Directives with which he was previously foiled, and as *Starbug* returns to the ship, it is diverted to Bay 47 – Quarantine. Lister, Cat and Kryten are to remain there, in accordance with Space Corps Directive 595, for three months. In the event, it takes only five days before arguments and fights break out between the captive trio. However, worse is yet to come, as Rimmer makes an unexpected appearance in a red and white checked gingham dress and army boots, carrying a ventriloquist's puppet that he calls Mister Flibble. The holo-virus, it seems, can be carried by radio waves, and Rimmer contracted it when he spoke to Lanstrom.

Completely insane, Rimmer orders that his shipmates should spend two hours W. O. O. as punishment for their behaviour. W. O. O. means WithOut Oxygen but fortunately for all concerned, another dose of the good-luck virus gives Lister the fortune he needs to provide an escape route. Pursued through the corridors of *Red Dwarf* by the fanatical Rimmer – who has now, like Lanstrom, developed hex vision, telepathy and telekinesis – Lister, Cat and Kryten are cut off from the hologram projection unit with which Kryten feels he can do something about Rimmer's current problem. However, Lister's luck comes into play again as the equipment necessary to set up a remote link just happens to be found lying beside them. Not a moment too soon, Kryten is able to reverse the effects of the holo-virus, although Lister believes his good luck must have worn off when he discovers that Rimmer is, in fact, perfectly okay. Finally, a startled Rimmer wakes to find himself confined to quarantine, and supervised by his three crewmates, who have clothed themselves in a matching set of red and white checked gingham dresses . . .

5: DEMONS AND ANGELS.

Broadcast date: 19 March 1992.

Guest cast: None.

Kryten has developed another incredible device – a triplicator, which can create two extra copies of anything that is placed within its field. There are only three drawbacks. Firstly, the copies have a lifespan of one hour only. Secondly, whilst one is infinitely superior to the original, the other is infinitely worse. And finally, when Kryten attempts to reverse the procedure, *Red Dwarf* explodes – which is a bit of a problem for all concerned. Although the crew escape in *Starbug*, they soon realise that they don't have long to live. Even if they had enough fuel to reach a habitable planet, it would do them little good, as they only have enough oxygen for seven minutes. Rimmer and Kryten don't need oxygen of course, and Rimmer wonders if the jettisoning of Lister and Cat's corpses would lighten their load enough to reach safety. However, his plans are abruptly curtailed when Kryten points out that, as a hologram relying on emergency power only, he himself has less than four minutes of run-time left. Lister takes charge of the situation, and suggests a search of the wreckage for any oxygen or fuel tanks. What they find instead is something quite remarkable. Where once there was one *Red Dwarf*, there are now two – products, obviously, of the triplicator. Kryten surmises that instead of reversing the triplicating process, the machine actually reversed its field, thus re-creating *Red Dwarf* and everything on it. It was obviously the tremendous power drain required by this that caused the original to explode. Of course, these two new ships will be 'high' and 'low' versions of the original, and they will both fade away in one hour's time, but as each ship should have a triplicator of its own, Kryten feels that it should be no problem to reverse the procedure and merge the two vessels back into a perfect copy of the original. Of course, things don't go quite that smoothly. The two *Red Dwarf* s come complete with their own crews, and on the first ship, Lister, Rimmer, Cat and Kryten encounter spiritually enlightened versions of their own selves. The real difficulties begin, however, when the originals and their 'high' copies fly over to the 'low' ship, and instantly come under fire from the homicidal maniacs who have been formed from the dark sides of their own natures. Pacifists to the end, the 'high' Cat and Kryten attempt to reason with their counterparts, and are mercilessly slain. Lister is captured, and a spinal implant allows his 'low' self to dictate his every movement by remote control. He is forced to knife the 'high' Lister to death, and likewise to kill the 'high' Rimmer by crushing his light bee. Meanwhile, Rimmer, Cat and Kryten have made their way to the cargo bay with both triplicators, but they only have two minutes to evacuate the 'low' ship before it disappears.

Lister arrives at the last instant, but rather delays things by trying to murder the Cat. Kryten's chloroform pads put him out of action, a little less painfully than the Cat's attempt, which consisted of a knee to the groin. With only seconds to spare, the four originals pilot *Starbug* out into space, and watch as both the 'high' and 'low' ships vanish, to be replaced as planned by their own vessel, back in full working order. However, there is still the problem of the spinal implant to contend with. With Lister still acting like a homicidal maniac, it becomes obvious that, despite the disappearance of the 'low' ship, the remote control unit and its operator have survived – and a quick blast of bazookoid fire brings the 'low' Lister out of hiding. Still smarting at the damage the controlled Lister did to his neckline, the Cat is delighted when he gains possession of the control unit. Kryten can remove the implant easily enough, but the Cat pleads with him to leave it in situ – just for one more week.

6: BACK TO REALITY

Broadcast date: 26 March 1992.

Guest cast: Timothy Spall (Andy), Lenny Von Dohlen (Cop), Anastasia Hille (New Kochanski), Marie McCarthy (Nurse), Jake Sharian (New Lister).

On a recon mission to an ocean planet, the *Red Dwarf* crew discover the wreckage of the SSS *Esperanto*, from which a marine seeding experiment once took place. Quite remarkably, it seems that the entire crew have committed suicide, even down to a haddock, which closed its own gills and suffocated itself. The reason soon becomes obvious, as Lister, Kryten and the Cat begin to suffer bouts of depression, caused by the presence of a substance which, Kryten theorises, is some kind of ink, such as might be squirted from a particularly large and dangerous version of a squid. From his safe haven back in *Starbug*, Rimmer is able not only to confirm Kryten's conjecture, but also to pinpoint the monstrous creature itself – no hard task, as it is frighteningly close, and getting nearer. One hurried return to the 'Bug later, Holly lifts off for an immediate retreat, but the squid is too quick, and its deadly ink surrounds the fleeing vessel. Even as it does, *Starbug* veers out of control and into a quite spectacular crash. The vessel is completely destroyed and, needless to say, everyone on board suffers an immediate death. That means only one thing, of course. Game Over. Lister, Rimmer, Cat and Kryten suddenly find themselves alive and awake, and plugged into 'Red Dwarf – the Total Immersion Video Game' in which, after playing for four years, they have accumulated the phenomenal score of 4 per cent. Leisure World attendant Andy gleefully points out the areas they missed. Had they found the Captain's message, hidden in microdot form in the letter 'i' on one of Rimmer's swimming certificates, they would have discovered that Rimmer was in fact a hand-picked special agent for the Space Corps, on a secret mission to destroy *Red Dwarf* and guide Lister to his destiny as the creator of the Second Universe. Andy is quite amused that, having missed that blatant clue, the group had been stuck with the prat version of Rimmer for four years. And how could Lister not have got Kochanski – the whole object of the game for him? Dejected, the foursome head for the recuperation lounge, passing on the way the group who are to replace them as Lister and company in the next game. The question on everybody's addled minds is now – who are they really? The Cat, for one, is not very pleased with the answer. He is Duane Dibbley, a 'no-style gimbo with teeth that druids could use as a place of worship'. Kryten, however, is quite happy with his new half-human form and his identity as Jake Bullet, an agent for the Cybernautic Division of the Police Department. Of course, says Rimmer, the Cybernautic Division could be traffic control ... Most ironic of all, Lister and Rimmer turn out to be half-brothers. The twist is, Lister's new persona of Sebastian Doyle is a wealthy man, whilst brother Billy is a homeless tramp. Dispirited by this information, Dibbley, Bullet and the Doyles set out to reacclimatise themselves to the fascist world in which they apparently live. However, they barely manage to get to the car park, and Sebastian's limousine, before they find themselves on the wrong end of a policeman's gun. Oh, and the Cybernautic Division does turn out to be traffic control. Big trouble! Only the sight of Sebastian Doyle saves the group from a fate exactly the same as death. The old Lister learns with horror that he is really the Head of this totalitarian state's Ministry of Alteration – where people are altered from being alive to being dead. The news doesn't sit well with him. Nor is Kryten particularly pleased when, to save a young child from becoming the next victim of the fascist system, he is forced to shoot the cop down in cold blood. The group flee, but they realise they won't get far. In fact, none of them have gone very far at all. Back on *Starbug*,

Holly watches with concern as Lister, Rimmer, Cat and Kryten veer madly around the cockpit, trapped in a shared hallucination caused by the Despair Squid's ink. Inevitably, the events they are 'witnessing' take their toll, and the four huddle together, ready to bid goodbye to life in the same way as the crew of the Esperanto. Finally, and in the nick of time, Holly is able to communicate with Kryten by broadcasting on a higher frequency, persuading him to make the moves which, in real life, will release a dose of lithium carbonate – a mood stabiliser – into the cockpit. A confused crew come back to reality, where Holly assures them that her limpet mines have seen off their attacker. All that is left then is for all to thank their good fortune, and to make their weary way back to *Red Dwarf*.

RED DWARF VI

Regulars: Rimmer – Chris Barrie. Lister – Craig Charles. Cat – Danny John-Jules. Kryten – Robert Llewellyn. Written by Rob Grant and Doug Naylor. Produced by Justin Judd. Directed by Andy de Emmony. A Grant Naylor Production for BBC North.

1: PSIRENS

Broadcast date: 7 October 1993.

Guest cast: Jenny Agutter (Professor Mamet), Samantha Robson (Pete Tranter's Sister), Anita Dobson (Captain Tau), Richard Ridings (Crazed Astro), C. P. Grogan (Kochanski), Zoe Hilson and Elizabeth Anson (Temptresses). Featuring the hands of Phil Manzanera.

Lister wakes from deep-sleep on *Starbug*, to find he has amnesia.

Kryten fills in some details, and Lister is appalled to learn that he's a curry-eating slob. He also discovers that he can't play the guitar, although Kryten assures him that, once he regains his memory, he'll believe he can. A synaptic enhancer helps restore his mind, whilst Rimmer's hologram is rebooted. The crew have been out of action for two hundred years, ever since *Red Dwarf* was apparently stolen. Kryten has woken them because they finally have a chance of recovering it. The ship has taken a detour round an asteroid belt, but the smaller *Starbug* can slip through unharmed, thus closing the gap between them.

They head into the belt, but find themselves navigating through a spaceship graveyard. A message written with intestines and blood warns them of psirens, shape-changing GELFs which lure unwary travellers to them and suck their brains out through straws. Two temptresses appear on the screen, begging for someone to fertilise their planet of three thousand women. Cat volunteers and only the common sense of the others saves him. The psirens then try their charms on Lister, presenting an image of his lost love Kochanski. He too resists, and Kryten also exposes a giant flaming meteorite as a similar illusion. A second such hazard is all too real though, and *Starbug* plummets down onto an asteroid. The landing stanchion is buried, so Lister goes out to repair it – to be confronted by the image of Pete Tranter's sister, whom he lusted after through puberty. A second GELF arrives, in the form of Kryten and a battle breaks out over his brains. He escapes, but unfortunately two Listers return to *Starbug* and the others have to work out which is which. The guitar test eventually separates them: having copied Lister's mind perfectly, the GELF believes it can play well and thus does so. Cat and Kryten shoot the creature without hesitation, and it flees into the ship's depths. When Kryten finds it, it emulates Professor Mamet, his creator, whom he is programmed to obey. It orders him into the waste compactor.

Meanwhile, Rimmer's power-pack runs down and he fades away. Then Lister and Cat discover a brand-new drinks machine, realising too late that it's a less than cunning psiren disguise. Producing a straw, the creature prepares to feast. But it has reckoned without Kryten's versatility. Emerging from the compactor as a cubic mass of trash, he drops onto the intruder from a great height.

2: LEGION

Broadcast date: 14 October 1993.

Guest cast: Nigel Williams (Legion).

Twenty-four hours behind *Red Dwarf*, and *Starbug* is losing ground. Worse, space weevils have invaded the food stores and the only meat left is . . . space weevil. Lister's 'crunchy king prawn' meal is fortunately interrupted, when an imminent threat sets Cat's nostril hairs vibrating. A heat-seeking missile has locked onto the ship and neither the blue alert bulb nor Rimmer's surrender seem likely to stop it. When the 'missile' hits, it forms an energy globe round *Starbug*, guiding it to a space station where the exploring crew are confronted by a being called Legion. Legion proves both his skills and his good intentions by removing Lister's appendix (which was on the verge of peritonitis) and converting Rimmer's soft-light drive into a hard-light one. The visitors are then guided into a hall filled with the finest pieces of art created. Legion is clearly a remarkable being, and Rimmer sees the value in signing him up to join the crew. Unfortunately, this means showing him that they aren't the uncouth morons Lister seems to be, and a skirmish with Mamosian anti-matter chopsticks does nothing to help. In the event, Legion has other plans anyway. The Dwarfers, he states, must remain with him until they die.

Legion shows his captives to their luxurious 'cells'. Features of Lister's room include eight-packs of lager, sugar puff sandwiches and a spare pair of sneakers in the ice box, whilst

Rimmer's is perfect down to the over-starched pyjamas and nocturnal boxing gloves. Likewise Kryten, faced with dirty floors and a mop, is in hog heaven. However, despite the opulence of their surroundings, they are still prisoners – and Lister's cunning escape plan, culled from the film *Revenge of the Surf-Boarding Killer Bikini Vampire Girls*, does nothing to change that. In fighting off Lister, Legion loses his face-plate and the truth becomes obvious. His features are an amalgam of the *Red Dwarf* crews' own; Legion is a gestalt entity, a being made up of the essences of others. The various scientific and artistic triumphs around him were achieved during his previous incarnation, composed of five of the most brilliant minds of the 23rd century. Since their deaths, Legion has been unable to live and he is now forced to maintain his existence through his present guests. However, Kryten knocks out Lister and Cat, removing their personalities from Legion's mix. Rimmer, with his new invulnerable form, is more problematic: even smashing him over the head with a vase doesn't help, and the hologram finally has to reach inside himself and remove his own light bee. Left with only Kryten to draw on, Legion becomes the android's double, sharing his regard for human life and thus compelled to carry the *Starbug* crew to safety. He even leaves them with a star-drive, which could make the journey to *Red Dwarf* in nanoseconds. Despite a healthy scepticism from the crew, it actually works. But due to a faulty connection, it doesn't take *Starbug* with it.

3: GUNMEN OF THE APOCALYPSE

Broadcast date: 21 October 1993.

Guest cast: Jennifer Calvert (Loretta), Denis Lill (Simulant Captain/Death), Liz Hickling (Simulant Lieutenant), Imogen Bain (Lola), Steve Devereaux (Jimmy), Robert Inch (War),

Jeremy Peters (Pestilence), Dinny Powell (Famine), Stephen Marcus (Bear Strangler McGee).

Starbug has strayed into a rogue simulant hunting zone. The crew switch to silent running, to avoid detection; however, this means prying Lister away from the Artificial Reality machine in which he acts out his sexual fantasies. Shut-down comes too late: the ship is detected by a battle-class cruiser and hailed by its xenophobic occupants. Knowing that simulants loathe humans, Lister and Cat concoct a ruse involving Kryten's detachable eyeballs, their own chins and the act of lying upside down beneath a camera. The simulants are not impressed, and when their captain teleports onto *Starbug*, he discovers the truth of the so-called Vindalooan people. These four pathetic specimens, he decides, will prove no sport at all. He guns them down, and they wake three weeks later in a *Starbug* which has been upgraded and fitted with laser cannons. The simulants are expecting a game of cat and mouse, and as the Cat states, the only way to win that is by not being the mouse. To their enemies' surprise, *Starbug* attacks, and a fluke hit brings the simulant ship down. However, the captain transmits an Armageddon Virus into *Starbug*'s navi-comp. Locked onto a suicide course and only thirty-eight minutes from a large moon, the Dwarfers have one chance of survival. Kryten contracts the virus himself and, inside his own mind, struggles to create a dove program to eradicate the infection. The others patch into his dreams and view his misadventures as a sheriff in the Old West, where the virus is represented by the 'Four Apocalypse Boys'. However, it is stronger than Kryten predicted. His systems can't cope, and his dream persona turns to drink. For once, one of Cat's suggestions proves good: using the Artificial Reality console, the crew beam themselves into Kryten's dreams, as characters from an AR game. Lister is Brett Riverboat, knife thrower; Rimmer is Dangerous Dan McGrew, barefist fighter; and Cat is the gunslinging Riviera Kid. The trio's newfound skills stand them in good stead when Rimmer precipitates a bar-room brawl, and they are able to drag Kryten to safety.

Time runs out quickly. The Apocalypse Boys – War, Famine, Pestilence and Death – ride into town, determined to rid themselves of Kryten. When the sheriff's new protectors face them, Death decides to even the odds. The virus spreads to the AR machine, and their special skills are erased . . . as Rimmer discovers during his all too physical confrontation with War. Outnumbered and outgunned, Lister, Rimmer and Cat leave the game. Everything is up to Kryten now, but the others have bought him the time he needs. He tells the Apocalypse Boys to go for their guns, then brings them down with his own dove program and 'spreads peace through the system'. Returning to the real world, Kryten only has to feed this antidote into the navi-comp. He does so, even as *Starbug* disappears beneath the molten surface of the moon. Tense seconds later, it explodes back into the atmosphere, and heads for the hills to a quartet of triumphant cries: 'Yeeee-haaaa!'

4: EMOHAWK – POLYMORPH II.

Broadcast date: 28 October 1993.

Guest cast: Hugh Quarshie (Computer), Martin Sims (GELF), Ainsley Harriott (GELF Chief), Steven Wickham (GELF Bride).

Rimmer's petty-minded enforcement of Space Corps drills is halted by a real-life emergency. A computer-operated Space Corps External Enforcement Vessel charges the *Starbug* crew with looting derelicts. Frontier law decrees that the penalty is death – and, being totally guilty, the Dwarfers can't persuade their accuser otherwise. They flee towards a GELF zone, gambling that the vessel will not follow them. Struck by pulse bolts, they nevertheless make the trip successfully, and land safe but not sound on a GELF moon. *Starbug*'s auto-repair systems can handle most of the damage, but the oxy-generation (O/G) unit is a charred mess. The crew set out towards the nearest GELF settlement, and Kryten is pleased when they are afforded the creatures' warmest welcome: not being skinned alive. Presentation of a cornucopia of gifts, from Swiss watches to Levi jeans, buys the Dwarfers entry to the *watunga* – or hut – of the Kinitawowi tribe. There, the real negotiations begin. The tribe have an O/G unit . . . but the price for it is Lister.

She may be the looker of the family, but Lister is not pleased at the thought of marrying the tribal chief's daughter: a warty yeti lookalike whose name sounds like a footballer clearing his nose. After some persuasion though, he agrees to walk down the aisle. The plan is a simple one: leaving with the O/G unit, Kryten and the others will repair *Starbug* and come back for their colleague. However, when his new bride demands her conjugal rights, Lister brings his planned escape forward. Pursued by outraged GELFs, the crew return to *Starbug* and make a hasty departure. However, the chief's pet emohawk – a domesticated polymorph – has sneaked on board. Like its larger cousin, it steals emotions: it takes Cat's cool and Rimmer's bitterness, turning the pair into Duane Dibbley and Ace Rimmer respectively. Ace seals Lister and Kryten in the engine room and prepares to sacrifice himself and Duane by opening the airlock, expelling the emohawk from the ship. However, his captives break free in time to prevent his foolish sacrifice. Armed with liquid dilinium, the quartet pursue their quarry on the engine decks, where Dibbley is the first to encounter the monster, disguised as his thermos flask. The emohawk metamorphoses into a grenade and Ace saves everyone by using his hard-light body to cushion the explosion. Lister freezes the creature with dilinium. By extracting DNA strands from the emohawk and reinjecting them into his colleagues, Kryten can return them to normal. However, Ace requests a twenty-four hour stay before his return to negativity and snidiness. Duane can't wait to get back to being the stylish Cat since, as Duane Dibbley, he never knows when the next klutzy thing is going to happen. His accidental triggering of the dilinium and the consequent freezing of his crewmates proves the point.

5: RIMMERWORLD

Broadcast date: 4 November 1993.

Guest cast: Liz Hickling (Rogue Simulant).

Despite cheating at his medical examination, Rimmer doesn't get the results he'd hoped for. Kryten advises a program of relaxation and the regular grinding of Chinese worry balls to stave off a stress-related electronic aneurism. Unfortunately, rest doesn't seem to be on the cards. *Starbug*'s refrigeration unit has packed in, and unless the crew wish to survive indefinitely on Kryten's fungus scrapings, they have to steal fresh supplies from the Simulant ship they shot down a few weeks ago. Rimmer argues that the expedition beggars logic. Not only might one of the xenophobic killers still be functioning, but the ship's superstructure has been weakened and the whole thing will soon disintegrate. Lister, however, breaks more bad news: the reserve fuel tank has been punctured and fuel is urgently needed. The crew board the Simulant ship and, using its teleporter, transport goods onto *Starbug*. But, true to form, one Simulant Lieutenant has survived the crash. She confronts Lister, Kryten and Cat, and even Lister's request for a date isn't enough to save them from death. Undetected, Rimmer might be their key to survival – but he's more interested in saving his own neck. Diving into an escape pod, he unwittingly sets off a shipquake and, taking advantage of the distraction, his colleagues teleport back to their ship. Unfortunately, they also jump a timeline, and find themselves a few days back into their own past. Kryten corrects the fault, and *Starbug* jets out of the ship even as it falls to pieces. Retrieving Rimmer is not so simple. His pod was looted by the Simulants from a seeding ship, and it's heading for the nearest S3 planet. That turns out to be on the other side of a nearby wormhole, which creates a rather interesting time dilation effect. Although it will take only an hour or so for *Starbug* to follow the pod's path, almost six hundred years will pass for Rimmer.

Rimmer arrives on the barren planet which he christens Rimmerworld. Thanks to a pair of eco-accelerator rockets in the pod, he is able to transform it into a lush paradise in seven days. His attempts at genetic cloning start off less successfully; his perfect female mate turns out to be an exact copy of himself. He resolves to try again – and six hundred years later, *Starbug* lands on a planet which, according to Kryten, displays thousands of life-signs. Almost immediately after arriving, they are set upon by armoured Rimmer clones. They take the captives to their leader, who wears the letter 'H' as a holy sign but, as Cat detects, is not the real Rimmer. The trio are accused of displaying un-Rimmerlike behaviour such as bravery, charm and compassion. They will be executed at dawn, and in the meantime, they are taken to a cell which they share with a certain cloaked figure who has been there long enough to wear a pair of Chinese worry balls down to the size of ball bearings. Rimmer has been in prison for five hundred and fifty-seven years, having been overthrown by his own snidy, double-dealing clones. Lister decides it's time they left, and formulates a daring escape plan involving knotted sheets and cunning disguises. Kryten suggests they use the teleporter instead, but another callibration fault takes them temporarily into their own future . . . where, apparently, the crew are bemoaning the fate which awaits Dave Lister!

6: OUT OF TIME

Broadcast date: 11 November 1993.

Guest cast: None.

Starbug has lost *Red Dwarf*, and relations are becoming strained. Even Rimmer's weekly moral meetings offer no help. Then the ship runs into a storm front and a nasty jolt wounds Lister and reveals a startling fact: he's a 3000 series android, made to look realistically human and technically of a lower rank than Kryten. Kryten takes the news badly. All these years he's been looking up to Lister – worse, scrubbing his gussets. Taking command of the ship, he ensures that his former idol goes about his new cooking and cleaning chores diligently. However, Kryten soon realises that *Starbug* is passing through pockets of unreality and distorting the perceptions of its crew. Restored to the helm and waited on by a mortified android, Lister guides the ship through the reality minefield, which first causes the Cat to disappear then fits the entire crew out with animal heads before stealing *Starbug* from around them. Kryten theorises that this is a defensive device fitted to a Space Corps test ship, something with a prototype drive so powerful that no one must get their hands on it. The test ship will be at the epicentre of the field, so to prevent the crew from being distracted by more hallucinations, he places Lister and Cat in suspended animation and guides *Starbug* in himself. One quick looting mission later, the Dwarfers have their own time-drive – as a quick trip to take in the heady medieval atmosphere of deep space proves.

Returning to their own time, the crew receive an SOS message from what appears to be another *Starbug*. It transpires that on board the ship are their own future selves. Their time-drive has malfunctioned, and they need to copy components from the newer machine. Kryten is wary of communicating with them, worried about the crew seeing their own future. However, they can't ignore a plea for help. Kryten volunteers to meet the future versions himself, as he can wipe his brain of what he learns. However, the discovery that something horrible has happened to Lister proves more than he can cope with. The future crew board the ship, and Lister, Rimmer and Cat are sealed on the obs deck to avoid meeting them. However, Lister patches the medi-scan through to the monitors and watches delightedly as a balding Cat, an obese Rimmer and a wig-wearing Kryten arrive on board. Then he sees himself: merely a brain floating in a tank!

Kryten learns that, having found the long-sought star-drive, the future crew are now epicures, travelling through time and enjoying the best that mankind has to offer. Unfortunately, most of the best is in the hands of ruthless dictators, and Kryten is startled to learn that they consort with the likes of Louis XVI and Adolf Hitler. Lister, too, has heard enough. He shoots his way off the ops deck and demands that the visitors leave. They are forced to agree, but upon returning to their ship, they broadcast this warning: if they can't have the time-drive, then no one can. They will fight for it to the death. Lister is prepared to engage them, as is Cat – and Kryten would rather die than wear that toupee. To everyone's astonishment, even Rimmer announces that he's 'Better dead than smeg!' They go in hard, but the fight is decidedly one-sided. Lister drops first, then Cat, then Kryten, whose last words indicate that there might yet be a way out. Seizing upon this hope, Rimmer grabs a bazookoid, heads for the time-drive and fires, just as *Starbug* explodes . . .

TO BE CONTINUED

BOHEMIAN RHAPSODY.

Is this the real life? Is this just fantasy? Or are we just cheating by mentioning an obviously non-canonical appearance in this section? Actually, a mixture of all three – as in the midst of 1993's Comic Relief event, sharp-eyed Dwarf fans were treated to an unexpected appearance by their heroes.

'Comic Relief asked us to do all kinds of things, actually,' Rob Grant says. Doug Naylor adds: 'We were going to do *Red Dwarf* and the Daleks at one point, but because the schedule was so horrific, there just wasn't time to do that.' Fortunately, the telethon organisers had a solution: the possé could still make their way onto our screens by appearing in a specially filmed video of the twice chart-topping Queen hit, 'Bohemian Rhapsody'.

The idea was a simple one, but effective on screen. Any celeb who fancied him or herself a pop star just set the cameras rolling and bopped along to the song. The impromptu performances were then collected and edited into one definitive video – in which you never knew quite who was going to turn up next. Amongst the stars on parade were the assembled casts of *Drop the Dead Donkey*, *Birds of a Feather*, *Jeeves and Wooster* and *Eldorado*. Nor was it only comedy shows which were spotlighted; the residents of Brookside Close contributed a few lines, as did such luminaries as Noel Edmonds, Andi Peters and Esther Rantzen. They even had Gordon the Gopher in there!

The *Red Dwarf* crew made their surprise appearances (seven in all, but who's counting?) towards the end of the montage, seated in the cockpit of *Starbug* and miming with gusto. 'We thought it was just a mime thing,' explains the show's most celebrated musician, Danny John-Jules. 'But in the end we watched it back and of course everyone else was bloody singing it. It looks like maybe we can't sing, or we don't want to sing!' Rob Grant confirms that that isn't the case: 'We've got a quite melodious crew really, with one exception I think . . .'

For those who keep an eye out for such things, 'Bohemian Rhapsody' was the television premiere of the *Red Dwarf VI* crew – that is to say, our first glimpse of the modified *Starbug* set and of Cat and Rimmer's new costumes. The sequence was shot after recording of 'Psirens' (on Saturday 20th February 1993, for those people who really have to know that sort of thing too), although the audience of the night remained unaware of this additional attraction, having already left the studio. Fortunately, Lister had been required to play guitar in the episode, thus the prop was handy for Craig Charles to make use of.

There was one problem though, which led to Robert Llewellyn's Kryten appearing sans nose. In what has become an end-of-recording tradition, the plastic proboscis was ripped from Robert's face by co-star Craig, neither realising that there was more filming to be done. Not even a red nose was available to cover the deficiency, and in the end only a dab of red paint could be found to make the mechanoid look more in keeping with the occasion.

Despite such hiccups, Danny at least enjoyed making the video. 'It was such an easy feeling – we just rolled cameras, played the playback and went for it from top to bottom, and they took out whichever bits they wanted to use. It wasn't like we had to rehearse it or anything, we just did it in one take.'

SECTION FOUR:

THE
INDEX

Capitals denote items which have their own entries elsewhere in the index.

A

A TO Z OF RED DWARF, THE: The book inside which RIMMER kept his diary hidden.

A TO Z OF THE UNIVERSE, THE: A comprehensive guide being compiled by HOLLY, including street names, post offices, steeples and everything.

ABORT SEQUENCE X1X: The AUTO-DESTRUCT system override, for which only Senior Officers have security clearance. Since all the Senior Officers are dead, HOLLY should really have thought to update this.

ACE: RIMMER's childhood nickname – which unfortunately, none of the other kids would use, no matter how much he let them beat him up. They preferred instead to refer to him as BONEHEAD.

ADVANCED MUTUAL COMPATIBILITY ON THE BASIS OF PRIMARY INITIAL IDENT: The state experienced by KRYTEN and CAMILLE upon their meeting each other for the first time. Humans would refer to the sensation as 'LOVE at first sight'.

AENEID, THE: After reading a comic book version of Virgil's epic poem, featuring the story of the Wooden Horse, LISTER came to the conclusion that the adage 'Beware Greeks bearing gifts' should be amended to 'Beware Trojans, they're complete SMEGheads'.

AFTER-EIGHT MINTS: At the last count, there was only one of these left on board RED DWARF – and everyone is too polite to take it.

AGORAPHOBICS SOCIETY: LISTER claimed to belong to this group in order to explain his presence – along with RIMMER's and the CAT's – in a shower cubicle together. The real explanation of course, is that they had just travelled back in time via a STASIS LEAK, and had found themselves there by accident.

AIGBURTH ARMS: A Liverpool Public House which was the setting for a great deal of DAVE LISTER's misspent youth.

AIR, JANE: A Mapping Officer on board the NOVA 5. The RED DWARF crew discovered her body when they answered a distress call from the ship's MECHANOID, KRYTEN. See also GILL, ANNE and JOHNS, TRACEY.

ALBANIAN STATE WASHING MACHINE COMPANY: An organisation which boasts technology in advance of STARBUG's. Nothing unusual there.

ALBERT: LISTER's pet mould, which he intended to grow to a height of two feet. Albert was tragically killed when KRYTEN washed out the cup he was living in.

ALEXANDER THE GREAT: RIMMER believes that in a past life, he was in this Emperor's household as the CHIEF EUNUCH.

ALICE: RIMMER's cousin; daughter of his UNCLE FRANK, and twin sister of his cousin SARAH. RIMMER wasn't sure if she fancied him or not. Chances are she didn't!

ALIEN INVASION FLEET: Fortunately this turned out to be one of LISTER's old sneezes congealed on the radar screen.

ALIENS: Theoretical creatures from other worlds. Despite scientific evidence to the contrary, RIMMER believes in their existence fervently, and uses them to rationalise any phenomenon he cannot himself explain. His fondest hope is that he will run into the alien QUAGAARS and that they will use their advanced technology to provide him with a new body. Of course, both the race and the technology are products of his own imagination.

ALISON: A fictional sister, for whom RIMMER requested NAPOLEON's autograph when the two met in a BETTER THAN LIFE fantasy. Apparently, her name was shortened to Arnie!

ALLMAN, THOMAS: An unfortunate who was adjudged unworthy of having existed by the INQUISITOR and was consequently erased from history.

ALL-NATIONS AGREEMENT: That great preserver of democracy which, amongst other things, stipulates the right of POWs to non-violent constraint, and makes sure the Chinese don't take too many car park spaces.

ALPHABETTI SPAGHETTI: Allegedly used as some form of sex aid by LISTER and the POLYMORPH, when the latter was in the form of MRS RIMMER.

AMATEUR HAMMOND ORGAN RECITAL NIGHT: Wednesdays – the day on which RIMMER leads the SKUTTERS in playing his favourite instrument, much to the annoyance of the rest of the crew.

AMNESIA: This condition deserves a mention here; we just can't remember why.

ANEURISM, ELECTRONIC: The unpleasant fate awaiting RIMMER if he can't avoid stressful situations.

ANDROID HOME BREW: A sort of cross between Vimto and liquid nitrogen, this intoxicant was designed by HOLLY in order for KRYTEN to properly celebrate his last day party.

ANDROIDS: (1) Otherwise known as MECHANOIDS. These mechanical creatures were built by humans purely to serve. Each has been programmed to believe in the fictional notion of SILICON HEAVEN, as an encouragement for them to obey their masters.

ANDROIDS: (2) KRYTEN's favourite soap opera. This GROOVY CHANNEL 27 production featured Android 14762/E as KELLY, Android 97542/P as BROOK, Android 442I53/2 as Simone, Android 72264/Y as Gary, Android 24/A as Brooke Jnr, Android 980612/L as Bruce and Android 791265/B as the Android in the Bus Queue. The show was produced and directed by KYLIE GWENLYN.

ANDY: A Brummie twonk who was actually the product of a group HALLUCINATION. He was the the LEISURE WORLD staff member who greeted DUANE DIBLEY's party as they emerged from the RED DWARF TOTAL IMMERSION VIDEO GAME, and happily ridiculed their performance.

ANGER: The emotion the POLYMORPH stole from RIMMER. It coaxed it from him by taking on the form of MRS RIMMER and waxing lyrical on the tricks that LISTER could get up to with ALPHABETTI SPAGHETTI.

ANORAK: An essential component of DUANE DIBLEY's tasteful attire – and the final nail in the CAT's coffin!

APPENDIX: Of course, LISTER couldn't have had his appendix taken out twice, hence these four possible explanations:
1) When LEGION claimed to have removed said object to prevent PERITONITIS, he was really engaging LISTER's trust through an insidious illusion.
2) So confused was he by LISTER's pasting of eight months' memories into his mind, that RIMMER only thought those eight

months included an appendectomy.

3) LISTER made a mistake whilst working on RIMMER's mind, so that someone else's recollection of the operation strayed into his mind.

4) Rob and Doug screwed up.

ARCHANGEL GABRIEL, THE: Fearful for his existence, when attempting to justify himself to THE INQUISITOR, RIMMER claimed to have had a vision of this heavenly apparition and to have become an instant convert.

ARIES: LISTER's star-sign. So now you know.

ARKS: The means by which the CAT PEOPLE left RED DWARF. There were two of these; one for the CAT faction which believed the CARDBOARD HATS on FUCHAL should be red, and one for those who believed they should be blue. Unfortunately, the Blue-Hats, who were in the first of the arks, used LISTER's LAUNDRY list as a star chart and crashed straight into an asteroid.

ARMAGEDDON VIRUS: A computer virus programmed into STARBUG's navi-comp by the defeated SIMULANTS, who were obviously sore losers. *See* DOVE PROGRAMME.

ARMIES DU NORD: Amongst RIMMER's most prized possessions were a full set of miniature replicas of this army, hand-carved by the legendary DUBOIS BROTHERS. However, when he and LISTER were marooned on an ICE PLANET, they had to be burnt to ensure LISTER's survival.

ARMSTRONG, NELLIE: The first woman on the moon in the female dominated PARALLEL UNIVERSE.

ARNOLD J RIMMER - A TRIBUTE: The video RIMMER made of his own death, which featured an extensive eulogy and poetry readings – by himself.

ARROWS: Weapons from which CAT's sense of smell can glean a great deal of information. On the GELF moon of the

KINITAWOWI, he was able to determine that one such projectile had been shot from a bow.

ART COLLEGE: Attended by LISTER...for ninety-seven minutes.

ARTICLES: Presumably working hand in hand with the SPACE CORPS DIRECTIVES, these are the guidelines by which QUEEG insisted RED DWARF be run. In particular, Article 5 states that in the event of the ship's computer being guilty of gross negligence leading to the endangerment of personnel, the back-up computer (QUEEG himself) should take over its position. When this happened, the crew initially saw the move as a good one – until QUEEG invoked Article 497, which required them to work in order to earn credits for their food. Of course, as QUEEG was really HOLLY all along, it is disputable how much of what you have just read is in fact true.

ARTIFICIAL REALITY MACHINE: Similar to TIV technology. Well, exactly the same really. The DWARFERS picked up an AR console from a derelict spacecraft, and LISTER used it to play such role-playing GAMES as GUMSHOE and STREETS OF LAREDO. More precisely, he used it to simulate SEX, notably with LORETTA. And with the ball girl in Wimbledon. She might have been jail bait, but at least she had great pixels.

ASTEROID SPOTTING: A pastime enjoyed by RIMMER, who sometimes asks KRYTEN to take him out in *STARBUG* for this purpose.

ASTEROIDAL LICHEN STEW: Along with DANDELION SORBET and SPACE NETTLE SOUP, this culinary delight prompted LISTER to risk life and limb in pursuit of better food supplies.

ASTRO-NAVIGATION AND INVISIBLE NUMBERS IN ENGINEERING STRUCTURE MADE SIMPLE: A book owned by ARNOLD RIMMER – for all the good it ever did him.

ATHLETES' FOOT: Suffered by LISTER and left untreated when RIMMER borrowed his body. The best treatment he has found for it so far has been RIMMER's abortive attempt at making a lemon meringue pie.

ATTACK OF THE KILLER GOOSEBERRIES: A film of which HOLLY was reminded when, his consciousness having been projected into a WRIST WATCH, he discovered a large hole in LISTER's pocket.

AUNTIE MAGGIE: One of RIMMER's relatives, whose birthday fell on July 17th.

AUTO-DESTRUCT: All spaceships seem to include this facility, which must make most space travellers rather nervous. When a crazed SKUTTER wired RED DWARF's destruct system to a food DISPENSER, it was fortunate that HOLLY had previously had the foresight to remove the bomb. It was just a pity that she neglected to mention the fact to anyone.

AUTO-PILOT: Well, in actual fact 'it's Muggins here that has to do it,' as HOLLY is quick to remind us.

AUTO-REPAIR: *See* SELF-REPAIR UNIT.

AWOOGA: The distinctive sound of RED DWARF's klaxon alarm, or at least HOLLY's verbal equivalent. As the CAT says, when the Awooga waltz starts it's time to do a quick step to cover.

B

BACKLOG: See BLACK BOX.

BACKWARDS EARTH: EARTH after THE BIG CRUNCH, on which time was running backwards. It was visited by the RED DWARF crew in the year 3991.

BANANA AND CRISP SANDWICHES: LISTER found one of these in ADOLF HITLER's briefcase, after using the TIMESLIDES to steal it from him; having been temporarily restored to life, RIMMER ate it.

BANANA BOMB: A drink enjoyed by LISTER in his BETTER THAN LIFE fantasy.

BANANA, GIANT INFLATABLE: An essential component of the tasteful decorations in LISTER and RIMMER's original bunk room.

BANANA YOGHURT, FAMILY-SIZED TUB OF: A prominent feature of one of the CAT's more enjoyable dreams. He apparently shared the interior of the tub with three beautiful girls.

BANGALORE BELLY: The condition to which LISTER put down what was actually a near-fatal case of peritonitis.

BARRINGTON, FIONA: A girl RIMMER got off with at the age of 15, in his father's green-house. RIMMER thought he'd got lucky, in fact he'd got his hand in warm compost.

BAR-ROOM TIDY: A non-violent reverse pub brawl, as indulged in by the RED DWARF crew on BACKWARDS EARTH.

BATTERING RAM: A use to which KRYTEN was not too pleased at being put. His six foot long, fairly sturdy construction – and his flat head! – made him the ideal device to enable the others to move around the ship when the electric doors ceased to operate. The experience so damaged his brain that he temporarily took to referring to LISTER as Susan.

BAXTER, BING: An American quiz show host, who LISTER associated with CONFIDENCE. When his own CONFIDENCE took on physical form, it assumed Baxter's voice.

BAY 47: Not only was this the location of QUARANTINE, but was also the place where the car belonging to SEBASTIAN

DOYLE was parked – an amazing coincidence or what?

BAZOOKOIDS: Heavy-duty weapons with a heat-seeking setting. These are standard issue on RED DWARF, and have been employed by the crew against creatures such as the POLYMORPH and RIMMER's SELF-LOATHING.

BEADLEBAUM, HARRY: A simple carpenter's son who went on to own the biggest chain of PIZZA stores in history.

BEANBAGS: Allegedly made by GELFS from the skins of their victims.

BEARDSLEY, PETER: An actor who starred in what LISTER considered to be the definitive remake of the film CASA-BLANCA. It is unknown whether or not he was in any way related to the twentieth century footballer of the same name. *See also* BINGLEBAT, MYRA.

BEER MILKSHAKE: See MARIJUANA GIN.

BELLINI, BARBRA: An officer aboard a prison ship, which was taking a group of SIMULANTS to JUSTICE WORLD. When a MUTINY led to the deaths of the entire crew, the one surviving SIMULANT abandoned ship in Barbra's personal ESCAPE POD. Needless to say, it was later picked up by the crew of RED DWARF, whose hopes for a date were rather thwarted.

BENTLEY V8 CONVERTIBLE: The vehicle belonging to his brother, in which RIMMER claimed to have lost his virginity to a girl called SANDRA.

BERMUDA TRIANGLE: This is, of course, one of the great mysteries of the universe ... how did that song ever get to be a hit?!

BERNI INN: One of the biggest advantages of being THREE MILLION YEARS into deep space is that the nearest example of this type of restaurant is sixty billion miles away.

Craig Charles gets ready for action.

SMEG HEAD!

Chris Barrie as the neurotic dead man, Arnold J Rimmer.

Danny John-Jules stars as the fashion-concious Cat.

Right: Norman Lovett, the original Holly, pictured unusually with arms and legs.

Below: Hattie Hayridge, Holly Number Two, showing here how black clothes can reduce the need for full amputation.

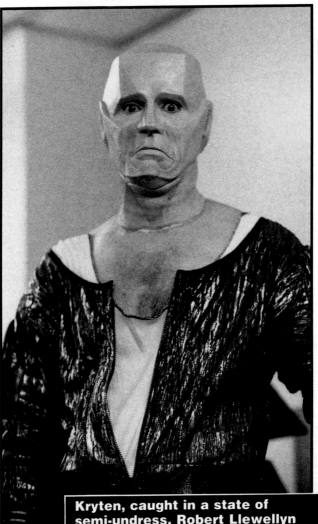

Kryten, caught in a state of semi-undress. Robert Llewellyn plays the laundry-loving mechanoid.

Visual effects supremo Peter Wragg, with the Self-Loathing creature not quite seen in 'Terrorform'.

The eponymous *Red Dwarf* itself, designed by Peter Wragg. More of the show's award-winning vessels follow.

WHITE MIDGET

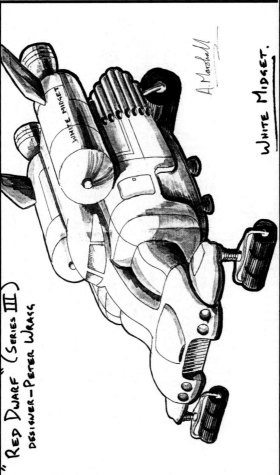

"RED DWARF" (SERIES III)
DESIGNER – PETER WRAGG

WHITE MIDGET.

A. Marshall

From the drawing board of Alan Marshall: the original design of the unused White Midget spacecraft for series III.

SSS ESPERANTO

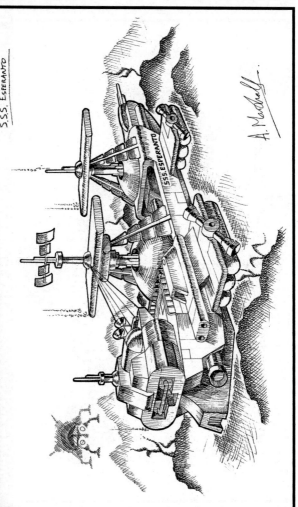

THE WRECK OF THE
S.S.S. ESPERANTO

SSS ESPERANTO

A. Maskell.

BETTER DEAD THAN SMEG: Even RIMMER agrees!

BETTER THAN LIFE: A fantasy GAME that allows the players to enjoy a shared illusion, in which everything they desire comes true. This was experimented with by LISTER, RIMMER and CAT. See also TOTAL IMMERSION VIDEO.

BEXLEY: LISTER's second son; see JIM for more details. Currently living in a PARALLEL UNIVERSE, Bexley will – if we can believe the FUTURE ECHOES – return to his death in the RED DWARF drive-room in his mid-twenties.

BHINDI-BHAJI: The companion of TARKA-DAL . . . actually the CAT.

BIG BLACK TOM: The real culprit responsible for FRANKENSTEIN's so called VIRGIN BIRTH.

BIG CRUNCH, THE: When the universe finally stops expanding, this reverse Big Bang will occur and time will begin to flow backwards.

BINGLEBAT, MYRA: An actress who starred in what LISTER considered to be the definitive remake of the film CASA-BLANCA. See also BEARDSLEY, PETER.

BINKS: A Commander aboard ENLIGHTENMENT who was not greatly impressed by the crew of RED DWARF. He curtailed his insults, however when LISTER threatened the use of a HOLOWHIP.

BIOLOGY CLASSES: One of the many lessons to which LISTER never paid any attention at school. In this one, he was more concerned with turning to page 47 of the text book and drawing little beards and moustaches on the sperms.

BIO-SUITS: The vitally important items of life saving protective apparel which LISTER, CAT and KRYTEN did not wear in the VIRAL RESEARCH DEPARTMENT.

BIRTHDAY PRESENT: Surprisingly, RIMMER once gave

LISTER a \$£5 BOOK token, though he had already borrowed \$£15 from LISTER to buy it with. He never paid it back, either.

BLACK BOX: RED DWARF's indestructible FLIGHT RE CORDER, which was buried temporarily on an unnamed planet. All space ships are required to have these and even KRYTEN possesses his own version, albeit smaller and considerably less useful.

BLACK CARD: An imaginary object called into existence by RIMMER when he wished to end a conversation with LISTER. *See also* WHITE CARD.

BLACK HOLE: A dangerous spacial phenomenon which sucks time and matter out of the universe. HOLLY evacuated RED DWARF when she thought it was about to run into five of these, but they turned out to be specks of GRIT on the monitor screen. She protested that black holes are actually quite difficult to spot in space, what with them being completely black.

BLACK-RIBBED KNOBBLER: LISTER's greatest ever catch when CONDOM FISHING was a magnificent two-pound specimen of this type.

BLOBS, HUGE GREEN: The best description we have of the race to which the PLEASURE GELF, CAMILLE and her husband HECTOR belonged.

BLUE ALERT: Engaged primarily to keep RIMMER happy, this emergency state serves to ensure that all crew members remain on their toes. On STARBUG it consists of a blue light flashing the word 'alert' on and off, and its effectiveness is thus questionable. *See also* RED ALERT.

BLUE-GREEN PLANETOID: Where RED DWARF was parked when last seen.

BLUE MIDGET: The smaller of the two types of shuttle-craft which the RED DWARF carries. *See also* STARBUG and WHITE MIDGET.

BLU-TACK: The means by which LISTER's posters are stuck to the wall of his bunk room. In fact, the Blu-Tack belongs to RIMMER, who attempted to take it with him when he moved out.

BOB: The name by which KRYTEN refers to one of the SKUTTERS.

BODY SWAP: *See* MIND SWAP.

BOG-BOT FROM HELL: *See* KRYTEN.

BOG ROLL: When an entire roll was used up in one day, RIMMER was convinced that ALIENS were responsible.

BONEHEAD: RIMMER's real childhood nickname. *See also* ACE.

BONGO: One of ACE RIMMER's friends in his own dimension. Bongo looked suspiciously like KRYTEN did when he attained human form – and both bore a startling resemblance to JIM REAPER. Amazing, eh?

BOOKS: According to RIMMER, LISTER has read the same number of books as Champion the Wonder Horse – zero. LISTER even admitted it on one occasion. Of course, neither were including any with lift-up flaps or where the main character is a DOG called Ben. His reading opportunities were further curtailed when he and RIMMER were marooned on an ICE PLANET, and LISTER had to burn many of their books to survive. These included *Biggles Learns to Fly*, LOLITA, *The Caretaker* by Harold Pinter and the complete works of WILLIAM SHAKESPEARE. Other books owned by RIMMER include THE A TO Z OF RED DWARF (actually a hollow shell in which his diary is kept), HOW TO PICK UP GIRLS BY HYPNOSIS, *1001 Fabulous Chat-up Lines* and ASTRO NAVIGATION AND INVISIBLE NUMBERS IN ENGINEERING STRUCTURE MADE SIMPLE. LISTER is also the proud owner of the POP-UP KARMA SUTRA – ZERO GRAVITY EDITION. Finally,

HOLLY claims to have read every book ever written, particularly enjoying the works of AGATHA CHRISTIE and particularly disliking Kevin Keegan's book, FOOTBALL – IT'S A FUNNY OLD GAME. It was once alleged that his entire store of knowledge came from THE JUNIOR COLOUR ENCYCLOPEDIA OF SPACE. *See also* CAT BOOKS.

BOOTLE MUNICIPAL GOLF COURSE: LISTER lost his virginity at the age of twelve to MICHELLE FISHER, by the tenth hole of this course – and he wasn't even a member of the club.

BOXER SHORTS: LISTER was quite upset when KRYTEN laundered his boxer shorts, transforming them into the bendable variety, but not quite as upset as he later became when he discovered that the pair he was wearing was actually a POLYMORPH.

BOXING, FEMALE TOPLESS: A sport greatly enjoyed by LISTER – as a spectator, of course.

BRAINS: PSIREN snacks, best enjoyed with the aid of a straw.

BRANNIGAN: The ship's psychiatrist, whose personality RIMMER temporarily took on when the HOLOGRAM SIMULATION SUITE was damaged.

BREAKFAST: LISTER shows a preference towards onion-covered cornflakes with tabasco sauce and chilled VINDALOO juice.

BREASTS: After messing around with KOCHANSKI's HOLOGRAM DISC, RIMMER was shocked to find himself left with one of these wobbly extremities. However, he was in no great hurry to be rid of it, unlike LISTER who developed a couple of large ones following RIMMER's misuse of his body during a MIND SWAP.

BROOK: A character in the ANDROIDS soap opera, presumably married to KELLY, who was shocked to discover that

Brooke Jnr was not his ANDROID. He was played by ANDROID 97542/P.

BROWN, CAROLE: An executive officer, whose mind was brought temporarily back into service for a failed attempt to abort the AUTO-DESTRUCT sequence.

BSc, SSc: The qualifications which RIMMER likes to quote himself as having. In fact, they stand for Bronze Swimming Certificate and Silver Swimming Certificate. In RED DWARF – THE TOTAL IMMERSION VIDEO GAME a microscopic message which CAPTAIN HOLLISTER had hidden in the letter 'i' on one of the certificates provided a blatant clue to the GAME's solution.

BUCHAN: A science officer on RED DWARF whose scientific knowledge was given to RIMMER via the MIND-PATCHING process. See also McQUEEN.

BULGARIA: A country not visited by any members of the RED DWARF crew whilst on BACKWARDS EARTH.

BULLET, JAKE: The macho-sounding detective from Cybernautics, who was actually responsible for traffic control – or would have been if the policeman hadn't been merely an imagined persona of KRYTEN.

BUTCH ACCOUNTANT AND THE YUPPIE KID: RIMMER's favourite type of Western, at least as far as LISTER can tell from his behaviour at the LAST CHANCE SALOON.

C

CADET SCHOOL: It is no surprise whatsoever to learn that RIMMER once attended such an establishment. The school in question was run by a Training Officer called CALDICOTT, and RIMMER's fondest memory of his time there was the occasion on which he beat him at RISK. Whilst there, he also enjoyed a brief liaison with a fellow cadet called SANDRA although, despite his claims, he never actually lost his virginity to her.

CADMIUM 2: The type of RADIATION that wiped out the entire crew of RED DWARF.

CALDICOTT: RIMMER's Training Officer at CADET SCHOOL.

CALLISTO: A moon of Jupiter, on which PETERSEN purchased a Build-It-Yourself MARILYN MONROE kit.

CAMERON MACKINTOSH AIR-COOLED DIESEL: A rarity which RIMMER was delighted to discover during his ten-day vacation on the DIESEL DECKS. Apparently, the item in question was a 184 – almost identical to the 179!

CAMILLE: A PLEASURE GELF with whom KRYTEN fell in love – even when she revealed her true form as being that of a HUGE GREEN BLOB. However, when her husband HECTOR arrived on the scene, the ANDROID took inspiration from CASABLANCA in persuading her to leave with her spouse.

CAPTAIN AJ RIMMER, SPACE ADVENTURER: How RIMMER wished to be referred to, in order to impress the crew of the NOVA 5. He also wouldn't have minded being called ACE or Big Man.

CAPTAIN'S TABLE: To RIMMER especially, the ultimate honour was to be invited to dine here. Unfortunately, he managed to ruin the occasion. *See* GAZPACHO SOUP.

CARDBOARD HATS: An intrinsic part of the CAT PEOPLE's view of Heaven, based on LISTER's own ambitions as related to FRANKENSTEIN. The hats were to be worn in the HOT DOG AND DOUGHNUT DINERS on FUCHAL. Unfortunately, nobody could agree on whether they should be red or blue, and vicious HOLY WARS broke out. LISTER was particularly saddened by this, as the hats were supposed to be green anyway.

CARGO BAY: The site of one of LISTER's more unpleasant experiences, when his safety harness snapped and he cracked his spine in three places. RIMMER found the whole incident extremely amusing, and said so. LISTER perhaps got his own back by smashing one of the STARBUGs into the cargo bay doors, although KRYTEN did rather a better destruction job with STARBUG 1 shortly before that. The cargo ramp here is also frequently used by LISTER and CAT when playing soap-sud slalom.

CARGO DECKS: The storage areas of RED DWARF, in which the CAT PEOPLE evolved and lived. They are situated two thousand levels from LISTER and RIMMER's sleeping quarters in the officers' block, and take over two days to reach on foot.

CASABLANCA: A FILM much admired by LISTER, who considered the definitive version to be that which starred PETER BEARDSLEY and MYRA BINGLEBAT. He used the FILM as an integral part of his teachings when he instructed KRYTEN in the art of LYING. KRYTEN obviously enjoyed it, for he shared it with CAMILLE, who decided that it would be 'their movie'. However, when her husband HECTOR turned up, KRYTEN borrowed a trick or two from the film to persuade his love to return to her husband.

CAT: The only one of the CAT PEOPLE remaining aboard RED DWARF, and presumably the sole surviving member of the entire species.

CAT AND MOUSE: Despite cartoon propoganda, CAT maintains that the only way to win such a game is by not being the mouse.

CAT BOOKS: The literature of the CAT PEOPLE, made up of scents instead of words.

CAT PEOPLE: The race which evolved from LISTER's pet

cat FRANKENSTEIN.

CAT PRIESTS: Keepers of the word of CLOISTER, these religious leaders wore the HOLY CUSTARD STAINS, the SACRED GRAVY MARKS and the CARDBOARD HATS which were his icons. LISTER met one of the Priests on RED DWARF only moments before he died, and was able to convince him that his faith had been justified.

CGI: No we don't know what it stands for, but see SEBASTIAN DOYLE anyway.

CHASM OF HOPELESSNESS: An area of the PSY-MOON located not too far from the SWAMP OF DESPAIR and quite close to the WOOD OF HUMILIATION.

CHEN: One of LISTER's friends and drinking partners aboard RED DWARF.

CHESS: The GAME chosen by QUEEG in the final showdown with HOLLY, despite HOLLY's alternative suggestions, which included draughts, Monopoly and snakes and ladders. HOLLY was not exactly a novice at chess, however. He and fellow computer GORDON had been involved in a tournament that spanned THREE MILLION YEARS, though only one move had ever actually been made.

CHICKEN: The disguise chosen by HOLLISTER for a FANCY DRESS PARTY, which earned RIMMER eight years' PD when he mistook his commanding officer for a drug-induced HALLUCINATION. Later LISTER was transmogrified into such a bird by the DNA MODIFIER, and learnt exactly why they cluck so much (see also HAMSTER). For no apparent reason the EMOHAWK transformed itself briefly into said fowl during its visit to STARBUG. Currently, there are no live chickens on board, thus precluding the enforcement of SPACE CORPS DIRECTIVE 68250. However, if you plan to travel by XPRESS LIFT in the future, it's worth mentioning that the chicken served up on board tastes slightly worse than its container.

CHICKEN MERENGO: The entry which some people argue should have been in the index last time. We disagree.

CHICKEN, ROAST: The form which RIMMER thought his fictional ALIEN race the QUAGAARS had taken, when one was discovered in what turned out to be one of RED DWARF's GARBAGE PODs.

CHICKEN SOUP NOZZLE: An integral part of Z SHIFT's duty roster was to keep these items clear of blockages.

CHICKENS, REHYDRATABLE: When LISTER and RIMMER inventoried the ship's stores, they discovered that there were 140,000 of these on board.

CHIEF EUNUCH: RIMMER believes that, in a past life, he occupied this role in the court of ALEXANDER THE GREAT. LISTER believes it too. Even today, RIMMER claims that he can't look at a pair of nutcrackers without wincing.

CHILD PSYCHOLOGIST: LISTER had to see one of these at age six, in order to cope with the death of his stepfather. Having been told that his dad had gone to the same place as his dead goldfish, he spent hours with his head down the toilet bowl trying to communicate with him.

CHINESE WORRY BALLS: Given to RIMMER to aid him in stress management, they were more like Chinese Worry Marbles by the time he was rescued from RIMMERWORLD.

CHIPS: These items control certain aspects of ANDROID behaviour. We know, for instance, that KRYTEN has, amongst others, a guilt chip, an anxiety chip, a sanity chip and a good taste chip.

CHLOROFORM: A particular type of anaesthetic which KRYTEN is a dab hand at administering. On RIMMER's instructions, he chloroformed LISTER and CAT so that their bodies could be swapped with RIMMER's without their agreement. The technique came in more useful, however, as a painless way of halting LISTER when he became a remote controlled homicidal maniac.

CHOCOLATE WRAPPER: The item used by LISTER to take notes whilst revising for the Chef's EXAM. RIMMER saw it as conclusive proof that he was not displaying quite the right attitude.

CHRISTIE, AGATHA: A novelist whose works were so enjoyed by HOLLY that he arranged for his memory banks to be erased so that he could read them all over again.

CIGARETTES: One of LISTER's many vices, which he indulges in despite RIMMER's objections and the No Smoking sign that he has deliberately placed in their bunk room. RIMMER has made use of the habit in the past, however, by hiding LISTER's supply and giving them back to him at the rate of one for every day that he obeyed orders. By the time LISTER uncovered the hiding place, he had earned the grand total of four and three quarters.

CINEMA: An area of RED DWARF is allocated for this use. It is frequented by the SKUTTERS, in defiance of RIMMER's orders, by LISTER, who apparently visits it every Sunday afternoon, and it was also where KRYTEN took CAMILLE to see CASABLANCA.

CINZANO BIANCO: The nickname which LISTER claimed to have been given by his fellow POOL players at the AIGBURTH ARMS so called because, once he was on the table, they couldn't get him off.

CLEARANCE ZONE: The area of JUSTICE WORLD in which the honesty of visitors is assessed, before they are allowed to proceed any further.

CLIFTON, FIELD MARSHAL: The dignitary who invited

RIMMER to dine with him during his BETTER THAN LIFE fantasy.

CLITORIS: Acronym for the Committee for the Liberation and Integration of Terrifying Organisms and their Rehabilitation Into Society. This was one of the names put forward by RIMMER in his anger-free campaign against the POLYMORPH. See also THE LEAGUE AGAINST SALIVATING MONSTERS.

CLOAK: A device fitted aboard *STARBUG*, with the ability to render the shuttle-craft invisible.

CLOISTER THE STUPID: According to legend, the CAT PEOPLE's deity, who will return to lead them to the Promised Land of FUCHAL. Unfortunately for the CATS, Cloister is really LISTER, and the whole thing's been a bit of a mistake.

COCKPIT COMPUTER: The mechanism which ran ACE RIMMER's dimension-spanning LIGHT SHIP. Possessed of Artificial Intelligence and a female personality, it was smitten with ACE's manly charm.

COFFEE: LISTER likes to take his double caffinated with four sugars.

COLUMBO: According to RIMMER, the man in the dirty mac who discovered America.

COME JIVING: Presumably a future version of 'Come Dancing'; it has been commented that the CAT could have passed for a finalist in this competition.

COMPLAINTS: Rimmer filed 247 against Lister – including one of MUTINY.

COMPUTER RASH: A weak excuse used by HOLLY to explain the lipstick marks which covered his face while he was 'working' with HILLY.

COMPUTER SENILITY: The 'illness' with which HOLLY

became stricken during his THREE MILLION YEARS alone. KRYTEN successfully cured this by raising the now female HOLLY's IQ to a staggering 12,000. Unfortunately, a side-effect of the experiment was that her operational life-span was drastically reduced. Fortunately the closure of a WHITE HOLE negated the 'repair' anyway, so it was back to square one for the loopy computer.

COMPUTER SLUG: A small item on which HOLLY can record information. The slug – and therefore the data – can then be plugged into any other computer.

CONDOM FISHING: An activity in which LISTER indulged in his younger days. As the local canal was devoid of FISH, condoms were all he and his friends could catch – although he is particularly proud of the 2lb BLACK-RIBBED KNOBBLER he was once able to land.

CONDOM, TRIPLE-THICK: DUANE DIBBLEY likes to keep one with him at all times. Well, you never know.

CONFIDENCE: One of the imaginary beings who LISTER and CHEN theorised lived inside their heads. He became frighteningly real when LISTER caught a mutated PNEUMONIA virus which allowed his HALLUCINATIONS to become solid. Confidence was modelled after all the things that LISTER associated with confidence – he looked like a player from the LONDON JETS, and sounded like BING BAXTER. He died when he took off his helmet in space, in an attempt to convince LISTER that he didn't need oxygen to breathe. *See also* PARANOIA.

CONFIDENTIAL REPORTS: CAPTAIN HOLLISTER kept one of these on each member of his crew, presumably on their PERSONAL DATA FILES. RIMMER, of course, took his death as an opportunity to review his own, and he wasn't too pleased by what he found!

CONTRACEPTIVE JELLY: The substance for which

LISTER once swapped RIMMER's toothpaste as a practical joke.

COPACABANA: A hit song of the 20th century, an instrumental version of which was selected by KRYTEN's CPU to keep him company when severe damage caused it to go temporarily off-line.

COUNTRY AND WESTERN CHANNEL: Sadly, some things never change.

COWS: One of the types of animal that LISTER wanted to breed when he got his farm on FIJI.

CRANE, NIRVANAH: A Flight Commander aboard the HOLOSHIP ENLIGHTENMENT, who fell in love with RIMMER. As crew member 4172 she was selected by STOCKY as RIMMER's opponent in a contest for a position aboard the HOLOSHIP. The computer's prediction that she would be RIMMER's best chance proved accurate, since she was prepared to sacrifice her own existence so that he might replace her in the crew and thus fulfil the potential she believed he possessed.

CRAPOLA, INC.: The company which, much to LISTER's regret, manufactured the TALKIE TOASTER.

CROCHETED HATS: The colourful items of head wear that, thanks to a handy knitting pattern magazine, thoughtfully provided by RIMMER, LISTER made during his five-day stint in QUARANTINE.

CROSSBOW: The means by which the hallucinating KRYTEN intended to kill himself and the others, believing it to be a handgun.

CROSSWORD BOOK: The means by which RIMMER hoped to 'kill a couple of centuries' when LISTER intended to go into STASIS, leaving him alone for THREE MILLION YEARS.

CRUNCHIE BARS, FUN-SIZE: The most important task of Z SHIFT (as commanded by ARNOLD RIMMER) was to ensure that the VENDING MACHINES didn't run out of these objects.

CUFFLINKS: A fashion accessory favoured by the CAT – even on space suits.

CURRY: A type of food very much favoured by DAVE LISTER, who has diligently introduced the CAT to its wonders. Of course, he is always willing to sample other types of food too. One June, for instance KRYTEN recalls him trying a PIZZA. Unfortunately the meal was missing that one certain something – curry sauce! See also VINDALOOS.

CUSTER, DEREK: The heroic figure who, along with companions Kit and Titan, rescued RIMMER from RIMMER-WORLD.

CYANIDE CAPSULES: These are provided as standard equipment in XPRESS LIFTS, due to the unlikeliness of escape in the event of an accident.

CYBER-PARK: The existence of one of these on LEGION's space station would have allowed his 'guests' to visit any time period and indulge in any fantasy with anyone they chose. Seems they escaped a bit too soon.

D

DAILY GOAL LIST: The list which RIMMER set himself every day – and always failed to complete.

DAMAGE REPORT MACHINE: The one on RED DWARF was last reported to be damaged. The one on STARBUG exploded.

DANDELION SORBET: The perfect dessert to follow

ASTEROIDAL LICHEN STEW.

DANDRUFF: A flake of this was the only thing RIMMER could find that contained any of his cells and could therefore be used to form a clone body via the DNA MODIFIER. Unfortunately, one sneeze from CAT ruined his ambitions.

DARTBOARD: A vital piece of equipment contained aboard *STARBUG*.

DAVRO: See LEGION.

DAY-GLO ORANGE MOONBOOTS: The noxious and fetid items of footwear which once set off a chemical alarm. LISTER believed they would help him score with the crew of the NOVA 5; the girls never realised how lucky they were to be dead.

DEADIES: A derogatory slang term for dead people who have been re-incarnated as HOLOGRAMS.

DEATH: Leader of the FOUR APOCALYPSE BOYS in KRYTEN's ARMAGEDDON VIRUS inspired dreamscape. He looked suspiciously similar to the SIMULANT captain responsible for said virus, and his motto was: 'Have infection, will travel.'

DECIMALISED MUSIC: HOLLY's notion for improving music. Innovations include replacing the octave with a decative, adding the notes H and J and incorporating woh and boh into the musical scale. He christened his invention HOLL ROCK.

DECOYS: STARBUG's way of confusing oncoming missiles; used once and unsuccessful.

DEEP-SLEEP: A form of suspended animation available on STARBUG. Unlike STASIS, which freezes time, deep-sleep merely reduces the ageing process, albeit dramatically.

DEGANWY: The site of a school summer camp which LISTER once attended. This was run by his Geography teacher, MISS FOSTER.

DEFENSIVE SHIELDS: See DEFLECTOR SHIELDS.

DEFLECTOR SHIELDS: A rather useful defensive system, not possessed by STARBUG.

DESCARTES: A French thinker whose philosophical astuteness is often confused with that of POPEYE the sailor man.

DESPAIR SQUID: The product of an experiment into accelerated evolution by Planetary Engineers. This enormous cephalopod emitted a venom which not only caused HALLUCINATIONS but induced a state of extreme melancholy. As a result of coming into contact with the squid's ink, the crew of the SSS ESPERANTO were compelled to commit SUICIDE, a fate also suffered by the other marine life on the unnamed world.

DEVELOPING FLUID: A batch of this substance mutated over THREE MILLION YEARS in storage, and KRYTEN discovered that it could make photographs apparently come to life. Using the fluid, he was able to develop TIMESLIDES.

DEVIANCY, GROSS: On RIMMERWORLD, this meant displaying charm, bravery and honour, as opposed to double-dealing, and two-facedness. DEREK CUSTER and friends were charged on eight counts and CAT believed he must be Public Enemy No. 1.

DIARIES: Both LISTER and RIMMER possessed one, but only RIMMER had the good manners to read his bunkmates's diary behind his back. The diary belonging to RIMMER proved useful in locating the STASIS LEAK.

DIARRHOEA: The illness for which LISTER requested sick leave no less than five hundred times during his eight month stint with the JUPITER MINING CORPORATION.

DIBBLEY, DUANE: The styleless, buck-toothed geek who took a party into RED DWARF THE TOTAL IMMERSION VIDEO GAME. In reality the person the CAT imagined himself to be when under the influence of the DESPAIR SQUID's ink. As a preference CAT chose death over a life spent in plastic sandals and an anorak. However, an encounter with an EMOHAWK and the subsequent theft of the CAT's cool and style resulted in a tempory return for the DUKE OF DORK.

DICE, FURRY: Optional extra found in BLUE MIDGET and in RIMMER's BETTER THAN LIFE fantasy JAGUAR. *STARBUG* used to have a set as well, but the elastic snapped when the shuttle-craft collided with ACE RIMMER's ship. HOLLY seemed quite pleased about the incident, and commented that the cockpit was now a lot more tasteful.

DICK: A fictional character who featured in the elementary books of the CAT PEOPLE.

DIESEL DECKS: The setting for a ten-day hiking vacation which RIMMER took, along with two SKUTTERS. The subsequent slide show presentation threatened to melt KRYTEN's intelligence circuits.

DIMENSION THEORY OF REALITY: The theory developed in ACE RIMMER's dimension that stated that a ship travelling at the theoretical SPEED OF REALITY could break the barrier into PARALLEL UNIVERSES. It obviously worked, as ACE was able to visit our own universe, meeting his counterpart here.

DISCO LIGHTING: LISTER claims it is only due to inefficient examples of these that he has dated worse than the warty yeti lookalike he encountered on the GELF MOON.

DISPENSER 172: The DISPENSER which fell foul of the now infamous CHICKEN SOUP NOZZLE blockage!

DISPENSERS: Also known as VENDING MACHINES, these handy, time saving apparatus dispense food to – and presumably also prepare food for – the crew of RED DWARF.

DIVA-DROID INTERNATIONAL: A corporation which manufactured MECHANOIDS such as the KRYTEN Series III (otherwise known as the Series 4000) and HUDZEN 10 models.

DIXON, REGGIE: One of the many musical artistes whose only actual fan seems to be ARNOLD RIMMER. His albums apparently include the unappetising 'Tango Treats'.

DNA: RIMMER searched long and hard for an example of his own, in the hope that the DNA MODIFIER could then provide him with a body. One sneeze from CAT, and that hope was lost. However, using equipment discovered in ESCAPE POD 1736 he was able to populate RIMMERWORLD with an army of clones; it is likely that either the genetic code was present in his LIGHT BEE's programme or that it is possible to synthesise DNA using material from his hard-light body.

DNA MODIFIER: A machine which could turn any living thing into any other living thing by altering its molecular structure. Amongst other things, it turned LISTER into a CHICKEN and KRYTEN into a human. It also formed a MUTTON VINDALOO BEAST out of a curry.

DOBBIN: The drummer with SMEG AND THE HEADS, who later joined the police-force and the masons.

DOG: Much to the CAT's frustration, his PARALLEL UNIVERSE counterpart was not female, and if that wasn't bad enough, was a dog! Although evolved into humanoid form and reasonably intelligent, the dog still retained many canine characteristics, and was particularly scruffy, smelly and flea-ridden, with a predilection for sniffing others' behinds.

DOG FOOD: Having been forced to eat some when marooned on an ICE PLANET, LISTER realised why DOGS licked their testicles.

DOGS: When CAT first learnt about these creatures, via a photograph of LISTER's stepfather's dog, HANNAH, he became intent upon finding one to chase. LISTER disabused him of this notion by claiming that they were eighteen feet long with teeth as big as your leg. Upon divorcing his parents as a teenager RIMMER was granted access to the family dog every fourth weekend. *See also* DOG.

DOGS' MILK: Used for necessity when the cows' milk ran out. Dogs' milk has the distinct advantage of lasting much longer – because, as Holly quite rightly pointed out, no bugger'll drink it!

DOLLARPOUNDS: Never mind the ECU – the dollarpound ($£) is the standard unit of world currency in the twenty-third century. RIMMER was the proud owner of twenty-four thousand of them, but when LISTER became marooned on an ICE PLANET, he had to burn the lot just to stay alive.

DOM PERIGNON '44: LISTER drank this in his BETTER THAN LIFE fantasy – out of a pint mug, of course.

DONALD: A hypnotherapist who regressed RIMMER to a previous incarnation as ALEXANDER THE GREAT'S CHIEF EUNUCH.

DONATELLA, DON: No, not a mutant turtle, a ZERO GEE FOOTBALL player in the ROOF ATTACK position.

DORKSVILLE: RIMMER's suggestion for a town to be named after KRYTEN following his creation of the TRIPLICATOR.

DOUBLE POLAROID: A euphemism for the strange appendage KRYTEN found on his body after turning human – so called because, after a quick look through an electrical appliance catalogue, he had to take two photographs to fit it all on so that he could show it to LISTER.

DOVE PROGRAM: In order to create this antidote to the ARMAGGEDON VIRUS, KRYTEN linked himself to STARBUG's computer. To better cope with the task at hand, his subconscious saw fit to perceive it as a Wild West confrontation.

DOWNTIME: KRYTEN's equivalent of sleep.

DOYLE, BILLY: One of DUANE DIBBLEY's party and the brother of the highly successful SEBASTIAN DOYLE, this down-at-heel vagrant was actually how RIMMER perceived himself when under the influence of the DESPAIR SQUID's ink.

DOYLE, SEBASTIAN: The Section Chief of CGI and Head of the MINISTRY OF ALTERATION in a FASCIST state. The mass murdering VOTER Colonel Doyle was a HALLUCINATION of LISTER's; in this hated guise he was pushed to the brink of suicide.

DREAM RECORDER: The machine which automatically records the dreams of everybody on board RED DWARF. It enabled LISTER to ascertain the fact that KOCHANSKI dreamt about him three times. CAT also used it to re-live those dreams in which he'd had a particularly good time.

DRIVE PLATE: Had RIMMER repaired this item efficiently, he might well have prevented the leakage of lethal CADMIUM 2 RADIATION that wiped out the entire crew of RED DWARF.

DRIVE ROOM: The bridge, by any other name. It was here that RIMMER met his death, whilst he was busy explaining to CAPTAIN HOLLISTER why he had failed to mend the DRIVE PLATE. LISTER's son BEXLEY is also destined to die here in his mid-twenties, following an accident with the NAVI COMP.

DROID ROT: An unfortunate disease which had caused the deterioration of KRYTEN's third SPARE HEAD.

DUBOIS BROTHERS: The legendary toy makers, who hand carved RIMMER's treasured ARMIES DU NORD.

DUKE: (1) Another of the nicknames that RIMMER would rather like to have (see also ACE). When he first met CAMILLE, he claimed that his friends often used this, but asked her not to mention it in front of them, just in case they'd forgotten. See also IRON DUKE and CAPTAIN A J RIMMER, SPACE AD-

VENTURER.

DUKE: (2) *See* FRANK.

DUKE OF DORK: *See* DUANE DIBBLEY.

DUMPLINGS: The taste notwithstanding, RIMMER's dumplings can be distinguished from the usual sort by their unique ability to bounce. *See also* STOMACH PUMP.

DUNCAN: A friend of LISTER's who introduced him to the use of MIRRORS on his toe-caps for looking up girls' skirts. When LISTER was ten, Duncan had to move to Spain because of his father's job – a bank job, as it happens. LISTER never saw him again.

DUREX VOLLEYBALL: *See* GAMES.

DUST STORM: A self-explanatory space phenomenon, which RED DWARF ran into shortly after LISTER's CONFIDENCE and PARANOIA manifested themselves on board.

DWARFERS: A recently coined term referring to the displaced RED DWARF crew. Not to be confused with the word's 20th-century usage, which denotes a particularly unpleasant sexual practice.

E

EARTH: The birthplace of LISTER, to which he hopes one day to return – even if it's been taken over by giant ants or dolphins. KRYTEN was surprised to discover that the planet was far shorter than he'd expected(?!). *See also* BACKWARDS EARTH.

EASTBOURNE ZIMMER FRAME RELAY TEAM: Allegedly somewhat faster than STARBUG.

ECO-ACCELERATOR ROCKETS: 25th-century TERRA-FORMING devices which created RIMMERWORLD in six days.

E5A9O8B7: The machine code equivalent of the word 'LOVE', utilising Z80012, using hex rather than binary notation and converting to a basic ASCII code. Sweet-talking KRYTEN wooed CAMILLE with its use.

EJECTOR SEAT: STARBUG is fitted with this gadget, as KRYTEN accidentally discovered. During his 'driving test', he managed to eject his instructor – RIMMER – out into the CARGO BAY.

ELECTRONIC BIBLE, THE: The fictional work in which ANDROIDS are programmed to believe. This states that 'the iron will lie down with the lamp,' and explains the concept of SILICON HEAVEN.

ELLIS, MICHAEL: Or rather Leahcim Sille, who had the generous occupation of bank raider on BACKWARDS EARTH.

EMOHAWK: A POLYMORPH spayed at birth and half domesticated. The one sent to sort out the DWARFERS after they cheated its KINITAWOWI masters out of an O/G unit transformed itself into several items, as you might expect from a shape-changer, and we suppose you'd like a list, eh? Here goes then: a rabbit, a lamp, a stick, LISTER's deerstalker, a CHICKEN, a can of beans, a FROG, a paper dart/plane, a microphone, a slinky, a toy car, a THERMOS FLASK and a GRENADE

ENFORCEMENT ORB, CLASS A: The SPACE CORPS EXTERNAL ENFORCEMENT VEHICLE which intercepted STARBUG and accused its crew of looting.

ENIG: KRYTEN's enigmatic last word in a TIMELINE which, fortunately, was later wiped out of history. As it transpired, this seemingly incomprehensible message was meant to tip KRYTEN's slightly younger self off to the fact that the programming of THE INQUISITOR's TIME GAUNTLET worked on a variation of the ENIGMA DECODING SYSTEM.

ENIGMA DECODING SYSTEM: *See also* ENIG (though if you're reading this section in the correct order you should just have done so) and TIME GAUNTLETS.

ENLIGHTENMENT: A HOLOSHIP crewed by the hologramatic cream of the SPACE CORPS – 2000 of them to be exact.

EQUAL RIGHTS FOR MEN MARCHES: Demonstrations which took place in the female dominated PARALLEL UNIVERSE. These protest rallies consisted of thousands of men burning their jockstraps, in an attempt to achieve equality.

ERASURE: A fate suffered by HOLLY after his defeat at CHESS by QUEEG – except that it was all a joke!

ESCAPE POD: Looks rather similar to an ORE SAMPLE POD; identical, in fact. The one on STARBUG escaped when LISTER used the release mechanism as a bottle opener. It was presumably an afterthought anyway, as there were none present when the shuttle crash-landed on an ICE-PLANET. Perhaps the idea was inspired by the one which didn't contain BARBRA BELLINI.

ESCAPE POD 1736: Originally looted from a 25th-century seeding ship, RIMMER used it, much to the annoyance of the others, as his exclusive means of escape from the doomed SIMULANT battle-cruiser. Its programme took it to the nearest S3 PLANET where RIMMER used the TERRAFORMING devices aboard to create RIMMERWORLD.

ESCORT BOOTS: An unusual feature of JUSTICE WORLD. Visitors have to wear these items of footwear, which then transport them through to the CLEARANCE ZONE for their crimes to be assessed. Anybody who is granted clearance is able to step out of the boots and walk freely around the complex. Anybody who isn't is sentenced and taken by the boots into the

JUSTICE ZONE. CAT wasn't too happy at being made to wear something of such uncool design, describing them as 'Frankenstein's hand-me-downs'.

ESPERANTO: A language which RIMMER has devoted a great deal of time to learning over eight years. It is a great frustration to him that even LISTER is actually better at it than he is.

EXAMS: The means by which SPACE CORPS technicians of LISTER and RIMMER's ranks could better themselves and become Corps Officers. RIMMER was desperate to do so, and he sat the Engineering exam eleven times, failing each one. He also tried his hand at Astro-Navigation, but failed that too, on no less than thirteen separate occasions (although he'll only admit to ten – and then only if you count the time he had his spasm!). LISTER, meanwhile, had never had much time for academic subjects. However, when the opportunity arose to become RIMMER's superior, he grasped it with open arms. He sat the Chef's exam, and claimed to have passed. He was lying.

EXERCISE: A pastime in which RIMMER would like us to believe he frequently indulges (see also NECROBICS). His sham has been exposed both by his own identical 'twin' and by QUEEG, both of whom put him through punishing exercise routines which he was unable to take. LISTER, of course, has never put up any such pretence.

EXISTENCE: The imaginary Western town in which KRYTEN fought the FOUR APOCALYPSE BOYS – as in 'You are now leaving . . .'

EXPERIMENTAL PILE SURGERY: One of LISTER's ideas for a practical joke was to put RIMMER's name on the waiting list for this treatment.

EXPIRY DATE: All ANDROIDS are fitted with these in order for the manufacturers to sell newer models. In KRYTEN's case, the arrival of his triggered both his SHUT-DOWN DISK (with which he was easily able to cope) and the arrival of his replacement, HUDZEN (with which he had rather more trouble!).

EXTRA-BROWN RUBBER SAFETY PANTS: Required by RIMMER when entering a soon-to-disintegrate SIMULANT Battle Class Cruiser.

F

FALCONBURGER, BLAIZE: The American TV Presenter of LIFESTYLES OF THE DISGUSTINGLY RICH AND FAMOUS.

FAMINE: Corpulant member of the FOUR APOCALYPSE BOYS.

FANCY DRESS PARTY: One of these bashes was in full swing when LISTER, RIMMER and CAT went back in time to visit RED DWARF on 2 MARCH 2077. CAPTAIN HOLLISTER's chosen costume caused a great deal of problems for RIMMER. *See* CHICKEN.

FASCIST: The political party which was hoping for a third glorious decade in power when DUANE DIBLEY and co emerged from RED DWARF THE TOTAL IMMERSION VIDEO GAME.

FASCIST DICTATOR MONTHLY: A magazine read by RIMMER, which once featured ADOLF HITLER as Mr October.

FASTER-THAN-LIGHT DRIVE: We're not too sure about this one, but think it might be a drive which enables spaceships to travel faster than the speed of light.

FEAR: The emotion the POLYMORPH stole from LISTER. Consequently, LISTER thought it would be quite a good idea to strap a nuclear bomb to his head so that he could nut the smegger into oblivion.

FELICITUS POPULI: The good luck virus developed by the hologramatic Doctor HILDEGARDE LANSTROM. LISTER used it to good effect in combating a HOLO-VIRUS infected and totally psychopathic RIMMER.

FELIS SAPIENS: The highly evolved race of CATs. HUDZEN's corrupted data banks mistakenly identified the CAT as being of the species Felix Sapiens. *See* CAT PEOPLE.

FICTION SECTION: That area of the WAX-DROID THEME PARK in which Droids of fictional characters were kept. One of these was Father Christmas, who was posted to HERO WORLD to help in the WAX WAR.

FIELD MICRO-SURGERY: A skill in which, like most others it seemed, ACE RIMMER was particularly well-versed. It allowed him to save the CAT's leg from amputation after a particularly nasty accident in STARBUG.

FIFTH DIMENSION: The HOLLY HOP DRIVE took RED DWARF through this, and into a PARALLEL UNIVERSE. LISTER didn't quite understand the concept – he thought of the Fifth Dimension only as a pop group, who got to number six with 'Baby I Want Your Love Thing'.

FIJI: The place where LISTER dreamed of settling down with KRISTINE KOCHANSKI. His hopes were not diminished by the fact that it had flooded, and was three feet under water.

FILM FUN MAGAZINE: A periodical which the SKUTTERS collected. It was delivered to RED DWARF by mail order.

FILMS: SEE VIDS.

5517/W13 ALPHA SIM MODEM: An interface circuit with a built-in 599XRDP. HOLLY modestly claimed it was just intuition that led her to choose this perfect gift for KRYTEN's last day present.

FIRE-AXE, MEDIUM SIZED: The implement that RIMMER deposited in KRYTEN's spine when he acquired telekinetic abilities.

FISH: The CAT is obsessed by these creatures, and was delighted when RIMMER showed him how to get as many as he wanted from the DISPENSERS. RIMMER seems to be partially obsessed too, as his tenth attempt at passing the Engineering EXAM consisted of the words 'I am a fish', written five hundred times. See also HADDOCK, HERRING, KIPPERS, MIMEAN BLADDERFISH and GOLDFISH, ROBOT.

FISHER, MICHELLE: The girl to whom LISTER lost his virginity on BOOTLE MUNICIPAL GOLF COURSE at the age of twelve.

FISHING: An activity enjoyed by all of the crew – although the others would prefer it if RIMMER wasn't quite so insistent on joining their expeditions. LISTER also used to indulge in CONDOM FISHING when he was younger. Of course, that sometimes just isn't possible in deep space – which is where JUNIOR ANGLER comes in.

FLAMINGO-UP: Like a cock-up, only much much bigger.

FLIGHT RECORDER: Each STARBUG is fitted with one of these. When STARBUG 1 crashed on BACKWARDS EARTH, LISTER was able to use a homing device to locate its recorder.

FLIGHT SCHOOL: An academy run by the SPACE CORPS for aspiring TEST PILOTS. Of course, RIMMER had aspirations of attending – and of course, he never did!

FLINTSTONE, WILMA: A cartoon character much desired by LISTER and the CAT. Unfortunately, she'll never leave Fred and they know it.

FOOD ESCAPE: The fate which CAT suffered after being introduced to the DISPENSER and obtaining at least six FISH.

FOOTBALL – IT'S A FUNNY OLD GAME: A book by Kevin Keegan which, having read every book ever written, HOLLY considered to be the worst one. We can imagine!

FOSTER, MISS: LISTER's Geography teacher, who didn't believe that men were better than machines – one machine in particular.

FOUR APOCALYPSE BOYS: Dream-state manifestations of the ARMAGEDDON VIRUS, who wanted to wipe KRYTEN out of EXISTENCE.

FOUR-SIDED TRIANGLE: One of the instruments that HOLLY theorised would be used for playing DECIMALISED MUSIC.

14B: A small instrument used in the maintenance of RED DWARF, with uncanny similarities to the 14F.

14F: A small instrument used in the maintenance of RED DWARF, with uncanny similarities to the 14B.

1421: The year in which, on 16 August, the STARBUG crew arrived to drink in the heady medieval atmosphere of deep space, thanks to their newfound TIME DRIVE.

FOX FUR: The 'ferocious' creature with which CAT found himself engaged in battle in the reception area of the GANYMEDE HOLIDAY INN.

FRANK: Along with DUKE, one of the cowboys who, at JIMMY's behest, went for their pieces in the LAST CHANCE SALOON, only to be outgunned by the RIVIERA KID and out-fought by DANGEROUS DAN McGREW. See also FRANK TODHUNTER, FRANK RIMMER (1) and FRANK RIMMER (2).

FRANKENSTEIN: In legend, the HOLY MOTHER of the

CAT PEOPLE, whose miraculous VIRGIN BIRTH spawned their race. In reality, LISTER's pet cat, who was impregnated by a BIG BLACK TOM on TITAN.

FREAKY FUNGUS: The common name for TITAN MUSH-ROOMS.

FRENCH: A subject (presumably one of many) in which LISTER came bottom at school. When his grandmother found out, she nutted the Headmaster.

FRIDAY THE THIRTEENTH 1649: *See* VIDS.

FRIDGE: RIMMER's weapon of choice when LISTER's nostril hair plucking became too much to bear.

FROGS: Generally, these amphibious creatures go ribbit, ribbit – or noises to that effect. In THE SWAMP OF DESPAIR, however, they tend to comment on how useless RIMMER is. On WAXWORLD the soapy kind were a vital component of the torture which the WAX-DROID of Caligula had in mind for LISTER and CAT. The treatment also involved the removal of their trousers, although beyond that, we can only speculate.

FRONTAL LOBES: A SIMULANT's idea of a xylophone.

FUCHAL: The PROMISED LAND, to which the CAT PEOPLE believed CLOISTER THE STUPID would lead them. In fact, Fuchal is a corruption of FIJI, where LISTER wanted to take his pet cat FRANKENSTEIN.

FUCHAL DAY: A festival of the CAT PEOPLE, on which anybody who didn't eat hot dogs was stoned to death with stale doughnuts.

FURSDAY: *See* HAVE YOU GOT A GOOD MEMORY?

FUTURE ECHOES: Images of the future, which could be seen on RED DWARF as the ship broke the LIGHT BARRIER. The faster the ship travelled the further into the future the reflections originated.

G

GAMES: The loss of RED DWARF has presumably robbed LISTER and CAT not only of the equipment needed to play Scrabble, Table Golf, JUNIOR ANGLER, unicycle polo and a computer adventure game featuring GANDALF THE MASTER WIZARD, but also of the space necessary for DUREX VOLLEYBALL, soap-sud slalom and even tiddleywinks show-jumping. Poker is still an option (although perhaps not the strip version, as they once claimed to HARRISON), whilst further entertainment can be found in the POINTY STICK GAME and the weekly crap game. Holly used to enjoy CHESS, competing both against QUEEG and postally with GORDON, whilst RIMMER played war games – RISK, especially – cheated at draughts against the SKUTTERS, considered himself a master of hide and seek and indulged in the occasional round of GOLF. LISTER and CAT played GOLF too, during their BETTER THAN LIFE fantasy; BETTER THAN LIFE being, of course, the ultimate in TIV games. Less sophisticated TIVs such as GUMSHOE and STREETS OF LAREDO were made available to LISTER via an ARTIFICIAL REALITY MACHINE. The whole crew believed they'd been playing in RED DWARF – THE TOTAL IMMERSION VIDEO GAME, but this was actually a HALLUCINATION. LISTER is an avid spectator of ZERO-GRAVITY FOOTBALL and a self-proclaimed expert at POOL, and we're led to believe that the STARBUG crew will one day play canasta and mixed doubles with ADOLF HITLER and friends. One game to avoid is CAT AND MOUSE, especially with a ship full of genocidal rogue SIMULANTS, and particularly if you're the mouse. *See also* PARTNERSHIP WHIST.

GANDALF THE MASTER WIZARD. *See* GAMES.

GANYMEDE HOLIDAY INN: The hotel in which the CAT became locked in mortal combat with a FOX FUR, and where LISTER found KOCHANSKI, already married to his future self. Judging by the reception area, this Holiday Inn was a dead ringer for its twentieth century Manchester counterpart.

GARBAGE POD: The type of vessel in which RED DWARF ejected its waste into space. When one of them was picked up by the ship on its way back to EARTH, RIMMER was convinced that it was an ALIEN craft.

GARDEN: KRYTEN's dream was to have one of these, which he had planted himself. He left RED DWARF on a SPACE BIKE to achieve his ambition, but crashed straight into an asteroid.

GAZPACHO SOUP: An expensive dish, intended to be served cold. This caused RIMMER a great deal of humiliation as, having been offered the privilege of dining at the CAPTAIN'S TABLE, he insisted on sending this course back to be warmed up. He has never quite lived the incident down, and blames it in part for his subsequent lack of success.

GAZPACHO SOUP DAY: NOVEMBER 25TH – the day on which the GAZPACHO SOUP incident took place, forever commemorated in RIMMER's diary as the date of his greatest humiliation.

GAZZA: SMEG AND THE HEADS' bass player, who later went into insurance.

GELDOF: All right, here we go – the Lyons/Howarth theory of 'Red Dwarf' continuity, tucked away in the index where nobody (least of all our editor) will find it. Okay, so we know that LISTER and RIMMER came from the twenty-third century – yet RIMMER referred to CAPTAIN HOLLISTER as MR FAT BASTARD 2044, and when he and LISTER visit their own past in 'Stasis Leak', the date is given as being 2 March

2077. This date, LISTER says, falls only three weeks before the accident in which the crew of RED DWARF are killed – yet in 'Me^2', he says that November 25th was only six weeks before said event. The solution? Obvious, really. The development and common usage of inter-planetary travel has forced humans to re-evaluate their calendar, or possibly even to introduce several different versions of it (since years are different lengths on each planet, right?). By simply removing January and February (the last two months to appear, after all), we can solve half of those supposed discrepancies in one swoop. And the proof? The month of Geldof, which the HOLOGRAMATIC NEWSREADER does in fact refer to. So there we are. All sorted!? . . . Oh well, please yourselves.

GELFS: Acronym for Genetically Engineered Life Forms. Created by mankind with a variety of, mainly suspect, puposes in mind, GELFS come in all shapes and sizes with just as many abilities. The DWARFERS have encountered several varients, some more hostile than others. For details see CAMILLE, EMOHAWK, KINITAWOWI, HECTOR, MRS LISTER, POLYMORPH, PSIRENS.

GELF MOON: Home of the KINITAWOWI.

GELF ZONE: A region of space populated by (wait for it) GELFS.

GENETIC CLONING: The process by which all human life on RIMMERWORLD was created. *See also* DNA.

GENNY: Beautiful female persona of the POLYMORPH, used to purloin the CAT's VANITY.

GERONIMO: RIMMER's sole contribution to the conversation which took place while he was having sex with NIRVANAH CRANE.

GIANT FLAMING METEORITE: The technical term for a giant meteorite covered in flames.

GILBERT: (1) LISTER's manservant in the alternate past he created for himself with the TIMESLIDES.

GILBERT: (2) An ANDROID once known to KRYTEN which, becoming slightly deranged, preferred to be known as Ramases Niblick the Third Ker-Plunk Ker-Plunk Whoops Where's My Thribble.

GILL, ANNE: A Mapping Officer on board the NOVA 5. The RED DWARF crew discovered her body when they answered a distress call from the ship's MECHANOID, KRYTEN. *See also* AIR, JANE and JOHNS, TRACEY.

GIMBOID: A mild insult, presumably in common use at the time that LISTER and RIMMER left EARTH. *See also* GIMP and GOIT.

GIMP: Another mild insult, similar in meaning to GIMBOID and GOIT.

GIVE QUICHE A CHANCE: The motif emblazoned on RIMMER's T-shirt when he attempted to devise a peaceful solution to the POLYMORPH problem.

GOALPOST-HEAD: *See* RIMMER, ARNOLD.

GOD: RIMMER found the idea of God preposterous – but LISTER ended up as the God of the CAT PEOPLE. *See* CLOISTER THE STUPID and RELIGION.

GOIT: Another insult!

GOLDFISH, ROBOT: LISTER owned two of these pisciform automata, which the CAT found a constant temptation. He named them LENNON and McCARTNEY.

GOLF: A GAME enjoyed by LISTER and CAT during their BETTER THAN LIFE fantasy. Their scores would have been rather difficult to assess, due to CAT's rather unique style of play, which involved throwing the club rather than hitting the ball. RIMMER used to play golf himself, and was therefore quite annoyed when LISTER confessed that, in the process of losing his virginity, he had left a large buttock crevice in the tenth hole of the BOOTLE MUNICIPAL GOLF COURSE. Despite its vast size, RED DWARF does not possess its own course so LISTER and CAT now have to make do with Table Golf.

GONE WITH THE WIND: The XPRESS LIFTS 'in-lift movie' on the day that LISTER, RIMMER and CAT journeyed down to the STASIS LEAK on Level 16.

GOOD PSYCHO GUIDE: When LISTER finally gets around to writing this handy reference work, LEGION's institute will rate four and a half chainsaws.

GOOD SCHOOLS' GUIDE: A publication much perused by MRS RIMMER; not that it did ARNOLD RIMMER much good.

GOODBYE TO LOVE: A song sung by HOLLY prior to his fake ERASURE. But he's no Karen Carpenter and if he had been wiped, at least the others would have been spared from a further performance.

GORDON: The SCOTT FITZGERALD's eleventh generation AI computer, with an IQ of 8,000. Gordon is involved in a postal CHESS GAME with HOLLY, and is winning by virtue of the fact that so far only one move has been made.

GREER, JEREMY: The author of THE MALE EUNUCH.

GRENADE: The item with which the CAT expressed a wish to play 'fetch' when he met THE DOG in a PARALLEL UNIVERSE.

GREY, MILITARY: Indistinguishable from OCEAN GREY, this was the colour to which RIMMER attempted to change RED DWARF's internal corridor walls. No sooner had he begun the job than his double (*see* RIMMER, MRS (2)) changed them back.

GREY, OCEAN: The colour of RED DWARF's internal corridor walls.

GRIT: HOLLY mistook five specks on the scanner scope for five BLACK HOLES. Understandable, considering the similarity in colour.

GROINAL SOCKET: One of KRYTEN's more useful features, into which a multitude of attachments can be fitted, ranging from a vacuum cleaner to an egg whisk. Unfortunately, very few people will eat his omelettes! KRYTEN apparently experienced the nearest emotion he has had to sexual excitement when he accidentally welded the socket to a front-loading washing machine.

GROOVY CHANNEL 27: The funky TV channel which had a HOLOGRAMATIC NEWSREADER, which screened the minority soap opera ANDROIDS and whose weather girl performed obscene actions with her pointy stick – in LISTER's inagination, anyway. See POINTY STICK GAME.

GUIDANCE BEAM: The malfunctioning device which drew STARBUG to LEGION's military research base.

GUILT: The emotion the POLYMORPH stole from KRYTEN.

GUITARS: LISTER has possesed several guitars, which is just as well considering his crewmates' ongoing efforts to destroy as many as possible. Believing himself to be the ghost of Hendrix when it comes to performing, he is nevertheless banned from doing so unless he puts on a space suit and goes outside. He has become very protective about his remaining instruments, particularly the genuine Les Paul copy with five strings which was give to him by his stepfather. His attempts to preserve an earlier model led to RIMMER filing a charge against him for MUTINY. As of now, it seems there are no guitars left on STARBUG; the final one was broken in a particularly nasty crash, as the CAT would no doubt swear blind.

GUMSHOE: Chandleresque AR GAME which enabled participents to experience a realistic simulation of America's underworld of the 1940s. Naturally, LISTER used it to experience simulated SEX.

GWENLYN, KYLIE: The producer and director of the TV soap opera ANDROIDS. Her surname has also been used on occasion as a term of abuse.

H

HAÇIENDA: A club on MIRANDA, where RIMMER instigated a fight with McWILLIAMS and four of his friends, then promptly left.

HADDOCK: A species of FISH very similar to the one that was discovered to have committed suicide as a result of coming into contact with its fellow marine creature, the DESPAIR SQUID.

HAGGIS, IRRADIATED: There are 4691 examples of this foodstuff aboard RED DWARF. Now wasn't that worth knowing?

HAIRCUT LENGTH: It is a source of frustration for RIMMER that CAPTAIN HOLLISTER never put forward his suggestion of reducing the required SPACE CORPS haircut length by a quarter of an inch. He was acting with the best of motives too: every major battle in EARTH's history, RIMMER contends, was won by the side with the shortest hair. No wonder he didn't appreciate HOLLY's little hair related jape which, in RIMMER's own words, left him looking like 'a complete and total tit'.

HAIR DRYER: The device with which the CAT inadvertently deactivated every instrument in the scanning room, while the others were trying to track a UFO. It also came in useful for frying eggs when RED DWARF lost all power – except that it was powered by LISTER using an EXERCISE bike, and he was knackered long before the first egg turned white.

HALLUCINATIONS: LISTER became prone to these when he caught a mutated PNEUMONIA virus. Worse still, his hallucinations became solid. See CONFIDENCE, PARANOIA, HERRING and MAYOR OF WARSAW. RIMMER, meanwhile, is no stranger to hallucinations either, thanks to the voyage to TRIP-OUT CITY which an accidental dosage of TITAN MUSHROOMS induced him to take. The whole crew suffered from potentially fatal hallucinations when the four of them encountered the DESPAIR SQUID

HAMMOND ORGAN MUSIC: A type of music of which RIMMER is a big fan, enjoying especially the works of REGGIE WILSON in this field. Unable to touch such an instrument any more, he encourages the SKUTTERS to practise this skill instead. See also AMATEUR HAMMOND ORGAN RECITAL NIGHT and HAMMOND ORGAN OWNERS SOCIETY.

HAMMOND ORGAN OWNERS SOCIETY: The organisation in which RIMMER served as treasurer, a post of which he is extremely proud.

HAMSTER: The second animal into which LISTER was turned by the DNA MODIFIER. *See also* CHICKEN.

HANDMAIDENS: Although manacled to a pillar on the PSYMOON, RIMMER thought his luck was in when two of these scantily-dressed ladies began OILING his nearly naked body.

HANDSHAKE: A term used to denote a radio greeting between space ships.

HANEKA: The principle time measurement used by the KINITAWOWI. Its exact equality to the standard EARTH minute caused CAT all manner of mathematical problems.

HANNAH: A DOG belonging to LISTER's stepfather, which features prominently in the only photograph he has of him.

HAPPY DEATHDAY: The song sung to RIMMER on the anniversary of his death. When the celebrations were over, a few verses of 'Show me the way to go home' were considered in order.

HARD-LIGHT DRIVE: The revolutionary type of HOLO-GRAM drive which, created by LEGION, was bestowed upon RIMMER. Unlike his previous soft-light drive, this gave him a solid presence, thus necessitating the immediate use of a PUNC-TURE REPAIR KIT.

HARD-LIGHT REMOTE BELT: The means by which RIMMER sustains his hard-light hologramatic presence away from STARBUG.

HARLEY DAVIDSON: The type of motor-cycle chosen by LISTER as his mode of transport in his BETTER THAN LIFE fantasy.

HARRISON: A potential replacement HOLOGRAM, chosen when it was believed that RIMMER was to join the crew of the HOLOSHIP. She declined the offer, deciding that remaining dead was preferable to spending any length of time with LISTER, KRYTEN and CAT.

HAVE YOU GOT A GOOD MEMORY?: A quiz in a magazine which LISTER was annoyed to discover had been filled in by someone. As it turned out, it was him – well, who else would spell Thursday with an F?

HEAD SEX CHANGE OPERATION: Performed by an erratic HOLLY upon himself so that he resembled HILLY, his counterpart in the female-dominated PARALLEL UNIVERSE.

HEAD-BANGER HARRIS: The likeliest owner of the FREAKY FUNGUS that LISTER gave RIMMER.

HEADLINES: RIMMER's wall contains a selection of these, all of which are about people called either Arnold or RIMMER. None of them are about him, but the intention is to make it look like they are.

HECTOR: A HUGE GREEN BLOB who turned out to be the husband of CAMILLE.

HEIDEGER: See LEGION.

HERO WORLD: An area of the WAX-DROID THEME PARK in which Droids of history's heroes were kept.

HERRING: The type of FISH which rained down in the bunk room during LISTER's bout of a mutated PNEUMONIA virus which made his HALLUCINATIONS solid. This particular image was inspired by an incident in twelfth-century Burgundy.

HEX VISION: A lethal symptom of the HOLO-VIRUS. Fortunately, the RED DWARF crew never meet anyone who can shoot straight.

HIGHS: The perfect version of RED DWARF and its crew, patterned by the TRIPLICATOR. Aboard the High RED DWARF a pure, aesthetic life was earnestly adhered to, the pursuit of culture and beauty providing the prime motivation for its exalted crew – unlike those bastards, the LOWS.

HILLY: RED DWARF's on-board computer in the female dominated PARALLEL UNIVERSE. HOLLY fell madly in love with his counterpart, and later performed a HEAD SEX CHANGE OPERATION on himself in order to look like her.

HITLER, ADOLF: Leader of the runners-up in World War II and not such a bad chap after all, according to the future STARBUG crew who used to pop in for the odd GAME of canasta, or mixed doubles with the Goerrings. Our own LISTER met him twice, once (along with CAT) as a WAX-DROID and once thanks to the TIMESLIDES. On BACKWARDS EARTH, Hitler really wasn't so bad: his armies retreated to where they came from, bringing people to life in the process. *See also* FACIST DICTATOR MONTHLY.

HOLDEN, FRED (THICKY): A particularly stupid classmate of RIMMER's, who was destined to become a multi-millionaire and marry LADY SABRINA MULHOLLAND-JJONES, all due to his invention of the TENSION SHEET.

HOLDER: *See* LEGION.

HOL ROCK: The name which HOLLY applied to his own invention of DECIMALISED MUSIC.

HOLLISTER, CAPTAIN: The Captain of RED DWARF, who ordered that LISTER be confined to STASIS.

HOLLY: The RED DWARF's tenth generation AI hologrammic computer, now lost along with the ship.

HOLLY HOP DRIVE: A device constructed by HOLLY, which looked rather suspiciously like a box with start and stop buttons. It was theoretically capable of instantly transporting RED DWARF anywhere in the universe, but on the one occasion it was used, it actually deposited the ship in a female dominated PARALLEL UNIVERSE.

HOLOGRAM: A computer-generated light image of a person, into which his or her brain patterns can be projected. This technology is used primarily for bringing people back from the dead. HOLLY can sustain one HOLOGRAM at a time, and currently this is ARNOLD RIMMER, although in the past GEORGE McINTYRE and KRISTINE KOCHANSKI have also had this distinction.

HOLOGRAM DISCS: Also known as PERSONALITY DISCS. The pieces of equipment on which are recorded the details necessary to generate HOLOGRAMS of particular people. RED DWARF holds both discs and back-up discs for each of its former crew members.

HOLOGRAM PROJECTION SUITE: The room from which HOLOGRAMS are created, monitored and controlled.

HOLOGRAMATIC NEWSREADER: One of these late broadcasters was employed by GROOVY CHANNEL 27.

HOLOGRAMMIC PROJECTION CAGE: An apparatus which must be used to sustain a HOLOGRAM away from RED DWARF, when conditions make it necessary.

HOLOGRAMMIC PROJECTION BOX: The apparatus from which HOLOGRAMS are created. Not surprisingly, these are located in the HOLOGRAM PROJECTION SUITE.

HOLOSHIP: A computer generated space craft crewed by HOLOGRAMS. Composed of tachyons, it is entirely without mass or volume and as such is capable of travelling through worm holes and star gates. *See* ENLIGHTENMENT.

HOLO-VIRUS: A disease so unpleasant that it can kill people that are already dead. The main symptom of the illness is complete insanity, but there are potentially lethal side effects. By stimulating various unused areas of the brain it endows its victim with psychic powers such as telepathy, telekinesis, and HEX VISION, but the energy used to sustain these abilities drains the life force. The disease can be transmitted by radio waves as RIMMER found to his cost when he contracted the virus from Doctor LANSTROM.

HOLOWHIP: A weapon which can apparently be used by humans in order to inflict pain on HOLOGRAMS. Presumably, STARBUG's Munitions Cabinet doesn't contain one of these, but the threat of its use certainly had Commander BINKS worried. Alternatively the device can certainly be used by HOLOGRAMS on humans as LISTER painfully discovered aboard the LOW version of RED DWARF.

HOLY BOOK: The bible of the CAT PEOPLE, which told the story of CLOISTER THE STUPID and the parthenogenesis of the CAT race.

HOLY CUSTARD STAINS: Thanks to LISTER, these be came items of religious significance to the CAT PEOPLE, and were worn by the CAT PRIESTS. *See also* SACRED GRAVY MARKS.

HOLY MOTHER: The title by which the CAT PEOPLE refer to LISTER's former pet, FRANKENSTEIN.

HOLY WARS: The millennia-long battle that broke out between the CAT PEOPLE over what colour the CARD BOARD HATS in FUCHAL should be.

HOME SWEET HOME: The motto which is monogrammed on to RIMMER's pyjamas.

HOMING POD: The means by which HUDZEN arrived on RED DWARF.

HOODED LEGIONS, THE: Acolytes of the Dark One, RIMMER's SELF LOATHING. Encountered on the PSY MOON, they were the negative aspects of RIMMER's psyche personified. Counted among their number were Bitterness, Self Doubt, Mistrust and Loneliness.

HORSES: One of the types of animal that LISTER wanted to breed when he got his farm on FIJI.

HOT DOG AND DOUGHNUT DINER: LISTER's desire to open one of these on FIJI became the CAT PEOPLE's idea of Heaven.

HOT WAX DRIP UNSIGHTLY HAIR REMOVER: One of CAT's beauty aids, which he adamantly refuses ever to unplug.

HOW TO PICK UP GIRLS BY HYPNOSIS: A book used extensively, but to little avail, by RIMMER. *See* LORRAINE.

HOWDY DOODLY DOO: A term of greeting used constantly by TALKIE TOASTER. Like most other things about this appliance, LISTER found this particularly irritating.

HUDZEN 10: The state-of-the-art MECHANOID sent to replace KRYTEN. Thousands of years alone in deep space had taken their toll on his sanity CHIP, however, with near fatal consequences for the RED DWARF crew.

HUMMING: An activity in which LISTER indulges – maliciously and persistently, according to RIMMER.

I

ICE AGES: LISTER's preferred time unit for calculating the period since he last had SEX. 'Four' sounds so much better than the alternative, and in leap ice ages, it's only one.

ICEBOX: A handy storage space for LISTER's spare sneakers.

ICE PLANET: The unnamed world where LISTER and RIMMER were marooned for several days when STARBUG crash-landed.

INDLING SONG, THE: A song composed by LISTER, and much admired by the personification of his own CONFIDENCE – if by nobody else.

INFLATABLE INGRID: RIMMER's Polythene Pal who, unbeknownst to him, was LISTER's pal too. *See also* RACHEL.

IN-FLIGHT MAGAZINES: These are present in STARBUG, their only purpose being to provide an anaesthetic effect which keeps the body relaxed in the event of a crash. CAT found that one of them worked particularly well when KRYTEN had to re-set his broken leg.

INFULLIBLE: HOLLY claims to be the nearest thing to infullible – i.e., infallible.

INTELLIGENCE TEST: LISTER conned PETERSEN into

believing he'd passed one of these.

INTERSTELLA ACTION GAMES: Makers of AR role-playing games such as GUMSHOE and STREETS OF LAREDO.

INQUISITOR, THE: A self-repairing SIMULANT which, having survived to the end of time, concluded that GOD did not exist and that the purpose of life was to lead it in a worthwhile manner. Building a time machine, it travelled throughout eternity administering its own particular brand of punishment to those who did not live up to their potential. Those it considered unworthy were erased from history and replaced. Needless to say, the Inquisitor's arrival aboard RED DWARF prompted a certain degree of worry among the crew.

IO AMATEUR WAR-GAMERS: RIMMER was once a member of this group, and felt that his commanding role in the WAX WAR would have earned him their respect.

IO HOUSE: RIMMER's old school, at which he was rather less than happy. He always resented his parents for not sending him to a private school and, as with most things, he believes this to be one of the factors which prevented him from achieving his ambitions. It is not clear whether or not this school is actually based on the Jupiter moon of Io itself.

IONIAN NERVE-GRIP: The non-existent, painless method by which KRYTEN promised to render RIMMER unconscious. RIMMER became suspicious when KRYTEN actually smashed him over the head with a vase.

IQ: HOLLY professes to have an intelligence quotient in the region of six thousand, this being equivalent to that of either 6000 PE teachers or 12,000 car park attendants. In reality, an advanced case of COMPUTER SENILITY has reduced this figure greatly. Although KRYTEN did try to rectify the problem, the raising of HOLLY'S IQ to 12,000 also brought about an exponential reduction in her life-span, leaving her with only

3.41 minutes of run-time left.

IRANIAN JERD: According to the CAT, this animal can do fifty pelvic thrusts per second. He considers his own record to be somewhat higher.

IRON DUKE: The radio code-name which the unhinged RIMMER gave to himself during the WAX WAR.

J

JACKSON POLLOCK: Euphemism for being sick (as in 'I feel a Jackson Pollock coming on'). This was used by KRYTEN after hearing LISTER telling of the time he was sick off the top of the Eiffel Tower. The result was apparently sold as a genuine example of the pavement art of this painter.

JACQUENAUX, LIEUTENANT GENERAL BARON: The commander of RIMMER's treasured ARMIES DU NORD.

JAGUAR, E-TYPE: The mode of transport selected by RIMMER in his BETTER THAN LIFE fantasy – complete with FURRY DICE.

JAPANESE MEAL: NIRVANAH CRANE felt that RIMMER's sexual technique was akin to one of these – it came in incredibly small portions, but there were plenty of courses.

JAVANESE CAMPHOR-WOOD CHEST: Given to him by his father, this is RIMMER's most cherished possession – or at least it was, before it acquired a GUITAR-shaped hole.

JAZZ FM: A radio station favoured by KRYTEN, who can pick it up with his left NIPPLE NUT.

JIGSAW: LISTER possesses one of these, which shows RED DWARF itself. Having wiped his own memory of the day on which he finished it, its completion became a bizarre mystery to him.

JIM: Jim and BEXLEY were LISTER's twin sons both named after JIM BEXLEY SPEED. They were conceived in the female-orientated PARALLEL UNIVERSE, but born in our own, where the differing physical laws caused them to age eighteen years within three weeks of being born. They were returned to their home dimension, where they currently live with their 'father' DEB LISTER. In another such dimension – the one from which ACE RIMMER hailed – LISTER's counterpart, SPANNERS, had a Jim and BEXLEY of his own, by KRISTINE KOCHANSKI. Unscrupulous PSIRENS tried to lure our own LISTER to his death by claiming that his KOCHANSKI had likewise borne his children, this time by breaking into RED DWARF's sperm-bank whilst LISTER was in STASIS. See also BEXLEY.

JIMMY: A regular of the LAST CHANCE SALOON, whose expertise with a whip was no match for BRETT RIVERBOAT's knife throwning.

JOE: No other name given. A member of the RED DWARF crew, known to GEORGE McINTYRE.

JOHNS, TRACEY: A Mapping Officer on board the NOVA 5. The RED DWARF crew discovered her body when they answered a distress call from the ship's MECHANOID, KRYTEN. *See also* AIR, JANE and GILL, ANNE.

JOHNSONS BABY BUD: The most romantic thing RIMMER ever had down his ear.

JONATHAN: The middle name with which RIMMER claims to have been bestowed. In fact it's really Judas.

JOVIAN BOOGLE HOOPS: Yet another form of cutlery which KRYTEN is skilled in the use of.

JOZXYQK: A word used by CATS when they get their sexual organs trapped in something – if the CAT is to be believed when playing Scrabble.

JUMP-LEADS: The devices which RIMMER expresses an interest in attaching to KRYTEN's NIPPLE NUTS, should he fail to 'shape up'.

JUNIOR ANGLER: All the thrills and spills of fresh-water fly-fishing in your own home, and as such, a favourite game with LISTER and the CAT. CAT has, however, had to lay down the law, telling LISTER that Junior Angler is the nearest he's going to come to making love to him. LISTER was doubtless quite relieved.

JUNIOR COLOUR ENCYCLOPEDIA OF SPACE, THE: The source of all HOLLY's knowledge – or so QUEEG alleged.

JUNIOR D: When RIMMER was seven, his Headmaster considered keeping him down a year in this class, but decided against it. In a PARALLEL UNIVERSE, his decision was different, and the Head's foresight led to Arnold's development into Commander ACE RIMMER.

JUNK MAIL: Even in THREE MILLION YEARS' time, this still constitutes the greater proportion of all post. In the case of RED DWARF in particular, the problem was an even greater one, due to LISTER's habit of sending off for everything he possibly could, simply to ensure that he got some letters.

JUPITER MINING CORPORATION: The company to which RED DWARF belonged. The corporation ran merchant vessels on behalf of the SPACE CORPS, crewed by Corps personnel.

JUPITER RISE: The photograph which all the tourists take.

JUSTICE COMPUTER: The mechanism which administers JUSTICE WORLD.

JUSTICE FIELD: This covers the whole of the JUSTICE ZONE on JUSTICE WORLD, and once within its influence, it is impossible to commit a crime of any kind without the effects of that crime rebounding against you. In this way, prisoners are expected to get into the habit of not committing crimes and to continue this habit upon release.

JUSTICE WORLD: The site of a high-tech, completely automated penal colony. *See also* anything else in this index that starts with 'Justice'.

JUSTICE ZONE: That area of JUSTICE WORLD in which prisoners are kept, and which is covered by the JUSTICE FIELD.

K

KEELAN, CHARLES: A schoolmate of LISTER's, who later achieved a certain amount of notoriety by eating his wife.

KELLY: A character in the ANDROIDS soap opera, presumably married to BROOK. She shocked him with the revelation that her son, Brooke Jnr, was not his. She was played by ANDROID I 4762/E.

KENDALL, FELICITY: A twentieth-century personality, whose bottom was, not surprisingly, much admired by the RED DWARF crew. They once discovered a moon which bore a startling resemblance to said object, and spent a great deal of time flying around it.

KIDNEY: A form of punctuation, or perhaps just an accident, for a luckless GELF victim.

KING OF THE POTATO PEOPLE: Someone who was apparently unwilling to let the badly deranged RIMMER release the others from QUARANTINE.

KINITAWOWI: One of the friendlier GELF tribes: not skinning you alive the moment they set eyes on you is one of their warmest greetings.

KIPPERS: ACE RIMMER was perhaps partial to this particu-

JUSTICE WORLD

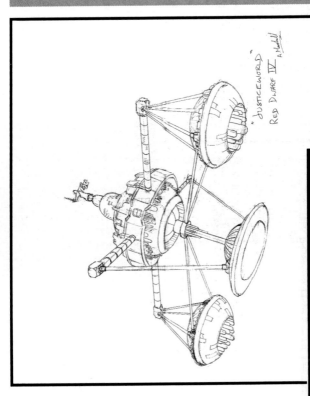

"JUSTICEWORLD"
RED DWARF IV A.Mudall

The imposing exterior of Justice World.

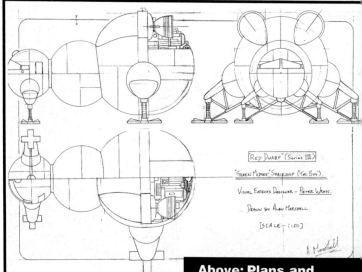

RED DWARF (Series III)

"GREEN MIDGET" SPACESHIP (THE BUG).

VISUAL EFFECTS DESIGNER — PETER WRAGG.

DRAWN BY ALAN MARSHALL.

[SCALE — 1:50]

A. Marshall

STARBUG

Above: Plans and elevations of what eventually became Starbug.

Below: A rough design of what became the series' premier vessel.

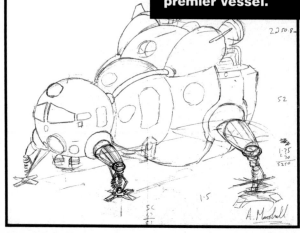

A. Marshall

A restful moment during the making of 'Timeslides'.

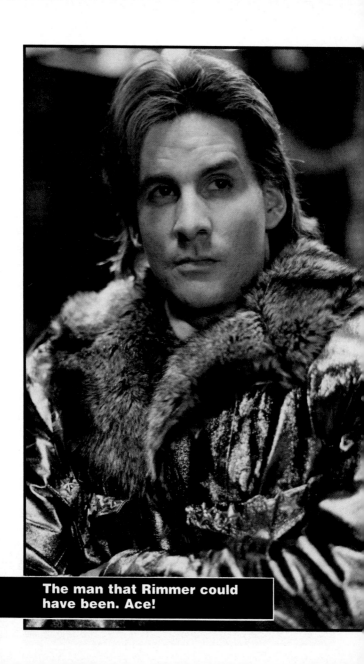

The man that Rimmer could have been. Ace!

Danny, Craig and Hattie share a philosophical moment.

'The End' is near for our heroes, plus guest actress C P Grogan.

Behind the masks: Robert llewellyn (below) and his predecessor David Ross (right), both happily bereft of Kryten's stifling rubber.

Matthew Devitt guest stars as someone the Cat didn't want to meet.

Suzanne Bertish guest-stars, as Rimmer finds his 'Parallel Universe' self too hot to handle.

The current cast discuss strategy in 'Demons and Angels'.

lar type of FISH, hence his oft-used phrase, 'Smoke me a kipper – I'll be back for breakfast!'

KITTY SCHOOL: A place of learning where CAT was taught the rudiments of the feline method of reading by smells and where, in religious instruction, he heard the story of CLOISTER THE STUPID.

KOCHANSKI, KRISTINE: A Navigation Officer on board RED DWARF, and the LOVE of LISTER's life, the girl of his dreams, the object of his desires, etc. So LISTER isn't about to let a couple of minor considerations – such as their relationship being something of a non-starter, and her being dead – stand in the way of true happiness. And in fact one day he will discover a way back through time and they'll be married. Ah . . . isn't it romantic? However, in the meantime he'd quite like to see Krissy's HOLOGRAM replace RIMMER's, but as RIMMER always considered her to be rather a snooty cow and has her disc well and truly hidden there isn't too much chance of that happening. *See also* PSIRENS

KRISPIES: A type of food favoured by CAT (aren't they all?!), and fed to him by LISTER.

KRYTEN 2X4B 523P: Formerly the service ANDROID on the NOVA 5, and brought on board RED DWARF by LISTER.

L

LABORATORY MICE: The only organisms on RED DWARF that had to obey orders from DAVE LISTER. Like every other form of life on the ship, these perished in the RADIATION leak, but the CAT still searches the CARGO DECKS in hope.

LAGER: A drink of which LISTER is a great admirer, particularly as milkshake flavouring or served hot with croutons. That proved to be his salvation when he faced the MUTTON VINDALOO BEAST, as after all, lager is the only thing that can kill a CURRY.

LANSTROM, HILDEGARD: A hologamatic Doctor at a VIRAL RESEARCH DEPARTMENT. The crew believed that she might be a valuable asset aboard RED DWARF so they considered having both her and RIMMER on a time share basis. Unfortunately the Doctor had fallen prey to her own genius and had been infected by the HOLO-VIRUS. The malady eventually killed her but not before she had made a good attempt upon the lives of our heroes.

LASER CANNONS: Useful devices fitted by considerate SIMULANTS to STARBUG, so as to provide themselves with a little sport. Had they carried out this alteration earlier, then one of CAT"'s amazing plans might actually have become feasible.

LAST CHANCE SALOON: Established in 1874, this was the best watering hole in EXISTENCE.

LAST, JAMES: Although we never saw him, LISTER claims that he was one of ADOLF HITLER's army of evil WAX-DROIDS. RIMMER is obviously an admirer of this musician, as LISTER recognised him from his companion's record collection.

LAUNDRY: CAT disgusted his shipmates with the revelation that he washes his clothes with his tongue! LISTER, meanwhile, carries out this chore with far less frequency. He did manage to get together a laundry list THREE MILLION YEARS ago, but this ended up being used to line the basket of his pet cat, FRANKENSTEIN. Unfortunately, the CAT PEOPLE later mis-interpreted its significance, believing it to be a star chart that would lead them to the PROMISED LAND of FUCHAL. One of the two ARKS in which they eventually left RED

DWARF tried to follow its directions, and collided with an asteroid. The laundry room, not surprisingly, also happens to be one of KRYTEN's favourite places.

LAXO: Good for indigestion and stomach upsets, but presumably no match for RIMMER's DUMPLINGS.

LEAGUE AGAINST SALIVATING MONSTERS, THE: One of the names put forward by RIMMER in his anger-free campaign against the POLYMORPH. *See also* CLITORIS.

LEARNING DRUGS: Illegal drugs that increase the capacity of the memory. RIMMER used them to improve his chances of passing his many EXAMS, although he never did so. LISTER did likewise, stealing the drugs from RIMMER's locker when he wished to enter the Chef's EXAM.

LECLERK, HENRY: A member of the REVOLUTIONARY WORKING FRONT, who was arrested in France whilst attempting to poison the source of all the world's Perrier water. Had he been successful, it was estimated that the entire middle class would have been wiped out within three weeks.

LEECHES: On the PSY-MOON they possessed the features of MRS RIMMER.

LEGION: A gestalt entity, composed in its first incarnation of five of the most brilliant minds of the 23rd century, amongst them HEIDEGER, DAVRO, HOLDER and QUAYLE. His later combination of LISTER, RIMMER, KRYTEN and CAT was something of a comedown.

LEGO: A toy which the six-year-old LISTER enjoyed playing with. The greatest boost to his collection came when his stepfather died, and sympathetic relatives bought him gifts. At the time, he hoped a few more people would die so that he could complete the set.

LEISURE WORLD INTERNATIONAL: A company which didn't exist, but which in the group HALLUCINATION induced by the DESPAIR SQUID became the home of twenty RED DWARF TOTAL IMMERSION VIDEO GAMES.

LEMMING: A type of animal once kept as a pet by RIMMER, until it sunk its teeth into him and he had to smash its head in, ruining his helicopter wallpaper.

LEMMING SUNDAY: The name applied by the press to the day RIMMER joined the SAMARITANS and five people committed suicide.

LENNON: One of LISTER's two ROBOT GOLDFISH. *See also* McCARTNEY.

LEOPARD: A type of LAGER; specifically the variety which LISTER used against the MUTTON VINDALOO BEAST.

LEVI JEANS: Even in the far distant future these items still retain, along with Swiss watches, strong bargaining power on the black market.

LICKETTY-SPLIT: RIMMER's preferred state of affairs – everything in order.

LICORICE ALLSORTS: Tragically, the only ones left on STARBUG are the black curly ones which no-one likes.

LIE MODE: KRYTEN's preferred mode for use whilst addressing RIMMER.

LIFESTYLES OF THE DISGUSTINGLY RICH AND FAMOUS: A TV show presented by BLAIZE FALCONBURGER, which once profiled LISTER when he altered the TIMELINES to make himself both rich and famous.

LIGHT BARRIER: The theoretical threshold which has to be crossed before attaining LIGHT SPEED. When RED DWARF did so, the action caused a series of FUTURE ECHOES to appear to its crew.

LIGHT BEE: A small, highly advanced device which 'buzzes around' inside RIMMER's hologramatic body, maintaining his form. When it isn't doing that, it can still hold his conscious personality – and LISTER found to his delight that it was small enough to swallow.

LIGHT SHIP: A vessel developed in the PARALLEL UNIVERSE of ACE RIMMER – if not in our own – which was capable of travelling at LIGHT SPEED.

LIGHT SPEED: Well, what does it sound like it means?!

LIGHT SWITCH: RIMMER's idea of a work of art.

LIMPET MINES: The explosives which HOLLY used to turn the DESPAIR SQUID into fried calamari.

LIQUID DILINIUM: A freezing agent used against the EMOHAWK

LISTER, DAVID: (1) The last human being left alive. God help Mankind!

LISTER, DAVID : (2) A version of LISTER that might have been born had a different sperm prevailed; he was brought into temporary existence when THE INQUISITOR attempted to remove all traces of the original from history. Unfortunately, for him, he was killed, but fortunately for the other LISTER, his dead hand proved useful for opening doors with.

LISTER, DEB: DAVE LISTER's counterpart in the female dominated PARALLEL UNIVERSE, identical to him in all but physical characteristics. She is the 'father' of his twin sons, JIM and BEXLEY, having slept with him after a drunken binge.

LISTER, MRS: Daughter of the KINITAWOWI chief, whose unpronounceable real name sounds like a footballer clearing his nose. Fortunately for the reluctant groom, the marriage was never consumated.

LITHIUM CARBONATE: A gas used as a MOOD STABILISER which reversed the near fatal effects of the DESPAIR SQUID's ink.

LITTLE JIMMY OSMOND: The only thing in the known universe for which HOLLY suspects that there may not be a logical explanation.

LITTLE TOMMY: The boy whom ACE RIMMER nursed back to health after an unspecified illness.

LIVVIES: A derogatory slang term employed by HOLO-GRAMS, to describe those people left alive.

LOLA: Barmaid at the LAST CHANCE SALOON.

LOLITA: Nabokov's erotic novel, and one of the books LISTER had to burn to keep warm when he and RIMMER were marooned on an ICE PLANET, though page 61 was spared the flames.

LONDON JETS: A ZERO GRAVITY FOOTBALL team supported by LISTER, who has the posters, the book and several shirts. Their ROOF ATTACK player, JIM BEXLEY SPEED, is LISTER's particular hero, after whom he named his twin sons, JIM and BEXLEY. It is also known that an un-named member of their team is the man he associates most with CONFIDENCE, as it is in this form that LISTER's own CONFIDENCE manifested itself.

LORETTA: Despite being a psychotic, schizophrenic, serial killing *femme fatale*, she was the sexiest computer sprite LISTER had ever seen. *See* GUMSHOE.

LORRAINE: A girl with an artificial nose, who initially fell for RIMMER's 'hypnotic' chat-up lines. She later came to her senses and, during the couple's first date, escaped through the toilet window. In order to avoid a second date, she claimed she had to move to PLUTO.

LOUIS XVI: According to history, a cruel despot who lived in obscene opulence whilst his subjects starved to DEATH. According to the future STARBUG crew, a charming, urbane and witty host with a cute wife, who held a banquet in their honour.

LOVE: Considered 'a short-term hormonal distraction which interferes with the pure pursuit of personal enhancement' the concept was abandoned, along with that of family, in the 25th century. RIMMER agreed with philosophy of the LOVE CELIBACY SOCIETY ie 'LOVE is a sickness that holds back your career and makes you spend all your money'.

LOVE CELIBACY SOCIETY: An organisation joined by RIMMER, due to his negative attitude towards the concept of LOVE. LISTER suspected, with much justification, that his true reason for joining was that nobody fancied him.

LOWS: The imperfect version of RED DWARF and its crew formed by the TRIPLICATOR. Aboard this vile, putrescent RED DWARF could be found all the abhorrent things in life: video nasties, weapons magazines, even toastie toppers. Its sadistic crew consisted of a one eyed LISTER, a clapped out KRYTEN, a sabre toothed CAT and a transvestite RIMMER; between them they were responsible for the death of their counterparts, the HIGHS.

LS: An abbreviation for LIGHT SPEED, as favoured by HOLLY.

LUGGAGE, ELECTRONIC: Another miracle of twenty-third century technology, made possible by the development of Artificial Intelligence circuits.

LUIGI'S FISH'N'CHIP EMPORIUM: Suppliers of LISTER's sausage and onion gravy sandwiches.

LUNAR CITY SEVEN: Presumably a real place, this conurbation is celebrated in a popular song which is particularly enjoyed by LISTER.

LYING: An action of which KRYTEN's programming rendered him incapable. With some help from the movie CASABLANCA, LISTER was able to overcome this 'difficulty'.

M

McCARTNEY: One of LISTER's two ROBOT GOLDFISH. *See also* LENNON.

McCAULEY, CAROL: A recipient of 'secret' love letters from RIMMER.

McCLURE, DOUG: Dinosaur battling star of most of the movies left on STARBUG. It is noteable that, when LEGION provided LISTER with his perfect environment, no such FILMS were present. *See also* VIDS.

McGEE, BEAR-STRANGLER: The meanest, toughest patron of the LAST CHANCE SALOON, and thus the one with whom RIMMER immediately picked a fight.

McGREW, DANGEROUS DAN: A barefist fighter with a great deal of stamina from STREETS OF LAREDO, this role-playing character was portrayed by RIMMER.

McGRUDER, YVONNE: The ship's female boxing champion, and the subject both of RIMMER's dreams and of his BETTER THAN LIFE fantasy. McGruder is the only woman he ever managed to sleep with, and even then, it was due in great part to the concussion she had suffered through being hit over the head with a winch. Apparently, she mistook him for somebody called NORMAN.

McINTYRE, GEORGE: A Flight Co-ordinator on board RED DWARF. He died and was brought back to life as a HOLOGRAM.

McQUEEN: A flight co-ordinator whose mathematical genius proved useful to RIMMER following a mind patching operation – at least it did until RIMMER's unsuitable mind rejected it. *See also* BUCHAN.

McWILLIAMS: A necrophiliac, according to RIMMER, who

voiced this opinion to McWilliams' face when he was with his four biggest friends in the HAÇIENDA club on MIRANDA. The outcome was a huge bar-room brawl, which RIMMER deftly avoided.

MACEDONIA: The site of ALEXANDER THE GREAT's palace, which was visited by RIMMER on a school trip. He later discovered that he might have led a past life there.

MAGIC CARPET: The means by which LISTER, CAT and KRYTEN hoped to visit the KING OF THE POTATO PEOPLE and plea for their freedom – and they say they weren't going mad?!

MAGIC DOOR: The term by which the CAT was able to comprehend the concept of the nature of the STASIS LEAK.

MALE EUNUCH, THE: A masculinist BOOK by JEREMY GREER.

MAMET, PROFESSOR: KRYTEN's creator about whom we know very little. However, a canny PSIREN knew enough to realise that assuming her appearance would render the mechanoid unable to refuse any command it recieved, even if it meant self-destruction.

MAMOSIAN ANTI-MATTER CHOPSTICKS: The impliments with which one is expected to consume MAMOSIAN CUISINE. If any of the DWARFERS hadn't been too polite to ask for a fork they might actually have tasted some of their meal.

MAMOSIAN CUISINE: A uniquely flavoured food, suitable for ANDROIDS, which made up the 24th-century banquet laid on by LEGION.

MAMOSIAN TELEKENETIC WINE: A drink which can be enjoyed without ever having to lift the glass. Theoretically, anyway.

MAN PLUS: What LISTER hoped to become, via the DNA MODIFIER, to combat the MUTTON VINDALOO BEAST. In fact, he ended up more like Man Minus.

MANTOVANI: One of RIMMER's musical idols.

MAPLE SYRUP: The comestible substance with which MELLIE promised to cover herself on ACE RIMMER's behalf.

MARCH 16TH: The date on which RIMMER spent twelve minutes, minus the time it takes to eat a PIZZA, having sex.

MARCH 2077: The month in which LISTER married KOCHANSKI and the crew of RED DWARF were wiped out – but see also GELDOF.

MARGUERITA, CHILLED: LISTER's favourite drink, no longer served on STARBUG due to the absence of tequila. KRYTEN broke out the last mini-bottle in anguish when he discovered his master's ultimate fate.

MARIJUANA GIN: No comment!

MATTER PADDLE: A prototype transporter discovered by KRYTEN in the research labs. This was capable of converting an individual into digital information and then transmitting him as light beams to another point in space. It could home in on any atmosphere-bearing planet within 500,000 light years. Unfortunately, when the crew used it, the one it homed in on turned out to be WAX-WORLD. The device was latter adapted, by KRYTEN, into a TRIPLICATOR.

MAXINE: The twin sister of LORETTA; she murdered PALLISTER and LORETTA took the rap knowing that PHILIP was her alibi. Something like that, anyway. *See* GUMSHOE.

MAYDAY: A distress call. RIMMER finds it difficult to understand why something like Shrove Tuesday or Ascension Sunday can't be used instead.

MAYOR OF WARSAW: According to RIMMER, this dignitary spontaneously combusted in 1546. When LISTER caught a mutated PNEUMONIA virus that made his HALLUCINATIONS solid, he remembered that tale, and the incident was re-enacted outside the bunk room.

MECHANOID MENU: Special ANDROID food, knocked up by HOLLY for what was supposed to be KRYTEN's last day of life. RIMMER recommended the barium hydro-chlorate salad nicoise and the helium 3 isotopes de la maison, with a small, radioactive fruit salad for pudding.

MECHANOIDS: *See* ANDROIDS (1).

MEDALS: LISTER was surprised to discover that RIMMER has four of these, although less so when he realised that they were for Three Years Long Service, Six Years Long Service, Nine Years Long Service and Twelve Years Long Service.

MEDICAL EQUIPMENT: LISTER's attempt use these items to make a meal a special occasion were met with some trepidation by CAT.

MEDI-COMP: The computer which runs RED DWARF's medical unit.

MEDI-SCAN: The means by which LISTER patched into the security cameras, thus obtaining a view of his future which KRYTEN had wished to keep from him.

MELLIE: One of ACE RIMMER's friends in his own dimension, this woman looked suspiciously like HOLLY's female form.

MENTAL EMETIC: A process used as part of the MIND SWAP operation.

MERCURIAN BOOMERANG SPOON: An often lethal type of cutlery.

MERMAID: One of the CAT's fantasies, as provided to him

by the BETTER THAN LIFE GAME, was a mermaid called MIRANDA. Naturally, she had the top half of a FISH and the bottom half of a woman. Well, the other way round would be stupid!

MILK RATION: The regular allowance of milk given to all crew members of RED DWARF before the accident that killed most of them. LISTER had to use his to feed his secret pet cat FRANKENSTEIN.

MILLENIUM OXIDE: A chemical substance, the presence of which alerted KRYTEN to the fact that there were SIMULENTS about.

MILLER, GLEN: RIMMER believed him to have been kidnapped by ALIENS – and he was worried that they might give him back!

MIMAS, SATURN: In ACE RIMMER's PARALLEL UNIVERSE, if not in our own, this moon is the site of the SPACE CORPS Test Base where he was stationed.

MIMEAN BLADDERFISH: An edible marine animal that, after borrowing LISTER's body, RIMMER selected as the FISH course for his first colossal meal.

MIND PATCHING: An illegal and dangerous process to insert the mind of an individual into that of another, thereby giving the recipient access to the intelligence of the donor. RIMMER had no scruples about undergoing the operation if it would help him gain a place aboard ENLIGHTENMENT.

MIND PROBE: The device used in the CLEARANCE AREA on JUSTICE WORLD to ascertain whether any visitors have a criminal background.

MIND SWAP: The process by which an individual's mind is drained and stored on tape, leaving the body free to play host to another personality. Both LISTER and the CAT were unfortunate enough to have their bodies temporarily on loan to

RIMMER.

MINIMUM HAIRCUT LENGTH: RIMMER always favoured the reduction of this by a quarter of an inch, but he could never persuade CAPTAIN HOLLISTER to see the matter quite his way.

MINISTRY OF ALTERATION: The Government department headed by Colonel SEBASTIAN DOYLE. The Ministry of Alteration changed people; it changed them from living people to dead people.

MIRANDA: (1) The CAT's MERMAID girlfriend in his BETTER THAN LIFE fantasy.

MIRANDA: (2) The Uranian moon where, whilst on planet leave, RIMMER started a fight in the HAÇIENDA.

MIRRORS: CAT wouldn't be seen without one of these at least not by himself. So when he's at his coolest, he finds almost insurmountable difficulty in tearing himself away from them. LISTER was alarmed when his mirror started to reflect FUTURE ECHOES, and KRYTEN banned him from looking in them altogether when he contracted SPACE MUMPS, presumably thinking that the hideous sight would make him hysterical. LISTER s best use for mirrors so far was taught to him by his best friend DUNCAN, at the age of ten. This was to apply them to your toe-caps, thus allowing you to look up girls' skirts.

MISTER FAT BASTARD 2044: The title with which RIMMER felt CAPTAIN HOLLISTER should have been honoured.

MISTER FLIBBLE: RIMMER's right-hand man – or rather right-hand penguin – when he lost his sanity due to the effects of the HOLO-VIRUS. Sadly the holographic glove puppet vanished when RIMMER was cured.

MODO: A term of abuse, once favoured by RIMMER.

MOGADON CLUSTER: Origin point of the PAN-DIMENSIONAL LIQUID BEAST.

MONKEYS: The way in which the CAT sees human beings.

MONROE, MARILYN: Fifties sex symbol, of whom several posters adorn the locker doors in LISTER and RIMMER's bunk room. The CAT was obviously impressed by her, as not only has he been known to read magazines about the actress, but she also became one of his girlfriends in a BETTER THAN LIFE fantasy (*see also* MERMAID). Another of her fans was obviously PETERSEN, who purchased a Build-It-Yourself kit on CALLISTO. This was eventually assembled by LISTER as a last-day present for KRYTEN. Using only a screwdriver and a tub of glue, LISTER was able to construct a 'droid whose resemblance to the original Marilyn fooled absolutely no-one – except KRYTEN. Finally, Marilyn's likeness was also taken by one of the WAX-DROIDs on WAX-WORLD. Blimey, is she a regular character or what?

MOOD STABILISER: *See* LITHIUM CARBONATE.

MOONBOOTS: *See* DAY-GLO ORANGE MOONBOOTS.

MOON HOPPING: An activity indulged in by both RIMMER and KRYTEN, on occasion. A relatively harmless pastime providing the moon hopped on to is not of the Psy variety. See PSY-MOON – if you hadn't figured that out already.

MOONQUAKE: These destructive and dangerous occurrences are to be avoided at all costs. Unless they coincide with RIMMER's rendition of the SPACE CORPS ANTHEM, in which case they are likely to come as a great relief.

MORALE OFFICER: RIMMER's self-appointed position on STARBUG. He feels he can boost the spirits of his comrades by routinely insulting them on a weekly basis.

MORRIS DANCING: An activity enjoyed by RIMMER, who is frequently disappointed by his colleagues' refusal to accompany him.

MOTIVATOR: A type of alarm clock, presumably internal, used by RIMMER.

MOTORHEAD: A twentieth-century rock band whose music is considered, by the people of the twenty-third century, to be classical in content.

MUGS MURPHY: A cartoon character, whose screen exploits were mistaken by RIMMER for the classic FILM Citizen Kane.

MULHOLLAND-JJONES, LADY SABRINA: A jet-setting model, and eldest daughter of the Duke of Lincoln. She was married to FRED 'THICKY' HOLDEN, but in an alternative version of the past, she became LISTER's bird.

MURRAY, SAM: A Deck Sergeant who was an odd choice of candidate for the post of replacement HOLOGRAM. *See also* HARRISON.

MUTANTS: Anyone on RIMMERWORLD who wasn't the spitting image of RIMMER. *See also* NORMS.

MUTINY: RIMMER filed a COMPLAINT against LISTER on this charge – for jumping on his foot when RIMMER was trying to snap his GUITAR in half. He also warned KRYTEN that he was committing mutiny by diverting STARBUG in an attempt to rescue CAMILLE from an exploding planet. Apparently, this is just cause for an ANDROID to be dismantled. A more serious mutiny on board a prison ship carrying SIMULANTS to JUSTICE WORLD led to the escape of one of the creatures, who was later inadvertently picked up by RED DWARF.

MUTTON VINDALOO BEAST: Half man, half CURRY, this was what HOLLY ended up with when she tested out the DNA MODIFIER with one of LISTER's curries. The creature was impervious to BAZOOKOID fire but, fortunately, was no match for a can of LAGER.

MY INCREDIBLE CAREER BY ADMIRAL A J RIMMER: A BOOK which RIMMER would have liked to have written, and which featured in his BETTER THAN LIFE fantasy.

N

NAPOLEON: RIMMER idolises this man, describing him as his 'all-time favourite FASCIST dictator'. He would like little better than to travel back in time to the nineteenth century, and become one of his marshals. Ironically, when a WAX-DROID of Napoleon fought in the WAX WAR on WAX-WORLD, RIMMER never actually got to meet him. He was on the opposite side.

NAPS: The CAT has to take nine or ten of these per day, as preparation for his main evening snooze.

NASAL ALERT: An impending disaster which has set CAT's nostril hairs vibrating.

NAVI-COMP: An integral part of RED DWARF's guidance system, situated in the DRIVE ROOM. A malfunction in this unit is destined to cause the death of LISTER's son BEXLEY, at some time in the future. There are also smaller navi-comps fitted in RED DWARF's shuttle-craft.

NECROBICS: Hologramatic exercises for the dead, with which RIMMER once dabbled.

NEGATIVE EMOTIONS: POLYMORPH snacks. *See* ANGER, FEAR, GUILT and VANITY.

NEUTRAL AREA: The area of JUSTICE WORLD in which visitors are received. They are then fitted with ESCORT BOOTS and taken to the CLEARANCE AREA to be judged.

NEWS CHRONICLE: A newspaper which, during the 1940s, featured LISTER on its front page after the TIMESLIDES allowed him to meet ADOLF HITLER at that time.

NEWSWEEK: The fabulously wealthy LISTER appeared on the cover of this magazine after inventing the TENSION SHEET.

NEW TOKYO: A city on twenty-third century EARTH where RUBBER NUCLEAR WEAPONS had to be deployed against a rioting crowd.

NEWTON-JOHN, OLIVIA: According to HOLLY, anything is better than listening to an album by this singer.

NIGHT SCHOOL: RIMMER once attended such an establishment, where he did a film course. He apparently learnt nothing whatsoever.

NIGHT WATCHMAN: The job to which HOLLY was demoted when QUEEG took over the running of RED DWARF.

NIPPLE NUTS: One of KRYTEN's more useful features. He was particularly upset at their loss when he was changed temporarily to a human. The left nut was used mainly to pick up short-wave radio transmissions such as JAZZ FM, whilst the right one regulated his body temperature.

NIVARO, RANDY: The Second Officer aboard the HOLO-SHIP, ENLIGHTENMENT. His PROMOTION PROSPECTS were presumably pretty slim, due to his IQ being a mere 194.

NODNOL: A city on BACKWARDS EARTH, looking suspiciously like our own Manchester.

NORMAN: According to LISTER, this is the name by which YVONNE McGRUDER referred to RIMMER while the two were engaged in copulation. This no doubt has something to do with the concussion she was suffering at the time.

NORMS: Anyone on RIMMERWORLD who *was* the spitting

image of RIMMER.

NORWEB FEDERATION: An organisation invented by HOLLY, NORWEB standing for the (real) North Western Electricity Board. He claimed that they had been tracking LISTER through space to obtain payment for electricity used by a light he had left on in the bathroom, THREE MILLION YEARS ago. However, it was all a jape.

NOSTALGIA NIGHT, 1990S: A party which took place on RED DWARF shortly before the accident in which the entire crew were wiped out.

NOVA 5: A crashed spaceship from EARTH, aboard which KRYTEN was discovered, still functioning as servitor for the long-dead Mapping Officers JANE AIR, ANNE GILL and TRACEY JOHNS.

NOVEMBER 25TH: *See* GAZPACHO SOUP DAY.

NOW. . . : The only passage from SHAKESPEARE that RIMMER is able to quote.

NOW IRRADIATE YOUR HANDS: Correct procedure after using an ELECTRONIC TOILET.

O

OCEAN MOON: The culpable party in the case of STARBUG's ruptured reserve fuel tank.

ODOUR EATERS: LISTER was reputedly the only person ever to receive a refund from the makers of these items.

OFFICERS' BLOCK: That part of RED DWARF in which the quarters of all the officers were situated. LISTER mistakenly entered here while it was still contaminated by RADIATION, and contracted a mutated form of PNEUMONIA. Once they had finally got around to decontaminating the area, LISTER and RIMMER vacated their own rather basic bunk room and relocated to these more up-market surroundings.

OH BOY, WAS I SUCKERED: The message which, if not for the intervention of his crewmates, CAT would have ended up spelling out with his intestinal tract, following an encounter with BRAIN-sucking PSIRENS.

OILING: As mentioned under the entry for HANDMAIDENS, RIMMER thought his luck was improving when the two girls began to oil him. Unfortunately, he discovered that the process was intended merely to increase his electrical conductivity.

OM: A song by SMEG AND THE HEADS that was never the hit they expected, though LISTER changed that when he altered the TIMELINES and bought three million copies, sending the disc to number one in the charts.

OREGON: A ship on which, according to CAPTAIN HOLLISTER, a nasty problem was caused by a number of unquarantined RABBITS.

ORE SAMPLE POD: A Pod for transporting ore samples in; unless of course it's referred to as an ESCAPE POD.

OUTLAND REVENUE: The tax people, owed $£8500 by RIMMER. His BETTER THAN LIFE fantasy became corrupted when they arrived to collect.

OXY-GENERATION UNIT: The life-saving device which the DWARFERS purchased from the KINITAWOWI. The price: DAVE LISTER.

P

PADRÉ, THE: A good friend of ACE RIMMER's from his own dimension. He was the chaplain at the MIMAS test base and greatly resembled our own CAT.

PALLISTER: A character in the GUMSHOE murder mystery game, who unfortunately got the worst part.

PAN-DIMENSIONAL LIQUID BEAST: A visit from this creature ensured that Christmas wasn't merely the usual bout of cracker pulling and watching *The Great Escape*.

PARALLEL UNIVERSES: Dimensions similar but not identical to our own. ACE RIMMER hailed from one of these, in which one small incident during ARNOLD RIMMER's childhood had changed the course of his life drastically. In another such universe, to which HOLLY accidentally transported RED DWARF, the roles of the sexes had been completely reversed. It was there that DAVE LISTER and ARNOLD RIMMER met DEB LISTER and ARLENE RIMMER, their female equivalents. See also HILLY and THE DOG.

PARANOIA: One of the imaginary beings who LISTER and CHEN theorised lived inside their heads. He became frighteningly real when LISTER caught a mutated PNEUMONIA virus which allowed his HALLUCINATIONS to become solid. However, he was murdered by CONFIDENCE – his counterpart – who didn't want to see him holding LISTER back.

PARROT'S BAR: Situated on RED DWARF's G Deck, this is one of the more stylish relaxation areas on board the ship. As such, it is the site that KRYTEN chose for his first date with CAMILLE. As he told her when she left, they'd always have Parrot's . . .

PARTNERSHIP WHIST: An activity which, on the whole, KRYTEN finds preferable to SEX.

PAWN SACRIFICE: The radio code-name used by KRYTEN during the WAX WAR. This was presumably given to him by RIMMER, and it reflected the use to which he was put.

PD: The Punishment Detail on RED DWARF had the duty of painting the exterior of the ship.

PEEPHOLE BRA: A revealing item of lingerie which is a recurring object in RIMMER's unhealthy fantasies.

PERITONITIS: *See* APPENDIX.

PERSONAL DATA FILES: RED DWARF holds one of these for each of its crew members.

PERSONALITY DISCS: *See* HOLOGRAM DISCS.

PESTILENCE: Unhygenic member of the FOUR APOCA-LYPSE BOYS.

PETERSEN, OLAF: A catering officer aboard RED DWARF, and a great friend of DAVE LISTER. RIMMER thought of him as a Danish moron, and this opinion was only confirmed when Petersen's holographic arm accidentally replaced his own, and launched a vicious assault on his private parts.

PETE TRANTER'S SISTER: The object of LISTER's lust throughout puberty. He wanted nothing more than to squeeze her buttocks together, thus forming one juicy, giant peach. An unscrupulous PSIREN once turned this desire against him.

PHILIP: Private eye role assumed by LISTER when playing GUMSHOE.

PIANO: An instrument which KRYTEN wished to play. During his visit to our dimension, ACE RIMMER took the time to show him how.

PINKY AND PERKY: Names applied to the SKUTTERS by RIMMER.

PIPELINE 22: The place in which RIMMER chose to hide LISTER's CIGARETTES, and from which CAT recovered them.

PIZZAS: The type of food in which RIMMER likes to indulge after sex – which probably means he hasn't had that many. His preferred type is a large quatro-formaggio, with extra olives.

LISTER, on the other hand, doesn't care for pizzas at all – at least not unless they have CURRY on them.

PLANET OF THE NYMPHOMANIACS: It seems a terrible shame that this world was only a product of the HALLUCINATION caused by the DESPAIR SQUID. Still, perhaps somewhere in the universe . . .

PLATINI, HERCULE: Captain of the HOLOSHIP, ENLIGHTENMENT with an IQ of 212, going someway towards proving the old saying: 'nobody loves a smart arse'.

PLATO: According to everyone else, a Greek philosopher. According to HOLLY's data banks, the inventor of the plate.

PLEASURE GELF: A Genetically Engineered Life Form programmed to appear to each individual as the object of his or her desires. One such GELF was CAMILLE, who KRYTEN saw as an ANDROID, RIMMER saw as a hologram – looking very much like his sister-in-law JANNINE RIMMER – and LISTER saw as the last woman alive. The object of CAT's desires, it turned out, was himself.

PLUTO: A planet which was first conquered by a woman. And was possibly also visited by LORRAINE, in her attempts to avoid the affections of ARNOLD RIMMER.

PNEUMONIA: LISTER fell victim to a mutated form of this virus after entering the contaminated OFFICERS' BLOCK. The disease caused him to have HALLUCINATIONS, which then became solid.

POINTY STICK GAME: In order to play this you'll need a pointy stick and a TV weather girl. Beyond that you'll have to use your imagination.

POLYGRAPHIC SURVEILLANCE: The type of lie detection system used by the JUSTICE COMPUTER on JUSTICE WORLD, to assess whether or not LISTER was telling the truth when he acted as a witness during RIMMER's trial.

POLYMORPHS: The product of a failed genetic experiment. Originally developed for warfare, these emotion-devouring, shape-shifting mutants proved to be insane. Two of them found their way aboard RED DWARF, and, if you're really interested, some of the forms assumed by the first one included: a small ALIEN, a teddy bear, a plastic bucket and spade, some flowers, a toy truck, a flamenco dancer doll, a telephone, a model elephant, a top hat, a baseball mitt and ball, a boxer doll, a plant pot, a flashing beacon, a model Volkswagen, a roller skate, a TRAFFIC CONE, a light shade, an inflatable penguin, a yellow pig, a male doll, a po, a clock, some cheese, an old trainer, a small bucket, a pom-pom, a scrubbing brush, a metal pail, a small inflatable FROG, a Chinese ornament, a light bulb, a light stand, a yellow ball, a sock, a RABBIT, a BEACHBALL, a shami-kebab, boxer shorts, a SNAKE and a large creature with plenty of teeth. There are no prizes for spotting any we might have missed. *See also* EMOHAWK.

POOL: The GAME at which LISTER considers himself a master. He claims that his friends at the AIGBURTH ARMS knew him as CINZANO BIANCO, because once he was on the table, they couldn't get him off. His skills came in useful when he was called upon to pot a planet into a WHITE HOLE, thus sealing it up.

POPEYE: When KRYTEN became temporarily human, he borrowed from the wisdom of this cartoon character, with LISTER's encouragement. He decided 'I am what I am', and returned to his ANDROID form.

POP-UP KARMA SUTRA, THE – ZERO GRAVITY EDITION: A book owned by LISTER. Who else?

PORKMAN, DOCTOR BOB: Inventor of the condom that calls you back.

POST POD: The means by which the mail arrives aboard RED DWARF.

POT NOODLE: One of the few items of food left aboard STARBUG when it crash-landed on an ICE PLANET. Fortunately for LISTER, there was also a can of DOG FOOD present, which he could eat instead. LISTER did eventually find an edible pot noodle, aboard the HIGH version of RED DWARF.

POWER PACKS: If possible avoid the cheap Martian ones.

PREGNANCY: LISTER thought, quite justifiably, that this could never happen to him. But when he slept with DEB LISTER in the female-dominated PARALLEL UNIVERSE, he was shocked to discover that the laws of that universe made it a very real possibility. Needless to say, all happened as feared, and DAVE LISTER shortly became the proud mother of twin sons, JIM and BEXLEY.

PREHISTORIC WORLD: The area of the WAX-DROID THEME PARK directly between HERO WORLD and VILLAIN WORLD, in which Droids in the shape of prehistoric creatures were kept. KRYTEN was not too impressed by the likeness, but still ran for cover when he and RIMMER accidentally found themselves right in their midst.

PRINCE OF DORKNESS: See DUANE DIBBLEY.

PROJECTION ROOM: That area of RED DWARF where slide shows are presented. This is presumably avoided by most of the crew members, due to RIMMER's penchant for giving such shows on the subject of TELEGRAPH POLES.

PROMISED LAND: *See* FUCHAL.

PROMOTION PROSPECTS: CAPTAIN HOLLISTER described LISTER's as being zero – and RIMMER's as being comical.

PSIRENS: As if from a futuristic version of the legend from the country big on curly shoes and hummus, these GELFS telepathically altered the perception of space travellers in order to lure them to their deaths. They first tried to entice CAT by masquerading as a couple of temptresses needing seed spreaders on a planet inhabited solely by women. Gullible as ever, Cat would have fallen for it if not for the others' assurance that the girls were in fact BRAIN-sucking Psirens – even the brunette. More sophisticated disguises were used against LISTER and KRYTEN, including KRISTINE KOCHANSKI and PROFFESOR MAMET.

PSI-SCAN: A vital piece of equipment, which may well save the lives of all the crew yet, if only KRYTEN can get it to work properly. The model he has is a 345, which out performs the 346 in nine out of ten bench tests, and was consequently voted Psi-Scan of the Year Best Budget Model three years running.

PSI-VIRUS: *See* HOLO-VIRUS.

PSY-MOON: An artificial planetoid capable of structuring its landscape according to an individual's psyche. One such moon, its terrain derived from RIMMER's mind, was not a very nice place to visit at all – no indeedy.

PUDDINGS, HOMOGENISED: One of the many foodstuffs stored on RED DWARF's CARGO DECKS.

PULSE MISSILE: Launched on STARBUG by a SPACE CORPS EXTERNAL ENFORCEMENT VEHICLE.

PUNCTURE REPAIR KIT: Placed on stand-by status when RIMMER regained the ability to touch. See RACHEL.

PURPLE ALERT: An invention of HOLLY's deranged mind, this alert status is used for situations which are not quite bad enough to merit a RED ALERT, but which are a bit worse than a BLUE ALERT.

PUSHKIN, NATALINA: The First Officer aboard ENLIGHT ENMENT. She considered it worth mentioning that her IQ was 201.

Q

QUADRANT 4, SECTOR 492: The area of space where EN-LIGHTENMENT was discovered.

QUAGAARS: The name RIMMER made up for the race of ALENS he believed he had discovered.

QUARANTINE: A subject on which RIMMER has always been strict. When HOLLY picked up an unidentified object, he insisted on it undergoing the standard quarantine procedure a procedure which LISTER immediately broke. Likewise, when LISTER, KRYTEN and CAT came into contact with a HOLO VIRUS, RIMMER made doubly sure that they were confined. But since LISTER was the only official crew member, all three were made to share room 152. When LISTER broke the quarantine imposed upon KOCHANSKI's quarters following the RADIATION leak, he fell victim to a mutated strain of PNEU-MONIA.

QUASARS: After eleven attempts at passing his Engineering EXAM, and ten at Astro-Navigation, RIMMER was alarmed to find that he didn't actually know what one of these was.

QUAYLE: See LEGION.

QUEEG 500: RED DWARF's back-up computer, or so everyone was led to believe. In fact, Queeg was an elaborate hoax on HOLLY's part.

QUEEN OF SPAIN: The role which RIMMER was allowed to take when his brothers were playing THE THREE MUSKETEERS.

R

RABBITS: According to CAPTAIN HOLLISTER, these animals caused an unspecified problem for the crew of the

OREGON.

RACHEL: RIMMER's polythene pal, who spent THREE MILLION YEARS in need of a PUNCTURE REPAIR KIT. Said kit is now on stand-by, thanks to RIMMER's aquisition of a HARD-LIGHT DRIVE. However, as Rachel is presumably on RED DWARF whilst RIMMER is on STARBUG, she will have to wait a while longer for that repair job. *See also* INFLATABLE INGRID.

RADIATION: The crew of RED DWARF died when the ship was contaminated with this. *See also* CADMIUM 2.

RASTA-BILLY SKANK: The type of music favoured by Lister. Despite the fact that it carries a Government Health Warning.

REAGAN, RONALD: On BACKWARDS EARTH, KRYTEN wore a mask of this former US President, in order to look inconspicuous.

REALITY CONTROL: Something which THE INQUISITOR was a self-appointed administrator of.

REALITY MINEFIELD: Defence mechanism fitted to highly important SPACE CORPS test ships. Pockets of unreality are used to disorientate potential looters by creating false realities, such as the one in which LISTER was perceived to be a SERIES 3000 MECHANOID.

REAPER, JIM: An employee of the DIVA-DROID INTERNATIONAL Corporation, specifically Head of Sales, Space Division.

REAR ADMIRAL LIEUTENANT GENERAL: The rank by which MRS RIMMER knew her youngest son, due to his reluctance to admit to any EXAM failures.

RECHARGING SOCKET: KRYTEN is equipped with one of these, fitted with the standard three-pin adaption. It was a cause of consternation to him upon becoming temporarily human that, although he seemed to have located his new socket, he couldn't keep the recharging lead in there.

RECREATORS OF THE BATTLE OF NEASDEN SOCIETY: A group of which RIMMER was once a member. He felt that his commanding role in the WAX WAR would have earned him their respect.

RECUPERATION LOUNGE: Provided by the fictional LEISURE WORLD as a place to recover after playing one of their TIVs.

RED ALERT: One step up from a BLUE ALERT, and rarely engaged by the STARBUG crew, as it unfortunately means changing the bulb.

RED AND WHITE CHECKED GINGHAM DRESS: The mode of attire, complete with matching hat and army boots, that the HOLO-VIRUS infected, totally unhinged RIMMER selected for himself. The others later donned similar apparel in which to 'entertain' the now cured HOLOGRAM.

RED DWARF: A ship the size of a city, the postal address of which is apparently Deep Space, RE1 3DW. Of the myriad wonders it contains, we have seen the DRIVE ROOM, the medical unit, the CINEMA, the teaching room, the refectory, the science room, the HOLOGRAM PROJECTION SUITE (on Level 592), the scanning room, the observation room, the observation deck, the photographic lab, the supply pipes, part of the CARGO DECKS, the storage bay, the hold, the QUARANTINE bay (47), the Officers' Club and a drinking establishment called PARROT'S BAR – plus, of course, various parts of the habitation decks, particularly LISTER and RIMMER's original bunk room and the sleeping quarters in the OFFICERS' BLOCK to which they later relocated. We also know that the ship has a penthouse suite on A Deck and research labs on Z Deck, as well as its own CARGO BAY, PROJECTION

ROOM, science lab, ammunition stores security deck, brig and botanical gardens. Its thousands of corridors are coded by colours (including red, blue and white) and numbers. Current status: missing presumed stolen. *See also* STARBUG, SPACE CORPS, JUPITER MINING CORPORATION, WHITE CORRIDOR 159 and in fact most of the rest of this index.

RED DWARF SHUFFLE, THE: A rap routine performed by LISTER and the CAT, the self-proclaimed 'smart party'.

RED DWARF – THE TOTAL IMMERSION VIDEO GAME: The TIV in which after four years DUANE DIBBLEY's party managed to score an astonishing 4% (using, if you really want to know, number sixteen of the LEISURE WORLD INTERNATIONAL arcade's twenty machines). Their poor performance, it seems, was due in no small part to RIMMER who failed to realise that he was in fact a special agent for the SPACE CORPS who had had his mind erased. LISTER also fared particularly badly, as he not only failed to get KOCHANSKI, but also to become creator of the SECOND UNIVERSE. At least three of the 'players' were crestfallen to learn they had missed the opportunity to land on the PLANET OF THE NYMPHOMANIACS, but fortunately, for their egos, the whole experience had been a HALLUCINATION induced by the DESPAIR SQUID.

RED HOT WEST INDIAN PEPPER SAUCE: For the want of one more crate of this substance, LISTER kept the STARBUG crew on board a disintegrating SIMULANT cruiser for one second too long: the ship wasn't yet empty.

REHYDRATION UNITS: An internal mechanism which helps to keep ANDROIDS such as KRYTEN functioning.

RELATIVE TIME DILATION: The first visible effect of the WHITE HOLE that threatened RED DWARF. Simply put, this meant that time was running faster in some parts of the ship than in others.

RELIGION: Like all MECHANOIDS, KRYTEN is programmed to believe in the ELECTRONIC BIBLE and the concept of SILICON HEAVEN. LISTER is sceptical of this, confessing to being a pantheist, but not a frying pantheist. RIMMER on the other hand, doesn't have a religious bone in his hologramatic body, and considers Jesus to be nothing more than a hippy – well he had long hair and didn't have a job, after all! And perhaps it's just as well, considering where the CAT PEOPLES' belief in CLOISTER THE STUPID got them.

REMOTE PROJECTION UNIT: A device which enables RIMMER's HOLOGRAM to be sustained on STAR BUG and elsewhere away from RED DWARF.

REPORT BOOK: RIMMER's constant companion. See also COMPLAINTS.

REVENGE OF THE SURF-BOARDING KILLER BIKINI VAMPIRE GIRLS: LISTER's inspiration for his cunning plan to escape LEGION. By draping his clothing over a misshapen sculpture, he hoped to delude the entity as to his true position. Unfortunately, LEGION had seen the film too.

REVERSE BROTHERS, THE SENSATIONAL: A variety act formed on BACKWARDS EARTH by RIMMER and KRYTEN.

REVERSE THRUST TUBE: KRYTEN's suggestion that he be shot from this into the path of an oncoming missile was warmly accepted by RIMMER. LISTER, however, vetoed the idea, being unprepared to do his own ironing.

REVISION TIMETABLE: Meticulous as always, RIMMER found that after seven weeks painstakingly preparing this chart, he only had one night left in which to actually revise. He was not therefore very pleased when LISTER dropped a curry on it. On another occasion, he was even less happy to find that LISTER had swapped around the symbols, causing him to go swimming when he should have been taking his Engineering

EXAM.

REVOLUTIONARY WORKING FRONT: A fanatical left-wing group, opposed to the middle class.

RICHARD, CLIFF: A pop star who would doubtless have been going strong for centuries to come had someone not had the good sense to shoot him.

RIMMER, ACE: The ARNOLD RIMMER of a PARALLEL UNIVERSE, who had grown up to be totally different from his counterpart in our reality. Brave, handsome, resourceful and popular and holding the rank of Commander in the SPACE CORPS, he instantly earned our RIMMER's jealous hatred. Under that macho exterior, he was sure, lurked women's underwear.

RIMMER, ARLENE: ARNOLD RIMMER's female counterpart in the PARALLEL UNIVERSE, and just as sad an excuse for a human being as he is.

RIMMER, ARNOLD: A total failure in life, and now a total failure in death as well, as HOLLY has chosen to resurrect this sad character in HOLOGRAM form. References to RIMMER in this guide generally mean this one.

RIMMER DIRECTIVES: The fictional set of rules with which RIMMER sometimes counters KRYTEN's oft-quoted SPACE CORPS DIRECTIVES. Given the rule: 'In an emergency power situation, a hologramatic crew-member must lay down his life so that the living crew members might survive,' for instance, the corresponding Rimmer Directive is: 'No chance, you metal bastard.'

RIMMER, FRANK: (1) Presumably named after an uncle on his father's side (*see* RIMMER, FRANK (2)), Frank was one of ARNOLD RIMMER's three older brothers. He was 6'5" by the time he was eleven, due to his father's use of a TRACTION MACHINE to stretch his sons to the regulation height for joining the SPACE CORPS. We also know that he later got married and that he bore an uncanny resemblance to Arnold himself.

RIMMER, FRANK: (2) ARNOLD RIMMER's uncle, and the father of twin girls, ALICE and SARAH. He gave RIMMER his first French Kiss, albeit unintentionally. He had confused MRS RIMMERS' room with her son's.

RIMMER, HOWARD: One of ARNOLD RIMMER's three older brothers, Also in the SPACE CORPS.

RIMMER, JANNINE: ARNOLD RIMMER's sister-in-law, who was a model. In spite of their relationship to each other – or perhaps because of it – RIMMER fancied her a great deal. When CAMILLE mirrored his heart's desire, there was an uncanny resemblance between the two.

RIMMER, JOHN: ARNOLD RIMMER's eldest brother, who was a TEST PILOT in the SPACE CORPS by the time Arnold was seven.

RIMMER, MRS: (1) The only name by which we know ARNOLD RIMMER's mother, who both despised him and disappointed him with her constant sexual liaisons. She was impersonated by the POLYMORPH in order to arouse RIMMER's ANGER. She accomplished this by indulging in an indecent act which involved DAVE LISTER and ALPHABETTI SPAGHETTI.

RIMMER, MRS: (2) The nickname LISTER used for the double of himself that RIMMER once created. The second RIMMER had to be switched off when the two found that they were incapable of living together.

RIMMER WORLD: The lush and verdant paradise, created by RIMMER using ECO-ACCELERATOR ROCKETS. He then proceeded to spoil the place somewhat with the use of GENETIC CLONING.

RISK: A war GAME particularly enjoyed by RIMMER – so

much so that he even went to the trouble of noting down his every dice score in his 'Risk Campaign BOOK'. One of his fondest memories is of the campaign he won against his CADET SCHOOL Training Officer, CALDICOTT.

RIVERBOAT, BRETT: LISTER's STREETS OF LAREDO alter-ego, whose knife throwing skills were unparalleled.

RIVIERA KID, THE: A highly charismatic STREETS OF LAREDO character whose identity was taken, not surprisingly, by CAT. The Kid used a Colt 45 as his weapon of choice; his skill with it was matched only by his dancing ability.

ROBERT HARDY READS TESS OF THE D'URBER-VILLES: A chewed-up tape of Thomas Hardy's classic once provided an enjoyable musical experience for the CAT and LISTER.

ROCKET PANTS, ROBBIE: A fictional character whose jet powered trousers, the CAT considered, would provide a useful means of escape when the STARBUG was stuck on the PSY-MOON.

ROEBUCK, PORKY: Considered by RIMMER to be his best and only friend, until the fateful SPACE SCOUTS camping trip when Porky led the pack in an attempt to cook and eat RIMMER, choosing for himself the right buttock. RIMMER should have realised what sort of 'friend' Porky really was when he threw his shoes with the animal tracks into the sceptic tank – RIMMER was wearing them at the time. Porky's father was also one of the many intimate friends of MRS RIMMER.

ROGUE SIMULANT HUNTING GROUND: Best avoided really.

ROLL-OFF DEODORANT: An invention of BACKWARDS EARTH, this helps you stay wet and smelly for up to twenty-four hours.

ROOF ATTACK: The position in which LISTER's hero, JIM

BEXLEY SPEED, played for the LONDON JETS ZERO GRAVITY FOOTBALL team.

ROOM 008: The honeymoon suite of the GANYMEDE HOLIDAY INN.

RUBBER NUCLEAR WEAPONS: A twenty-third century crowd control device. These were put to use in NEW TOKYO, when discontented shoppers rioted outside a store which had sold out of BETTER THAN LIFE.

RUBBER PLANT: LISTER possessed one of these and, according to HOLLY, spoke more words to it than he ever did to KRISTINE KOCHANSKI.

RUBBER SHARES: In the alternative dimension of ACE RIMMER, his popularity was such that his return to EARTH always positively affected their value.

RUBBLE, BETTY: Next-door neighbour of WILMA FLINTSTONE. Although the CAT would go with Betty, he'd be thinking of Wilma.

RUDE ALERT: An impending disaster which has affected HOLLY's vocabulary units.

RUN FOR YOUR WIFE: A 20th-century play, which LISTER's older self advised him never ever to see.

S

SACRED GRAVY MARKS: Thanks to LISTER, these became items of religious significance to the CAT PEOPLE, and were worn by the CAT PRIESTS. *See also* HOLY CUSTARD STAINS.

SACRED LAWS: According to the Holy Bible of the CAT PEOPLE, CLOISTER left five of these commandments to his people, including 'It is a sin to be cool'. When CLOISTER – or rather LISTER – actually read them, he commented that he had already broken four of them himself – and that he would have broken the fifth if there had been any SHEEP on board!

ST. FRANCIS OF ASSISI: A WAX-DROID of this worthy formed part of RIMMER's army in the WAX WAR. RIMMER later attributed to him the quote 'Never give a sucker an even break!' although KRYTEN was convinced that, if he really did say that, it was strictly off the record.

SAMARITANS: An organisation to which RIMMER belonged for one morning. The five people to whom he spoke killed themselves. One unfortunate had actually dialled the wrong number, and only wanted the cricket scores. The event reached the newspapers, who dubbed the day LEMMING SUNDAY.

SAMMY THE SQUIB: Machine-gun-toting GUMSHOE persona assumed by KRYTEN in order to interrupt LISTER's Artificial Reality SEX session.

SAND PIT: The place where, as children, RIMMER's brothers playfully hid a landmine. RIMMER apparently escaped unscathed when it went off.

SANDRA: A girl from CADET SCHOOL to whom RIMMER claimed to have lost his virginity in his brother's BENTLEY V8 CONVERTIBLE.

SARAH: RIMMER's cousin; daughter of his uncle FRANK RIMMER (2), and twin sister of his cousin ALICE. Unlike ALICE, RIMMER was absolutely sure that Sarah fancied him. However, she probably didn't either!

SATSUMA: Not only can LISTER not understand Mandarin, he is also at a loss to comprehend this language.

SATURN TECH: An educational establishment where RIMMER took a maintenance course.

SAUSAGE, GOLDEN: One of the items by which, it is said, the CAT PEOPLE will know their GOD, CLOISTER. Several simulacra of this Holy item can be found in the CAT PEOPLES' former living areas on the CARGO DECKS, and it was with one of these that LISTER was able to convince the last CAT PRIEST of his identity.

SAUSAGE PATE, RECONSTITUTED: Another useful fact – RED DWARF currently carries seventy-two tons of this food-stuff.

SCARPER CITY: A good place to visit when a SPACE CORPS ENFORCEMENT VEHICLE arrives.

SCHOOL CABBAGE: The vegetable on which RIMMER lays the blame for his lack of sexual prowess, having been force-fed it at IO HOUSE.

SCOTT FITZGERALD, THE: The spaceship aboard which GORDON served as the primary computer.

SCOUTER: A surveillance device. True to form RIMMER insists that it is his responsibility, and his alone, to order its launch. The others of course take no notice whatsoever. *See also* SEARCH PROBE.

SCRAMBLE: From bed to battle stations, it takes LISTER and CAT one hour, seventeen minutes and thirty-nine seconds, though LISTER's sure it'd only take one hour and sixteen minutes if they were to cut out their fourth round of toast.

SCRUMPING: An activity in which LISTER indulged during his childhood in Liverpool. Apparently, he went scrumping for cars. He admits, however, that he was caught every time.

SCS PIONEER: A vessel which fell victim to PSIRENS and took up permenent residence in their SPACE-SHIP GRAVE-YARD.

SEARCH PROBE: A device with a similar purpose to a SCOUTER, although strictly speaking it's used for searching for things instead of scouting them. Presumably once you've found something with your SEARCH PROBE you can then send in your SCOUTER to have a scout round. Look, if you want detailed technical information buy a *Star Trek* manual or something.

SEAT TILT CONTROL: No longer squeaky, thanks to the generosity of a crew of xenophobic, genocidal crew of SIMULANTS.

SECOND DEGREE MURDER: The crime with which RIMMER was charged – on 1,167 counts – by the JUSTICE COMPUTER. He received a sentence of eight years for each count, making a total of 9,328 years of penal solitude. Fortunately for him, KRYTEN was able to reverse the computer's decision at the appeal stage, by proving that he was nothing more than a complete dork.

SECOND TECHNICIAN: RIMMER's rank aboard RED DWARF. Not the most impressive of positions!

SECOND UNIVERSE: *See* RED DWARF THE TOTAL IM-MERSION VIDEO GAME.

SECURITY CLEARANCE CODE: A very useful thing to have, unless you happen to be erased from history, when it becomes totally worthless, as LISTER himself discovered when – courtesy of the INQUISITOR – that particular fate befell him. His number is 000169 – another piece of vital information.

SEE YA LATER, ALLIGATOR: The song played – by his own request – at the funeral of GEORGE McINTYRE.

SELBY: One of LISTER's friends aboard RED DWARF.

SELF-CONFIDENCE: A positive aspect of RIMMER's psyche, believed to be dead and buried alongside his generosity, his humour and his charm. With RIMMER's SELF-CONFI-DENCE at its side it manifested itself as a dashing swordsman in order to do battle with THE HOODED LEGIONS, before hope succumbed too.

SELF-HYPNOSIS TAPES: RIMMER went through a phase of playing these every night, in order to learn such subjects as ESPERANTO and quantum theory whilst he slept. This irritated LISTER, as it simply meant that neither of them could get any sleep.

SELF-LOATHING: The emotion which dominated RIMMER's mental landscape. Personified as a hideous creature it became the ruler of the TERRAFORMed PSY-MOON, intent upon torturing the man who spawned it.

SELF-REPAIR UNIT: Considering his encounter with the waste compactor, it is fortunate for KRYTEN that he possesses one of these.

SELF-RESPECT: *See* SELF-CONFIDENCE.

SENSO-LOCK FEEDBACK TECHNIQUE: The technology which makes TOTAL IMMERSION VIDEO GAMES such as BETTER THAN LIFE possible.

SERIES 3000: A line of ANDROIDS deemed too human-like for comfort. They soon fell out of favour and were superceeded by the series 4000 who, equipped with heads resembling a freak formation of mashed potato, could never be taken for human.

SERIES 5000: A superior model ANDROID to KRYTEN, a mere series 4000; fortunately favourable trade-in terms are available.

SERVICE ROBOTS: Presumably another name for the SKUTTERS. LISTER mentioned that there were four of these aboard RED DWARF.

SET-SQUARE: The device which, much to KRYTEN's despair, LISTER didn't even bother to use when making triangular sandwiches.

SEVEN: A number with which HOLLY admits to having a blind spot. It is also the number of children with which

RIMMER's mind saddled himself during his BETTER THAN LIFE fantasy.

SEVENTH DAY ADVENT HOPPISTS: Due to a misprint in their Bible which they took literally, RIMMER's parents' particular form of religion was based on 'faith, hop and charity', and required them to hop each Sunday. According to RIMMER, this made it necessary for sou'westers and asbestos underpants to be worn when Sunday Dinner was being served.

SEX: An activity that most of the crew of RED DWARF would like to indulge in more often. Unfortunately, stranded alone in deep space, they have to be content with going for runs, watching gardening programmes and playing JUNIOR ANGLER. RIMMER in particular only ever had sex once in his life, this being with the concussed YVONNE McGRUDER. He was therefore delighted to discover that the regulations of the HOLOSHIP, ENLIGHTENMENT stipulated that sexual congress be undertaken at least twice a day. Having managed in death what he only managed once in life, he resolved to stay on the ship with his latest love, NIRVANAH CRANE, but the relationship was not to be. LISTER, meanwhile, thoroughly regretted his only sexual encounter since leaving STASIS. Taking place as it did with his alternate self in a PARALLEL UNIVERSE, it left him pregnant – with twins.

SEX DECK: An area on a HOLOSHIP put aside for the purposes of sexual recreation. Ship's regulations require crew members to indulge in sex at least twice a day.

SHAKE AND VAC: Unfortunately, there is none left aboard RED DWARF. The implications of this are unknown.

SHAKESPEARE, WILLIAM: Obviously not quite as famous a figure in the future as he is now. LISTER didn't even know who he was – and RIMMER thought his first name was Wilfred. Even so, his plays are obviously still regarded as works of art, hence RIMMER's objections when LISTER realised he had to burn the very last copy in existence to keep himself alive.

SHAKESPEARE, WILMA: The female dominated PARALLEL UNIVERSE's finest playwright, author of such classics as 'Rachel the Third' and 'The Taming of the Shrimp'.

SHAM GLAM: A style of dress fashionable when LISTER was a teenager.

SHAMI KEBAB DIABLO: A chilli-based culinary speciality of LISTER's, though whether he has prepared the dish since it was assimilated by the POLYMORPH is uncertain.

SHAPIRO, HELEN: The female singer to whom RIMMER bore a startling resemblance following HOLLY's re-styling of his hair in revenge for an insult.

SHEEP: One of the types of animal that LISTER wanted to breed when he got his farm on FIJI. Given that FIJI was now three feet under water, RIMMER commented that he could corner the market in wet-look knitwear. *See also* SACRED LAWS.

SHERIFF: A dream-state persona created by KRYTEN's subconscious in order to devise the DOVE PROGRAMME. By the time BRETT RIVERBOAT and co arrived in town the lawman had hit the bottle.

SHE'S OUT OF MY LIFE: The first song LISTER learnt to play on his GUITAR. It was taught to him by his stepfather.

SHINY THING: A particularly prized possession of the CAT's – in reality, a YO-YO.

SHIPQUAKE: An imminent disaster aboard a SIMULANT Battle Cruiser which threatened to bring the DWARFERS' 'shopping' expedition to a fatal conclusion.

SIGMA 14D: A desert moon designated by HOLLY to be the rendezvous point for the crew once she had safely navigated RED DWARF away from five (non-existent) BLACK HOLES.

SILICON HEAVEN: The final resting place for ANDROIDS and other machines with Artificial Intelligence – or so they are programmed to believe. The promise of a reward in an electronic after-life is all that guarantees machines' servitude to Mankind.

SILICON HELL: The place where the photocopiers go.

SIMULANTS: Created for a war which never took place, these xenophobic, genocidal maniacs are physically the same as ANDROIDS, but lack the same degree of restrictive programming. The main difference between the two types of artificial lifeform is that an ANDROID will never rip off a human's head and spit down his throat. The DWARFERS have encountered several SIMULANTS on their travels; most uniquely, THE INQUISITOR, who was of the self-repairing variety.

SINAL FLUID: RIMMER was the proud owner of a small flask, containing the fluid of General George S. Patton. He had retained possession of it even when a rival collector offered him \$£1000. However, he generously gave it to KRYTEN as a last-day present.

SINCLAIR ZX81: Although she was slow and wouldn't load for him, she was HOLLY's one and only love – at least until he met HILLY, who literally turned his head.

SINGING POTATOES: HOLLY claimed that his collection of these musical root vegetables helped him to retain his sanity.

SKATEBOARD: The sight of MICHELLE FISHER totally naked almost caused LISTER to drop his.

SKIPPER: ACE RIMMER's nickname for LISTER.

SKIVE HARD, PLAY HARD: The sometime motto of LISTER and his cronies, SELBY, CHEN and PETERSEN.

SKUTTERS: RED DWARF's rebellious SERVICE ROBOTS. A quirk of their design has left them able to make insulting gestures, which they reserve exclusively for RIMMER.

SLEEPING: The CAT's third favourite activity. Although he hasn't gone into detail about the first two, we can probably guess. *See also* NAPS.

SLIDE-BACK SUNROOF HEAD: A feature of the Series 4000 GTI ANDROID of which KRYTEN, as a mere Series 4000, was particularly jealous.

SLOBBING: LISTER's hobby, to the pursuit of which he devotes most of his time.

SMART SHOES: Shoes with Artificial Intelligence. LISTER claimed that PETERSEN had purchased a pair of these and that, bored with their job, they had taken him from Oslo to Burma whilst he was unconscious. He had tried to get rid of them, but they had always followed him back home. Eventually, they stole a car and drove it into a canal. No, we didn't believe it either – but RIMMER did.

SME HE: Not surprisingly on many occasions KRYTEN is sorely tempted to throw a few insults in RIMMER's direction. Unfortunately his restrictive programming makes it impossible for him to utter more than a syllable or two and the ensuing abuse is generally lost on the 'thick skinned' HOLOGRAM he really is a SMEG-head isn't he?

SMEG: A popular twenty-third century expletive, from which the insults 'smegger' and 'smeg-head' are derived. LISTER demonstrated just about every use of this formidable word in the phrase 'Oh smeg! What the smeggin' smeg's he smeggin' done? He's smeggin' killed me!' But as for its actual meaning – well, we're not going to delve into that here (or indeed anywhere). Try Black's Medical Dictionary if you're curious.

SMEG AND THE HEADS: LISTER's first band, in which he featured as lead vocalist. Also included in the line-up were DOBBIN on drums and GAZZA on bass.

SNAKES: LISTER's second worst fear.

SOCK SUSPENDERS: A type of clothing worn by ARNOLD RIMMER, which ARLENE RIMMER considered to be extremely provocative.

SOCKS: LISTER's are particularly odious, and indeed RIMMER contends that they have in the past set off the SPRINKLER SYSTEM. HOLLY has been known to put RED DWARF on alert when her sensors discovered one on the CARGO DECKS, and mistook it for a completely new lifeform. LISTER also bemoaned the fact that, amongst all of his socks, he doesn't have a complete pair – whilst RIMMER's favourite use for them is to roll them up and stick them down his trousers, thereby hoping to impress any girls he may happen to meet.

SOLAR ACCELERATORS: The power source used to sustain RIMMER's HARD LIGHT DRIVE for the five and a half centuries he spent on RIMMERWORLD.

SOLAR BATTERIES: STARBUG's power source.

SOLAR PANELS: Situated on the outer hull of RED DWARF, RIMMER found these useful as his original hiding place for KOCHANSKI's PERSONALITY DISC.

SOMEONE TO WATCH OVER ME: A Gershwin song that RIMMER always intended to share with someone special. Now it's just his song.

SOUTHPORT: The seaside town where RIMMER believed he had made love to LISE YATES six times in one night, when, in fact, she had done it with LISTER.

SPACE BIKE: Ridden by KRYTEN – straight into an asteroid.

SPACE CORPS: The organisation which RIMMER's father was desperate to join, but was prevented from doing so because of his height. He was adamant that all four of his sons should follow the career path which was closed to him, and he even had each of them stretched on a rack to ensure that they could. RIMMER, however, was only able to enter the Corps at THIRD TECHNICIAN level, aboard the mining ship RED DWARF. Although he gradually made his way up the ranks to SECOND TECHNICIAN, he was never able to pass the EXAMS which would have made him a fully-fledged offlcer. LISTER, meanwhile, joined the Corps by the same route, but was happy to remain as the lowest rank on board the ship.

SPACE CORPS ACADEMY: By far the best route to join the SPACE CORPS, as this involves intensive training and immediate entry at officer level. All three of RIMMER's brothers were able to fulfil the entry requirements for the Academy, but Arnold himself had to be content with joining the Corps by a less direct route. *See* SPACE CORPS.

SPACE CORPS ANTHEM: A song with twenty-three stanzas, all of which RIMMER insists on singing when claiming new moons, etc.

SPACE CORPS DIRECTIVES: The rules and regulations which SPACE CORPS personnel must obey, and which RIMMER persistently mis-quotes. *See also* RIMMER DIRECTIVES and ARTICLES.

SPACE CORPS DIRECTIVES MANUAL: A volume which RIMMER believed to be imaginary, since all the directives contained therein seemed to be levelled against him personally. However, upon being furnished with a holographic copy he saw to it that any rules and regulations that would make things less pleasant for the others were obeyed to the letter.

SPACE CORPS EXTERNAL ENFORCEMENT VEHICLE: Watch out, it's the space filth.

SPACE CORPS SPECIAL SERVICE: An elite branch of the SPACE CORPS to which ACE RIMMER belongs, naturally.

SPACE CRAZY: A state of mind to which some people can be driven by loneliness, during prolonged journeys through space. Having avoided it for THREE MILLION YEARS, it seems unlikely that LISTER or RIMMER will now fall victim to this illness.

SPACE MIRAGES: Judging by the sign which warns of their presence, these phenomena are probably well worth seeing.

SPACE MUMPS: A particularly unpleasant disease which causes an enormous swelling of the forehead. This lasts for about three weeks, after which the swelling bursts – much to the disgust of CAT, who was present when LISTER's bout with this illness ended.

SPACE SCOUTS: An organisation to which the young RIMMER belonged. He almost got eaten by his fellow scouts on a survival expedition.

SPACE-SHIP GRAVEYARD: Created by and inhabited by PSIRENS. The STARBUG crew stumbled across it whilst taking a shortcut through an asteroid belt.

SPACE WEEVILS: When these insectoid space vermin invaded STARBUG's food stores, they became ironically the only way of replacing the contents. Despite the near-cannibalism of the situation, LISTER enjoyed his weevil snack, believing it to be crunchy king prawn.

SPANNER: Because in life RIMMER had been a technician, his Deathday cake was baked in the shape of a spanner. HOLLY was relieved that RIMMER hadn't been a gynaecologist.

SPANNERS: The name by which DAVE LISTER was known in the PARALLEL UNIVERSE from which ACE RIMMER hailed. An accomplished Flight Engineer in the SPACE CORPS, he had also achieved LISTER's longed-for desire of marriage to KRISTINE KOCHANSKI. The couple even had twin sons, JIM and BEXLEY. Unlike RIMMER, who was insanely jealous of his other-dimensional counterpart, LISTER was extremely pleased to learn that at least somewhere he was doing so well for himself.

SPARE HANDS: KRYTEN has at least one of these and, like the SPARE HEADS (see below), it seems capable of independent thought and expression. With an eye mounted on one of the fingers it can find its way around too.

SPARE HEADS: KRYTEN has at least three of these although one of them is infected with DROID ROT. Capable of independent thought and speech, the heads take it in turns to become the ANDROID's main head for a month.

SPEAKING SLIDE RULES: Entrants for the Engineering EXAM are positively not allowed to use these instruments.

SPEED, JIM BEXLEY: LISTER's hero, a ROOF ATTACK player for the LONDON JETS ZERO GRAVITY FOOTBALL team. LISTER named his twin sons JIM and BEXLEY after this sports star.

SPEED OF REALITY: According to the DIMENSION THEORY OF REALITY, this was the theoretical speed at which ACE RIMMER had to travel to reach a PARALLEL UNIVERSE.

SPIDER-MAN COSTUME: If we are to believe LISTER, he possesses one of these for the purpose of making love in.

SPINAL IMPLANT: A remote control device with which the LOWS forced LISTER into carrying out a successful murderous attack on the HIGHS and then an attack on his own crewmates with the same purpose.

SPRINKLER SYSTEM: RED DWARF does have one, although fortunately the only things that have set it off thus far have been LISTER's SOCKS.

SPROUTS: The vegetable that formed the basis of a menu

devised by RIMMER, while the others were in QUARANTINE. A typical meal would consist of sprout soup followed by sprout salad with sprout crumble for desert. Perhaps it had slipped RIMMER's memory that sprouts make LISTER sick.

SQUIRRELS: One of the types of animal kept in RED DWARF's botanical gardens. After KOCHANSKI finished with him, LISTER expressed a desire to become one – and in retrospect, he was glad that the DNA MODIFIER wasn't around at the time.

SSS ESPERANTO: A Class D SPACE CORPS Seeding Ship – its mission: to introduce oceanic life into potential S3 PLANETS. The crew were impelled to commit suicide by one of the fruits of their labour, the DESPAIR SQUID.

STARBUG: A class two ship-to-surface vessel, withdrawn from service due to design faults. It nevertheless the shuttlecraft of choice for the RED DWARF crew, who use it in preference to the smaller BLUE MIDGET and WHITE MIDGET. Originally, there were at least two Starbugs; however, the effort to maintain both was enormous, as they suffered more crashes than a ZX81. Currently, the RED DWARF crew live upon one such vessel (registration Starbug 1), as they search in vain for their parent ship. Capable of travelling both underwater and through marshy terrain, and fitted with a cloak, a DECOY device and, lately, LASER CANNONS, the ship is at least capable of holding its own.

STAR-DRIVE: Appropriated from LEGION, this device should have enabled STARBUG to catch up RED DWARF in a matter of nano-seconds. The star-drive made the trip; unfortunately it didn't take STARBUG with it.

STASIS: The freezing of time around a person, causing him or her to become a non-event mass with a quantum probability of zero.

STASIS BOOTHS: *See* STASIS ROOMS.

STASIS FIELD: The area in which STASIS takes place.

STASIS LEAK: A phenomenon discovered by the RED DWARF crew on Level 16, which enabled them to travel back through time to 2 MARCH 2077. This is even harder to explain than STASIS itself, so let's just accept the CAT's theory that it was a 'MAGIC DOOR', okay?

STASIS PODS: A nest of these life-sustaining chambers was discovered at the VIRAL RESEARCH DEPARTMENT; one of them was occupied by HILDEGARDE LANSTROM who, unfortunately, turned out to be absolutely raving bonkers.

STASIS ROOMS: Also known as STASIS BOOTHS. The two rooms on RED DWARF in which the STASIS FELD can cause STASIS to take place. We hope that's all perfectly clear now.

S3 PLANET: A potentially habitable world, with a similar atmosphere to EARTH (Sol three). As such, it is eligible to be claimed by RIMMER on behalf of the SPACE CORPS.

STELLAR-FOG: Tightly-packed particles, posssibly from an exploding super-nova, in which the STARBUG crew encountered a REALITY MINEFIELD.

STOCHASTIC CAPABILITIES: The ability to predict the future through the examination of probabilities. STOCKY, the computer on board ENLIGHTENMENT, was able to do this to an accuracy of five per cent. KRYTEN's CPU has similar, though more limited, capabilities.

STOCKY: An incredibly advanced computer aboard the HOLOSHIP, ENLIGHTENMENT, so called because of its STOCHASTIC CAPABILITIES.

STOMACH PUMP: This was required by the CAT after sampling RIMMER's lamb and DUMPLINGS. One was also used by RIMMER himself in an attempt to rid his body of a dose of FREAKY FUNGUS.

STOPPING DISTANCES: Just as is the case with cars, these have to be meticulously learnt before a spaceship is flown. For instance, the stopping distance for half the speed of light is four years and three months. The thinking time is a fortnight.

STRAWBERRIES: The type of fruit that KRYTEN was able to recreate using the TRIPLICATOR. Upon sampling the fruit LISTER discovered that one of them was succulent and delicious. The other he wasn't too keen on; he didn't care for its taste, its texture or its maggots.

STREETS OF LAREDO: Artificial Reality Western game which enabled the other DWARFERS to patch into KRYTEN's mind, buying him time to create the DOVE PROGRAMME.

SUGAR PUFF SANDWICHES: One of the few things that LISTER doesn't mind eating without the addition of CURRY sauce.

SUICIDE: An option which CAT prefers to wearing unfashionable prison clothing. Also the way in which SEBASTIAN DOYLE and company attempted to end their lives when afflicted by a DESPAIR SQUID, and the fate of all those who phoned ARNOLD RIMMER during his SAMARITANS stint.

SUICIDE SQUID: *See* DESPAIR SQUID.

SUITS: Having managed to build up a vast wardrobe of fine apparel, CAT has now become very protective about, and close to, his fashion collection.

SUPER-MARKET TROLLEY ATTENDANT: LISTER's job before joining the SPACE CORPS. He left it after ten years, because he didn't want to be tied down to a career.

SUPPLIES: RIMMER took a fancy to two brunettes who worked in this section. He offered to take them to TITAN ZOO, but LISTER's sarcastic comments about him, and about his mother's resemblance to the exhibits there, put them off.

SUSPENDED ANIMATION: A term often used instead of

STASIS, although not meaning that exclusively. Does that help at all?

SWAMP OF DESPAIR, THE: An area of the PSY-MOON located not too far from the WOOD OF HUMILIATION and quite close to the CHASM OF HOPELESSNESS.

SWIMMING CERTIFICATES: *See* BSc, SSc.

SWIRLY THING ALERT: Rarely engaged, as the CAT hates to get so technical.

SYNAPTIC ENHANCER: Used to restore LISTER's memory following 200 years spent in DEEP-SLEEP. Believing RIMMER to be his best mate, LISTER was obviously in great need of a shot.

SYNTHE-SHOCK: What KRYTEN told LISTER he was suffering from when he belived he was a SERIES 3000 ANDROID.

T

T-COUNT: The hologramatic equivelent of blood pressure, with the T presumably standing for tachyon. Thanks to a stress-related nervous disorder, RIMMER's T-count tends towards the dangerously high side.

TAIWAN: The country of origin of TALKIE TOASTER; also, KRYTEN once believed, of a mechanical DAVE LISTER, although this was due to the effects of a REALITY MINEFIELD.

'TAKE US TO YOUR LEADER': Yep, LISTER actually said it!

TALES OF THE RIVERBANK: THE NEXT GENERATION: A follow-up to the more popular 'Tales of the Riverbank', which was a critical failure due to the absence from its cast of Hammy Hamster. Hammy apparently slid into depravity when his series was cancelled; he ended up suffering the ultimate humiliation, as he had to turn to 'Hamster-grams' to make a living.

TALKIE TOASTER: Manufactured by CRAPOLA INC. and made in TAIWAN, this remarkable toaster had been fitted with Artificial Intelligence and speech circuits. That turned out to be a mistake, as the appliance became obsessed with its job. According to LISTER, it threw a major wobbler if he didn't eat four hundred rounds of toast an hour. Eventually, he lost patience and smashed it to pieces with the aid of the WASTE DISPOSAL. He was therefore most disappointed when KRYTEN took it upon himself to repair it – although thankfully, the proximity of a WHITE HOLE altered time in such a way that the repair job never took place.

TANDEM: The type of bike stolen by LISTER and CAT on BACKWARDS EARTH – the scoundrels!

TARAMASALATA: Despite being happily married for 35 years, BONGO so admired ACE RIMMER that he offered to cover himself with this substance for his enjoyment. Unfortunately for him, MELLIE had already offered ACE dinner on her – MAPLE SYRUP, in her case.

TARANSHULAS: *See* TARANTULAS. LISTER, on the other hand, should see a dictionary!

TARANTULAS: RIMMER's all-time greatest fear in the whole world is to have one of these creatures crawling up his leg – so naturally, when his mind insisted on dreaming up bad things in BETTER THAN LIFE, this was one of them. This particular phobia is also shared by LISTER, who thought his fear had been realised when his leg was visited by KRYTEN's detached hand. However worse was to come when the LOWS, controlling his actions with a SPINAL IMPLANT, forced him to eat one; LISTER, as you can imagine, was not best pleased .

TARKA DAL: Monocular ambassador from the great VINDALOOIAN EMPIRE, as created and portrayed by DAVE

LISTER.

TATTOO: Despite the one to be found on his inner thigh, LISTER claims he doesn't really love PETERSEN.

TAU, CAPTAIN: Perhaps at some point in the past she really had been the Captain of the SCS PIONEER, but when encountered by LISTER and co she turned out to be another PSIREN.

TEAR GAS: A defence mechanism aboard RED DWARF as LISTER discovered first hand when, thanks to the INQUISITOR, he was without a SECURITY CLEARANCE CODE.

TEA STRAINER: Kept by LISTER's bed in order to strain the cigar buts out of his early afternoon LAGER.

TELEGRAPH POLES, TWENTIETH CENTURY: A collection of items in which RIMMER is particularly interested. He possesses an extremely large number of fascinating slides and photographs on the subject, which so far, the rest of the crew have not quite got round to letting him show to them.

TELEPORTER: A device found aboard a SIMULANT ship which enabled the DWARFERS to escape from said vessel before it exploded. Later they used it to extricate themselves from a prison cell on RIMMERWORLD, thus denying LISTER the opportunity to put into action his foolproof escape plan, utilizing loosened bricks, a pulley system with ropes hewn from hessian strands, a trip wire, uniform swapping and sword-fighting – though not necessarily in that order.

TELETHONS: If RIMMER had realised sooner that life was meant to be lived in a worthwhile manner, he might have used his own credit card number when pledging money during these charitable events.

TENSION SHEET: A small piece of air-bubble packing paper painted red, patented by THICKY HOLDEN, which earned him a great deal of money, along with the affections of the delectable LADY SABRINA MULHOLLAND-JJONES. Using the TIMESLIDES, LISTER changed history so that he would become the inventor instead, thereby creating a TIMELINE in which he lived a fabulously rich and famous lifestyle, eventually dying at the age of 98 whilst making love to his fourteenth wife in a private jet. RIMMER tried to beat him at his own game by doing likewise, but only managed to give away the secret of the device to a younger THICKY HOLDEN, thereby restoring the TIMELINES to normal.

TERRAFORMING: *See* ALIENS (not the entry, the film).

TEST PILOT: The job which RIMMER always desired in the SPACE CORPS. His father wanted this for him too, and both were bitterly disappointed when it became obvious that it wasn't to be. The ambition was achieved, however, by RIMMER's eldest brother, JOHN RIMMER – and, much to his chagrin, by ACE RIMMER, his counterpart in a PARALLEL UNIVERSE.

THERMOS FLASK: A vital componant of DUANE DIBBLEY's survival kit, along with extra strong spot cream, anti-dandruff shampoo and a TRIPLE THICK CONDOM; as such it presented a perfect disguise for the EMOHAWK.

THIRD TECHNICIAN: LISTER's rank aboard RED DWARF – the lowest of the low!

THREE MILLION YEARS: The length of time LISTER spent in STASIS. Also, according to HOLLY, the average length of time for second class mail.

THREE MUSKETEERS, THE: A childhood game enjoyed by the RIMMER brothers – even Arnold, although he always had to be the QUEEN OF SPAIN.

TIME DRIVE: Discovered on a 28th-century derelict at the epicentre of a REALITY MINEFIELD, it was fitted onto STARBUG converting it into a time-travelling vessel. A subsequent encounter with the future STARBUG crew revealed that it hadn't been the wisest choice of customising jobs.

TIME GAUNTLETS: The formidable weapons employed by the INQUISITOR. Programmed by a variation of the ENIGMA DECODING SYSTEM, they were able to utilise time itself in a number of potentially fatal ways.

TIME HOLE: An orange whirly thing in space, according to the CAT's picturesque terminology. Actually, a portal to another point in time and space, and the means by which the crew of RED DWARF travelled to BACKWARDS EARTH.

TIMELINES: The flow of history, which was altered to varying degrees by both LISTER and RIMMER using the TIMESLIDES. THE INQUISITOR sought to do likewise, though the old backfiring TIME GAUNTLET trick reversed his damage. KRYTEN's accidental misprogramming of a TELEPORTER later caused him and his colleagues to jump timelines, arriving both in their own past and in the future. The FUTURE ECHOES, the events of MARCH 2077 and the appearance of the future, time-travelling STARBUG crew map out a great deal of the DWARFERS' possible destiny; however, with such forays into the past and future becoming more prevalent, who knows where the timelines will ultimately lead?

TIMESLIDES: Using a mutated batch of DEVELOPING FLUID, KRYTEN was able to create slides into which you could actually step. By using photographs of the past, the RED DWARF crew were able to travel back in time – although it was not possible for them to step out of the confines of the original picture.

TITAN: The moon on which a BIG BLACK TOM impregnated LISTER's cat, FRANKENSTEIN.

TITAN DOCKING PORT: The docking port on TITAN, no doubt.

TITAN HILTON: A hotel, missing at least one of its blankets.

TITAN MUSHROOMS: A hallucinogenic fungus which was

inadvertently fed to RIMMER by LISTER. Colloquially known as FREAKY FUNGUS.

TITAN TAJ MAHAL: One of the many Indian restaurants which advertises during film intermissions.

TITAN ZOO: Another of this moon's many tourist attractions. LISTER inadvertently offended RIMMER when he mistook his mother's picture for a souvenir from this place. RIMMER also hoped to visit here with two brunettes from SUPPLIES.

TIV: Acronym for Total Immersion Video. See TOTAL IMMERSION VIDEO GAMES.

TODHUNTER, FRANK: A senior crew member on board RED DWARF. RIMMER despised him for his affluent background, and was convinced that he was breast-fed on GAZPACHO SOUP and champagne.

TOILET, ELECTRONIC: LISTER was pleased to find an 'electronic lavvy' in his hotel room during his BETTER THAN LIFE fantasy. This apparently did everything for its user, including removing his trousers. A less sophisticated version could be found in LISTER and RIMMER's original bunk room, although since moving to the OFFICERS' BLOCK, they have used the more private facilities available there.

TONGUE-TIED: A song and dance routine which featured in one of the CAT'S few non-erotic dreams. It was presumably based on a tune written by somebody else, as a musical version was once played at a disco attended by the RED DWARF crew.

TOPIC BAR: RIMMER considered that he was probably the only person ever to get one without a hazelnut.

TOTAL IMMERSION VIDEO GAMES: These GAMES require the wearing of headsets, which insert electrodes into the frontal lobes and hyperthalons. This process allows them to create a virtual reality image in the player's mind. BETTER THAN LIFE is the best-known example of this type of GAME.

Under the influence of the DESPAIR SQUID's venom induced HALLUCINATIONS, the crew believed they had been playing RED DWARF: THE TOTAL IMMERSION VIDEO GAME for four years.

TOTTENHAM HOTSPUR: A football team whose name is, to HOLLY at least, considered to be a term of abuse.

TOUPEES: Despite their enormous technical advances, mankind never developed a toupee that didn't look ridiculous. This didn't stop HOLLY from sporting a rug to impress the NOVA 5 crew, nor the future KRYTEN's attempts at concealing his resemblence to a damaged crash dummy; however, it did lead to a SPACE CORPS DIRECTIVE which forbade all personnel from wearing ginger toupees on duty. More usefully, a larger toupee helped solve the global warming problem when it was fitted over the hole in the ozone layer.

TRACE: According to RIMMER, space jargon for tracking down someone or something. Though HOLLY's never heard of it and is convinced that the HOLOGRAM made it up.

TRACTION MACHINE: The device with which RIMMER's father hoped to ensure that, unlike him, all of his sons would be tall enough to join the SPACE CORPS.

TRAFFIC CONES: Even THREE MILLION YEARS into deep space, you can expect to find one of these after a good night on the ale. But where the policewoman's helmet and the suspenders come from is anyone's guess.

TRIPLE FRIED EGG BUTTY WITH CHILLI SAUCE AND CHUTNEY: A 'state-of-the-art sarnie' enjoyed by LISTER, although HOLLY was more concerned about the state of the floor. A sort of cross between food and bowel surgery, LISTER claimed to have found the recipe in a BOOK on bacteriological warfare.

TRIPLICATOR: A replicating machine cannibalised from the

MATTER PADDLE by KRYTEN. Instead of creating two exact duplicates of an original, as intended, it created one improved perfect version and one flawed imperfect version. Set in reverse it constructed HIGH and LOW variants of RED DWARF – complete with crews – while destroying the original in the process.

TRIP-OUT CITY: RIMMER's bout with TITAN MUSHROOMS sent him on a voyage here. During its course, he attended inspection parade totally naked apart from a pair of mock leather driving gloves and blue swimming goggles. He also attacked two senior officers, believing them to be armed and dangerous giraffes.

TROUT Á LA CRÈME: The DISPENSERS' FISH of the Day when RIMMER instructed CAT in their operation. Six Trout á la Crèmes later, CAT suffered a severe FOOD ESCAPE.

2Q4B: The middle name that some poor sucker of an ANDROID got lumbered with.

U

UNDERPANTS: LISTER admits to only having one pair of these – and delights in the revelation that RIMMER keeps his on coat-hangers.

UNDERWATER HOCKEY: A game played at both international and inter-planetary levels, hence the England team's tour of TITAN.

UO: HOLLY's personalised abbreviation for Unidentified Object.

UP, UP AND AWAY: An IN-FLIGHT MAGAZINE carried aboard the STARBUG.

URINE RE-CYC: STARBUG's emergency supply, which had

been reused so often it was starting to taste like Dutch LAGER. Kryten tried to make it more palatable by making it into wine. Cynically, his comrades argued that a really fine wine shouldn't leave the drinker with a foam moustache.

V

VACUUM CLEANERS, SUPER-DELUXE: A type of electrical appliance of which KRYTEN is particularly fond. When he temporarily gained human form, he was confused by the strange effect that the sight of these caused in his groinal area. *See* DOUBLE POLAROID.

VALKYRIE WARRIORS, SCANTY-ARMOUR CLAD: A particular fantasy of CAT's, albeit one by which he is not quite as impressed as he is by his own image. The warriors in question generally have cleavages down which ski-ing is a very practical proposition.

VANITY: The emotion the POLYMORPH stole from CAT, playing havoc with his dress sense.

VEG, FRESH: According to LISTER, for health psychos, vitamin freaks and people who excercise. Consequently, not his favourite food.

VENDING MACHINE: Lister and CAT's reaction upon finding one of these on STARBUG's engine deck was pehaps none too clever – given that there was a perception-altering PSIREN on board at the time.

VIBRATING LEOPARD-SKIN WATER BED: LISTER's BETTER THAN LIFE fantasy came complete with one of these – in the shape of a GUITAR.

VIDS: The common term for video tapes, which by the twenty-third century will also be available in triangular shape, though it's unlikely these will ever replace the established VHS format (remember Betamax?). The Flintstones is a favourite of both LISTER and CAT, the latter being something of a cartoon devotee. LISTER is a fan of the series *St Elsewhere*, claiming to have seen every episode. He also enjoys classic movies such as CASABLANCA, which he introduced to KRYTEN who, although enjoying it greatly, is still an aficionado of ANDROIDS, though he did find 'Easy Rider', 'The Wild One' and 'Rebel Without a Cause' quite influential. RIMMER on the other hand is generally hard to please and critical of much that he sees; for example he found 'King of Kings' quite far fetched and had a few ideas of his own for not only adding credibility to the plot but making it more action packed to boot. When the others were held in QUARANTINE, and RIMMER was required, by SPACE CORPS DIRECTIVE 312, to provide entertainment, the video he selected was 'Wallpapering, Painting and Stippling – A DIY Guide'; the choice wasn't popular. New videos sometimes arrive via the POST POD; one such was 'FRIDAY THE THIRTEENTH 1649', which presumably had a storyline identical to parts 1-1648. More extreme video nasties were discovered aboard the LOW version of RED DWARF, including 'Revenge of the Mutant Splat-Gore Monster 'and 'Die Screaming With Sharp Things in Your Head'. Finally, for a bunch of lonely males far out in deep space, gardening programmes provide a useful antidote to overactive hormones. *See also* DOUG McCLURE.

VILLAIN WORLD: An area of the WAX-DROID THEME PARK in which Droids of history's villains were kept.

VINDALOOIAN EMPIRE: The home of the great TARKA DAL and BHINDI BHAJI . . . not.

VINDALOOS: LISTER is quite a glutton for this type of hot curry, and has been known to experiment with all types – including kippers and caviar! When under threat of death,

LISTER's first regret was that he had never eaten a prawn vindaloo; he has presumably now rectified the omission. *See also* MUTTON VINDALOO BEAST.

VIRAL RESEARCH DEPARTMENT: The place of work of Doctor HILDEGARDE LANSTROM, and the place she developed her theory of positive and negative viruses (see also FELICITUS POPULI). Unfortunately she also inadvertently created a HOLO-VIRUS, which ended her hologramatic existence.

VIRGIN BIRTH: The CAT PEOPLE believe that this miraculous event happened to LISTER's former pet, FRANKENSTEIN, spawning their race. In fact, the responsibility lay with a BIG BLACK TOM on TITAN.

VON STAUFFENBERG: The German Officer who planted a bomb in ADOLF HITLER's briefcase. By stealing the case, LISTER inadvertently saved the dictator's life.

VOTERS: The citizens of the imaginary totalitarian state in which DUANE DIBLEY and his friend found themselves living.

W

WALRUS POLISHING KIT, PORTABLE: Just the kind of junk that LISTER would send off for in order to receive some mail.

WAR: Violent member of the FOUR APOCALYPSE BOYS.

WASTE COMPACTOR: STARBUG's method of crushing waste before it is ejected into space.

WASTE DISPOSAL: One of the sections in which LISTER worked during his tour of duty on RED DWARF. Any waste was loaded into GARBAGE PODS and ejected into space.

WASTE DISPOSAL UNITS: By the simple addition of some rocket fuel and a THERMOS FLASK full of nitroglycerine, KRYTEN transformed one of these everyday shipboard devices into a rather useful garbage cannon.

WASTE GRINDER: A quicker method of WASTE DISPOSAL than the GARBAGE PODS, this machine simply grinds up rubbish and ejects it into space. CONFIDENCE used it to dispose of PARANOIA once and for all.

WATER-WINGS: Items of RED DWARF's survival equipment which KRYTEN sometimes finds useful.

WATUNGA: The KINITAWOWI word for hut. Sheesh, what an absolutely invaluable reference work this is.

WAX-DROID THEME PARK: The use to which the whole of the newly-named WAX-WORLD was put. Presumably a future version of a wax-works museum. *See* WAX-DROIDS for more information.

WAX-DROIDS: Animated wax-works, which the crew of RED DWARF encountered on WAX-WORLD. After millions of years untended, the Droids had broken free of their programming, and a brutal WAX WAR had begun between the exhibits in HERO WORLD and those in VILLAIN WORLD. The forces of good included Elvis Presley (to whom RIMMER gave the rank of Sergeant), Abraham Lincoln, MARILYN MONROE, Albert Einstein, Pythagoras, Stan Laurel, Mahatma Gandhi, Mother Theresa, ST. FRANCIS OF ASSISI, The Dalai Llama, Queen Victoria, Noel Coward, Jean Paul Satre and Pope Gregory, all of whom we were introduced to. Father Christmas was also present, having been posted from the FICTION SECTION, and LISTER claimed to have seen the execution of Winnie the Pooh – and we also know that JOHN WAYNE, Sir Lancelot, Joan of Arc, Nelson, Wellington and even Doris Day had already perished in battle. On the side of evil were such despots as HITLER, Goebbels, Goering, NAPOLEON,

Caligula, The Boston Strangler, Mussolini, Al Capone, Rasputin, Richard the Third and JAMES LAST. You can probably see now why we didn't have the room to give all of these their own entries in this index!

WAX WAR, THE: The wax-thirsty conflict which was ongoing when the RED DWARF crew arrived on WAX-WORLD. RIMMER took command of the forces of HERO WORLD and led them into glorious victory against VILLAIN WORLD. Unfortunately, every WAX-DROID on the planet was wiped out in the process.

WAX-WORLD: Home of the WAX-DROIDS; also a giant WAX-DROID THEME PARK.

WAYNE, JOHN: Movie cowboy, and idol of the SKUTTERS, who are not only avid viewers of his films but also members of his fan club. When they are not working, they enjoy re-enacting his wild-west battles in the corridors of RED DWARF.

WD40: The lubricant with which KRYTEN oils his neck hinges. He also found its aroma particularly attractive when he believed that CAMILLE did likewise.

WELCOME BACK PARTY: A party thrown for GEORGE McINTYRE immediately after his funeral, when he was brought back onto RED DWARF as a HOLOGRAM.

WEST SIDE STORY: A musical update of the 'Romeo and Juliet' story, and the nearest thing to a SHAKESPEARE play RIMMER has ever seen.

WHAT BIKE: A magazine read by LISTER, who else?

WHITE CARD: An imaginary object with which RIMMER signalled to LISTER that a conversation could continue. *See also* BLACK CARD.

WHITE CORRIDOR 159: Quite a problematic area of the ship, as far as LISTER and RIMMER are concerned. The DRIVE PLATE which, inefficiently repaired by RIMMER, caused a RADIATION leak was in this area. Also, this is where LISTER collapsed after catching a mutated strain of PNEU-MONIA. Most importantly, it was the site of that now infamous blockage of the DISPENSER's CHICKEN SOUP NOZZLE.

WHITE HOLE: The exact opposite of the more commonly known phenomenon the BLACK HOLE. White holes spew time and matter back into the universe. When the RED DWARF crew encountered one, they had to knock a planet into it to escape its influence.

WHITE MIDGET: A shuttle-craft mentioned by LISTER but never actually seen, as he set off in BLUE MIDGET instead.

WHO'S NOBODY: The imaginary BOOK in which the CAT considered DAVE LISTER should have an entry.

WICKED STRENGTH LAGER: Another of LISTER's favoured brands of LAGER. This one certainly lives up to its name, as it got him 'pished' after only two cans!

WILSON, REGGIE: A purveyor of HAMMOND ORGAN MUSIC – and, much to everybody else's dismay, a particular idol of ARNOLD RIMMER. His albums include Reggie Wilson plays the lift music classics, sounds of the super-market – 20 golden greats, Pop goes Delius and Funking up Wagner.

WINE BAR: One of LISTER's greatest embarrassments is that he once entered one such establishment. He considers himself lucky that he was able to reverse the slide into depravity, preventing himself from 'selling out' and becoming a 'class traitor'.

W.O.O.: When the seriously loony RIMMER decided to sentence the others to a period WithOut Oxygen, they, not surprisingly, considered that two hours was just a bit excessive.

WOOD OF HUMILIATION: An area of the PSY-MOON located not too far from the CHASM OF HOPELESSNESS and quite close to the SWAMP OF DESPAIR.

WORM-HOLE: A spatial phenomenon which enabled RIMMER's ESCAPE POD to reach what would shortly become RIMMERWORLD. Unfortunately, due to the effects of time dilation, it would take 557 years before DEREK CUSTER, Kit and Titan were able to mount a rescue.

WORMSKIN RUG: The non-existence of such an item is RIMMER's rebuff to the old CAT saying: 'It's better to live an hour as a tiger than a lifetime as a worm.'

WRIST WATCH: A mechanism into which HOLLY can project his/her consciousness, allowing the computer to provide guidance to the RED DWARF crew even when they are not on board the ship. Unfortunately, this proved to be rather an unpleasant experience, due to LISTER's predilections for scratching under his arms and putting his hands in his pockets. The latter was made worse by the presence of a large hole in his trousers, which gave the first HOLLY a view that reminded him of ATTACK OF THE KILLER GOOSEBERRIES. In later years, the addition of KRYTEN to the crew has eased the problem, as HOLLY can now project her consciousness to a monitor screen on his chest plate, instead.

X

XANADU: LISTER's disgustingly opulent home in an alternate past, named after the hit song by Dave Dee, Dozy, Beaky, Mick and Titch.

XPRESS LIFTS: The elevators provided for long journeys down to RED DWARF's lower levels. As the journeys take a long time, computerised hostesses and inedible food are provided – as are CYANIDE CAPSULES since, in the event of an accident, there is no means of escape.

Y

YADRETSEY: A BACKWARDS EARTH newspaper.

YAKKA TALLA TULLA: The SPACE SCOUT mistress who saved RIMMER from a cannibalistic attempt on his life by the rest of the pack.

YANKEE DOODLE DANDY: LISTER's 'party piece' is to belch this tune when drunk. He considers it stylish, but was disgusted when he witnessed a similar performance by DEB LISTER, his female counterpart in the PARALLEL UNIVERSE.

YATES, LISE: A girl with whom LISTER once had a particularly special relationship. As a death day present he transferred the slightly modified memories of the affair into RIMMER's mind. Until he discovered the truth RIMMER was ecstatic, if not a little confused – after all moving to Liverpool and becoming a total slob was a bit out of character and not many people need their APPENDIX out twice!

YO-YO: CAT was delighted to discover one of these on his travels, and kept it as his 'SHINY THING', despite the fact that he didn't have a clue what it was for.

Z

Z SHIFT: The small contingent of which RIMMER was in charge, aboard RED DWARF. We are led to believe that this consisted only of himself and LISTER – and we know that its most important task was ensuring that the DISPENSERS didn't run out of FUN-SIZE CRUNCHIE BARS.

ZERO GEE FOOTBALL: Short for ZERO GRAVITY FOOTBALL.

ZERO GRAVITY FOOTBALL: A GAME particularly enjoyed by LISTER, who supported the LONDON JETS. LISTER's hero, JIM BEXLEY SPEED, was an accomplished player in this sport.

ZERO GEE KICK-BOXING: What ZERO GEE FOOTBALL is to present-day soccer (or maybe that boring American thing), this sport is to present-day kick-boxing. Blummin' obvious really.

001100111011100011110011100111100: An old ANDROID saying which, loosely translated, means: 'Don't stand around jabbering when you're in mortal danger.'

ZOOM FUNCTION: A facility inherent within KRYTEN's optical system, the loss of which he was most upset about when he became temporarily human.

SECTION FIVE:

THE
CREATORS

ROB GRANT AND DOUG NAYLOR

The guiding force behind *Red Dwarf*, Rob Grant and Doug Naylor have been together since their school and college days in Manchester and Liverpool. Their professional writing career began with radio, and most importantly with the comedy sketch show *Cliché* and its sequel Son of *Cliché*.

From there, it was only a short step into television, with *Carrott's Lib* in 1984, following which they were taken on as head writers for the satirical puppet show *Spitting Image*. It was at this time that they decided that they wanted a programme to call their own – and the rest, as they say, is history.

Rob and Doug are the sole writers of *Red Dwarf*, having penned all thirty episodes to date, as well as the novels which the series has spawned (the latter under the cunningly deceptive pseudonym of Grant Naylor). In more recent seasons, they have also become more involved with other aspects of the programme. Their own production company – called, quite naturally, Grant Naylor – took control of *Red Dwarf* from Paul Jackson Productions after Series II, and more recently, the pair have taken on the roles of both executive producers and part-time directors (the latter, again under the Grant Naylor pseudonym) for *Red Dwarf* V.

The Grant Naylor company is also responsible for *The Ten %ers*, which graduated from a one-off in Carlton TV's *Comedy Playhouse* slot into a full series in 1994.

Unfortunately, both seem to have an aversion to having photographs of themselves taken, hence the absence of such from this book's photo section. However, you can see what Rob at least looks like by watching the episode 'Backwards': there's a shot of him on Manchester's Portland Street, wearing dark glasses and smoking a cigarette.

CRAIG CHARLES

'If I could do anything,' confesses Liverpool-born Craig, 'I'd like to be a footballer.' He's had some degree of success in that field too, having played both with Tranmere Rovers and with the Liverpool Youth Team. However, it is in the performing arts that he has really made a name for himself.

Even before he appeared in *Red Dwarf*, Craig had carved himself a solid reputation as a comedian and a poet, earning amongst other things a regular slot on the comedy programme *Saturday Night Live*. Not wanting to be tied down to just one area, he has now become known as a presenter as well, having hosted such shows as *Them and Us*, *Craig Goes Mad in Melbourne* and *Cyberzone*. In 1993, he also co-wrote his first book, *The Craig Charles Almanac of Total Knowledge*. 'I like to do lots of different things,' he says, 'and I work in a business which, if you're good at it, allows you to do that. But really I see my career as a far more performance-based thing than as a television presenter.'

It was on *Saturday Night Live* that Craig first worked with producer Paul Jackson, who subsequently remembered him when *Red Dwarf* came along. He was auditioned for the role of Dave Lister, the linchpin around whom the show revolves and as we all know by now, he went on to play the role with great success in all of the televised episodes of the programme. And in the future? Well, again in Craig's words: 'I'll carry on doing it for as long as the writing guys are writing good scripts, and as long as I'm happy with what they do to my character.'

Of course, if we wanted to be really, really pedantic about it (and we do) you can also count the roles of the second Polymorph ('Polymorph'), the Inquisitor ('The Inquisitor'), Lister's own 'high' and 'low' selves ('Demons and Angels') and even Rimmer (in 'Body Swap'). In Ace Rimmer's dimension, which we visited in 'Dimension Jump', Craig made a brief appearance as Lister's counterpart there, a Space Corps Engineer called Spanners, and in 'Back to Reality', he portrayed the fictional character of Colonel Sebastian Doyle.

Similarly, he was Brett Riverboat in 'Gunmen of the Apocalypse's' AR scenes, whilst he portrayed one quarter of Legion in 'Legion' and a psiren in, believe it or not . . . 'Psirens'!

He even contributed to *Red Dwarf*'s music, writing the infamous 'Om Song' for his own brother Emile (along with two members of thrash metal band Napalm Death) in 'Timeslides'. In addition, he wrote, sang and produced the song 'Cash', also heard in the episode, and the instrumental 'Bad News' to which Kryten is seen dancing in its opening moments. Unfortunately, a production slip-up meant that none of this was recorded in the credits.

CHRIS BARRIE

'I think he's a deeply sad character,' says Chris on the subject of Arnold Rimmer. 'There's the fact that he's dead and can't touch anything – and he probably had a sad life to start with. I think he is in many ways probably the saddest person amongst them all.' More surprisingly Chris also adds, '. . . and possibly the nicest – and he's become more like that over the years. His vulnerabilities are being brought out a lot more.'

Chris is certainly no stranger to playing such roles, as witness his more recent interpretation of Gordon Brittas, controller of BBC 1's *Brittas Empire*. Although portrayed very differently by Chris, Brittas has an uncanny number of similarities to Rimmer. For example, both characters had unsuccessful stints in the Samaritans, unintentionally persuading even the wrong numbers to do away with themselves.

Chris's background, however, is as an impressionist, his first professional performances being at London's Comedy Store in early 1982. From then on, it was only a matter of time before his talents were spotted, both for radio and for television. On the former, he lent his voice to Rob Grant and Doug Naylor's creation, Hab – Holly's forerunner – in *Son of Cliché*, whilst on the latter, he made his first appearance during Jasper Carrott's 1983 *Election Special*. More work with Carrott followed (working with Grant and Naylor once again), as well as a long and successful stint on *Spitting Image* (yep, and again!). Over the years, Chris provided the voices for a multitude of rubber celebrities, among them such luminaries as Ronald Reagan, George Bush and Prince Charles. Indeed, his work on Spitting Image only finished when a direct recording clash with *Red Dwarf* V made it impossible for him to do both.

Chris originally became involved with *Red Dwarf* when he read for the character of Lister. Instead, he was given the role of Rimmer, the show's other major protagonist, which he has of course played in every episode. If we wanted to be as pedantic with him as we were with Craig Charles (and don't you just know it . . .) we could mention that he too played a Polymorph in 'Polymorph', the Inquisitor in 'The Inquisitor' and Rimmer's 'high' and 'low' equivalents in 'Demons and Angels', as well as both Lister and the Cat in 'Body Swap'. Chris has also been seen as Arnold's brother Frank in 'Timeslides', his other-dimensional counterpart Ace in both 'Dimension Jump' and 'Emohawk - Polymorph II' and his own Self-Confidence, Self-Respect and even Self-Loathing (voice only) in 'Terrorform'. He played Sebastian Doyle's step-brother, Billy, in 'Back to Reality', bare fist fighter extraordinaire Dangerous Dan McGrew in 'Gunmen of the Apocalypse' and, variably, one quarter, one third and one half of Legion in 'Legion'. Finally, in the episode 'Rimmerworld', he played just about everyone!

DANNY JOHN-JULES

Now an accomplished actor with a string of credits to his name, Danny actually set out originally to do something different – he wanted to work in the field of music.

Even now, he enjoys doing musical productions such as *Starlight Express* and, more recently, *Carmen Jones* at London's prestigious Old Vic theatre. He even appeared in the stage show *Cats* – perhaps an omen of what was to come!

'I've been very lucky,' says Danny, 'because wherever I work, I get to sing songs.' And indeed he does, these ranging from the Cat's song and dance production 'Tongue Tied' at the beginning of 'Parallel Universe' to similar routines in such programmes as *Maid Marian and her Merry Men* and *Runaway Bay*. 'Even when I did *Jackanory*,' he says, 'I did a rap.'

Danny took the role of the Cat very seriously, doing a lot of research into the characteristics of felines, in preparation for the task. 'Apparently,' he tells us, authoritatively, 'there is a bit of cat in everyone. That's why I think the character appeals to everyone. I had a guy come up to me when I was doing Maid Marian down in Somerset, and he said, "The Cat – that's me. That's exactly what I'm like!" ' He certainly had the right idea at his audition; the first person to be seen for the part, he made a big impression by arriving in character.

Again, Danny has played the Cat throughout *Red Dwarf*'s run to date. He did also make brief appearances as Rimmer in 'Body Swap', the Inquisitor in 'The Inquisitor', Camille in 'Camille' and the 'high' and 'low' Cats in 'Demons and Angels', whilst in Ace Rimmer's universe, he played the Padre ('Dimension Jump'). He was also the buck-toothed geek Duane Dibbley in 'Back to Reality' and 'Emohawk – Polymorph II', various fractions of Legion in 'Legion' and the stylish Riviera Kid in 'Gunmen of the Apocalypse'.

HATTIE HAYRIDGE

It was never Hattie's intention to become an actress. Indeed, she worked as a secretary for eight years until, in her own words, 'I couldn't stand it anymore. I think that's what prompted my getting up on stage.'

The first stage appearance was an impromptu one, blamed by Hattie on eight Southern Comforts. Nevertheless, the club management were impressed enough to give her an immediate booking – and her career has never looked back since.

Naturally television appearances were not too long in coming. The first of these was on a benefits programme called *Advice Shop*, for which Hattie wrote and performed a short comic monologue each week. She later went on, of course, to make her debut in *Red Dwarf*, as her deadpan style of delivery made her perfect to take on the role of Holly's female equivalent, Hilly, in 'Parallel Universe'.

Unknown to all at the time, 'Parallel Universe' was only the start of Hattie's long association with the programme. As Season two drew to a close, the original Holly, Norman Lovett, announced his intention to leave *Red Dwarf*. Hattie, of course, was the logical choice to inherit the part – and thus, viewers were informed at the start of *Red Dwarf III* that the eccentric computer had undergone a head sex change operation, modelling himself after Hilly.

Hattie's first love, however, is still stand-up comedy. 'There are hundreds of female actors,' she says, practically, 'and there aren't many female stand-ups, so I'm better off staying as a stand-up than being an untrained actress.'

As well as playing Hilly and Holly, Hattie made a brief appearance as Mellie in the episode 'Dimension Jump' – the only time in the programme that we have seen anything more than her head on screen. She also played Holly's own 'high' and 'low' versions in 'Demons and Angels'.

Hattie unfortunately left *Red Dwarf* after season five, with her character being lost aboard the missing ship. The way might still be open, however, for a comeback.

ROBERT LLEWELLYN

A writer as well as an actor, Robert Llewellyn made his debut in both fields in the early eighties, when he joined a theatre company called 'The Joeys'. His credits include the television comedy lecture 'The Reconstructed Heart', which was screened in early 1992, and the stage play *Mammon, Robot Born of Woman*, which is where he was spotted for *Red Dwarf*.

Robert made his *Red Dwarf* debut at the beginning of the third season, when he took over the now regular role of Kryten. The role, of course, has its fair share of problems. 'I'm completely covered from head to foot in very thick heavy rubber and plastic costumes,' he complains, 'and the lights are quite astonishing temperatures. I find it quite physically demanding, because it's so hot and it's so uncomfortable. It really stretches your patience to the absolute limit.'

Nevertheless, Robert has stayed with the programme for four years now and even reprised his robotic role in the unfortunately unsuccessful American pilot episode – although the costume in that case was rather less cumbersome than the original. 'I've often pleaded for Kryten to have a human head,' he jokes, 'but when I see it afterwards, I think yes, it does work, it does look good.'

Fortunately for Robert, he has been able to appear sans make-up on three separate occasions, most notably in the episode 'DNA' when Kryten temporarily gained human form. His other human roles were those of Diva-Droid Executive Jim Reaper in 'The Last Day' and Ace Rimmer's friend Bongo in 'Dimension Jump'. Like most of the rest of the cast, Robert also made a brief appearance (with mask this time) as the Inquisitor, in the episode of the same name, as well as playing Kryten's 'high' and 'low' selves in 'Demons and Angels' and his fictional alter-ego, Jake Bullet, in 'Back to Reality'. He played the whole of Legion (plus various fractions) in 'Legion' and was also a psiren in 'Psirens'.

NORMAN LOVETT

Known to *Red Dwarf* fans as the first person to play the ship's senile computer Holly, Norman is primarily a stand-up comic – although he did once appear in his own BBC2 show, *I Lovett*.

Norman first went into comedy whilst in his early thirties performing his 'hang-dog' stand-up routine on the same bill as new wave bands such as 999 and The Clash. A stint in the Comedy Store followed, with television roles coming shortly afterwards. Perhaps the best remembered of these, besides *Red Dwarf* itself, is his portrayal of Ruby Wax's floor manager in her Channel 4 show *Don't Miss Wax*, for which he wrote his own material.

He initially became involved in *Red Dwarf* when he auditioned for the role of Arnold Rimmer. Instead he was offered the voice-over part of Holly, which he took, in his own words, 'because I needed the work, but I was quite upset because it was a voice-over – after Ruby Wax, I wanted to stay seen on television.' In the end, of course, his wish was granted. Eventually, however, Norman decided that it was time to move on from the series. This was due, in part, to the pressures of travelling from his home in Edinburgh to rehearsals in London to recordings in Manchester, but he did feel he had done all he could with the character. 'Holly couldn't be a lead character really,' he says, 'he was just an image on screen. With "Queeg", they did a Holly story, and realistically I don't think they could have done any more. So I felt it was a good time to leave, as opposed to getting stuck in it.'

As for the possibility of a return to *Red Dwarf*, well . . . 'I'd probably do a one-off if they asked me to do an episode. It would be quite nice to meet the others again, that would bring back memories.'

Remarkably, in all his time in *Red Dwarf*, Norman was the only cast member not to have appeared in more than one role, which is a pity, because we were really enjoying digging up such useless bits of trivia.

DAVID ROSS

If anything, David Ross actually had more problems with the Kryten costume than Robert Llewellyn has. As the first actor to play the android, David had to endure long and gruelling make-up sessions, made worse by his natural claustrophobia. 'I think altogether it took about nine hours to put it on,' he remembers. 'It's like having plaster on any part of you, it is terribly uncomfortable and, I suppose, wearing, due to just the strain of sitting there in a chair for that length of time. Then of course, come six o'clock, your audience are coming in and you've got to start doing your actual job!'

Another northerner, David Ross hails from Blackburn, and began his career on stage in Barrow-in-Furness. He later graduated from Manchester Polytechnic, and went on to act in a multitude of television, stage and radio shows, including the Granada comedy series *Yanks Go Home* and *Leave it to Charlie*. More recently, he has been seen as Mister Weller in the acclaimed drama serial *GBH*, and has earned a certain amount of notoriety by appearing naked in his first West End lead in Alan Bleasdale's play *Having a Ball*. Since then, he has been working extensively at the National Theatre.

It was through David's work in radio, however, that he was first introduced to Rob Grant and Doug Naylor, who later recruited him into the *Red Dwarf* team. Impressed by his first appearance, they subsequently wrote Kryten into the series as a regular character, only to find David was unfortunately unavailable, appearing as he was in the play *Flea in Her Ear* at the Old Vic. He did, however, make a brief return visit to *Red Dwarf* the following year, when he took over John Lenahan's first season role as the (renamed) Talkie Toaster, for the episode 'White Hole'. 'It's great to be able to say that you've played a toaster,' jokes David – who also has some very definite ideas about what he'd like to turn up as next. 'I'd like to maybe play a poker next time. I love pokers!'

ED BYE

Ed started his career in the BBC as a floor assistant, eventually becoming a director and working along the way on such shows as *Three of a Kind*, *The Young Ones*, *Jasper Carrott* and *The Late, Late, Breakfast Show*. However, he left the Corporation to work as a freelancer when Paul Jackson asked him to direct the comedy series *Girls on Top* for Central.

'It was all quite a bit hairy that,' he recalls, 'because I hadn't directed much comedy – I'd directed a lot of light entertainment stuff but no actual structured comedy. French and Saunders I'd worked with before, so that was all right, but Ruby Wax was difficult and she wanted to get me thrown off the show. Fortunately I married her after the series, so that problem went away.'

More work in comedy followed, including – perhaps unsurprisingly – a number of Ruby Wax's solo series. Then, inevitably (considering the title of the book you're reading), along came *Red Dwarf*, to which Ed was again introduced by Paul Jackson.

'I've always been a bit of a science-fiction freak on the quiet,'

Ed confesses, and so, after an initial meeting with Rob Grant and Doug Naylor (with whom he had worked briefly before on *Carrott* and *Three of a Kind*), the match was made.

Ed stayed with *Red Dwarf* for four of its six seasons to date, and both produced and directed the series – the first time he had done both together. 'I tend to produce and direct as much as I can,' he says now, 'because that way you have more control over the project.' In later years, of course, he enjoyed sharing the production chores with Grant and Naylor themselves. Ed assures us that his absence from the credits of *Red Dwarf V* was not by choice. 'I committed myself to doing *The Full Wax*, which was a BBC 1 show with Ruby – and she asked me to do that before we knew we had another series of *Red Dwarf*' He certainly isn't ruling out a return to the show in the future – but then, he does seem to be a busy man at the moment, with his skills very much in demand for shows such as Rik Mayall and Ade Edmondson's *Bottom* and *The Detectives*, a comedy spin-off from Jasper Carrott's show.

JOHN POMPHREY

Other than Grant, Naylor and certain cast members, lighting director John Pomphrey is one of only three credited people to have worked on *Red Dwarf* since its inception. He operates from BBC North in Manchester, where the series was originally made, and describes his assignation to the series as 'a lot of luck really. There were three lighting directors in Manchester at the time and it came up as a name – *Red Dwarf* – nobody knew what it was. The other two lighting directors had jobs at the time, and the guy in charge said to me "Do you want to do it?" '

John describes his job as 'working with the designer, creating the environment and making it look right. The business of lighting is the relationship between the camera, the performer and the lamp; it's no good if the camera's out there in front looking at you and I light from the side . . . all you'll see is a brightly lit ear and a dark face. I've got to guess where the director is going to put his shots by looking at the action.'

Sometimes, his job gives rise to unexpected problems. 'At the back of Shepperton there's a swampy area which we used in "Terrorform". We were getting ready for a night shoot and as we were setting up, two electricians and myself fell into the water. The lamps went in as well and all the scripts were soaking wet. It was awful, but it caused a lot of hilarity. This year we were shooting in a similar place and when the generator turned up there was a life jacket on the side especially for me!'

HOWARD GOODALL

Howard has been the *Red Dwarf* musical maestro since, quite literally, the beginning of episode one. His works include both versions of the opening music, the popular Tongue-Tied song (for which Grant and Naylor provided the lyrics), the well-remembered Hammond organ theme from 'Dimension Jump' (which, he admits, wasn't done on a real Hammond at all) and, of course, the ubiquitous 'Fun in the Sun' theme which has ended almost every episode. 'That was really based on one episode in the first series,' says Howard, 'which was all about him [Lister] wanting to go to Fiji – all that stuff about "goldfish shoals nibbling at my toes" was all to do with that, although if you see it now it doesn't bear any relation to what you're watching and I quite like that.'

A freelancer operating out of London, Howard's impressive list of credits covers such programmes as *Blackadder* (all four versions), *Mr Bean* and *Not the Nine O'Clock News*. 'I had a bit of a lucky break when I was at university. I did a lot of student reviews and the people at Oxford, the people doing reviews at the same time, were Rowan Atkinson, Richard Curtis and one or two others. So when Rowan left I was already doing his show and within about a year of his leaving we were doing *Not the Nine O'Clock News*.'

You won't see Howard on screen, but if you want to catch his voice, then listen to his stirling rendition of 'Do Not Foresake Me, Oh My Darling', which accompanied Norman Lovett's Holly into battle in the episode 'Queeg'. As for any chart aspirations, 'Well, actually I was in a band before I got into all this; it wasn't a very good band, we made an album and a couple of singles which were really crap.'

PETER WRAGG

Another stalwart of *Red Dwarf*'s entire run, Peter Wragg has won World Television Society Awards for his effects work on the show. 'On the first series,' he recalls, 'it was basically just *Red Dwarf* the spaceship, up and past, left to right, towards the camera, away from the camera and nothing else. But they were pleased enough with those shots that the following year, Rob and Doug asked if we could be a bit more adventurous. By the time we got to Season three, they had the confidence in myself and my assistants to say: "Well if we can provide a vehicle for you to demonstrate your talents then we will," and I think they've been very pleased with the results that they've got. I consider myself lucky that Rob and Doug were prepared to write more and more effects into the programmes as they went along, giving me the opportunity to do more.'

Peter's career began as a model maker with A P Films (later Century 21), where he worked on programmes such as *Thunderbirds* and *Captain Scarlet*. Live action shows such as *UFO* and *Doctor Who* followed, before he was chosen by the BBC to work on the then fledgeling *Red Dwarf*. Although he now works with several different *Starbug* models (to different scales and with different fittings), he gave us some clue as to why the eponymous red ship is no longer featured: 'We haven't got any models of it. The original one was literally about eight feet long, from scoop to engine, and that virtually fell to pieces over the years. So then we had to make another one for Season five, which wasn't quite as big – probably about five feet from nose to tail – but we had to make that so we could blow it up for "Demons and Angels".'

And the rest of the people who have made Red Dwarf what it is . . .

(Actors' and technicians' names in CAPITALS, actors' roles in **bold**, technicians' jobs in roman and series and episode titles in *italic*.)

ABINERI, JOHN: **Rimmer's Dad** (*Better Than Life*)
ABRAHAM, JAKE: **Second Lister** (*The Inquisitor*)
ADDIE, ROBERT: **Gilbert** (*Timeslides*)
AGNEW, MIKE: Production Manager (*Seasons 2 and 3*).
AGUTTER, JENNY: **Professor Mamet** (*Psirens*)
ALLEN, MARK: Graphic Designer (*Seasons 1 to 3*)
ANSON, ELIZABETH: **Temptress** (*Psirens*)
ARCHER, GILLY: Associate Producer (*Season 3*)
ASBURY, CLAIRE: Production Team Member (*The Last Day*).
ASH, DEBBIE: **Marilyn Monroe** (*Better Than Life*)
AUGINS, CHARLES: **Queeg** (*Queeg*), Choreographer
    (*Parallel Universe*)
AUSTIN, JEREMY: **Rathbone** (*Better Than Life*)

BAILEY, PAULINE: **Marilyn Monroe** (*Meltdown*)
BAIN, IMOGEN: **Lola** (*Gunmen of the Apocalypse*)
BAKER, MARK: Production Team Member (*Psirens, Out of Time*)
BALL, NICHOLAS: **Simulant** (*Justice*)

BANKS, MORWENNA: **The Lift Hostess** (*Stasis Leak*)

BARBER, FRANCES: **Genny** (*Polymorph*)

BARGH, CELIA: Production Team Member (*Season 4*)

BATES, PETER: Insert Editor (*Back to Reality, Season 6*)

BATES, RUPERT: **Trout á la Crème** (*Balance of Power*), **Chef** (*Balance of Power*), **Bodyguard** (*Timeslides*), **Hector Blob** (*Camille*)

BATHURST, ROBERT: **Todhunter** (*The End*)

BATTYE, JOHN: Vision Supervisor (*Thanks for the Memory, Queeg*), Vision Controller (*Stasis Leak*)

BAYNES, HETTY: **Cockpit Computer** (*Dimension Jump*)

BERTISH, SUZANNE: **Ms Rimmer** (*Parallel Universe*)

BEVAN JONES, HILARY: Producer (*Season 5*)

BEVERIDGE, ANGELA: Vision Mixer (*The Last Day*)

BIBBY, MEL: Designer (*Seasons 3 and 4*), Production Designer (*Seasons 5 and 6*)

BIRKINSHAW, JOANNA: Production Accountant (*Seasons 4 and 5*)

BLACKALL, PETER: Props (*Season 4*)

BLAKE, ROGER: **Noel Coward** (*Meltdown*)

BOWMAN, ANDY: Visual Effects Designer (*The Inquisitor*)

BRADLEY, PAUL: **Chen** (*The End, Balance of Power*)

BRADSHAW, STEPHEN: Assistant Designer (*White Hole*), Production Designer (*Seasons 5 and 6*)

BRIERS, LUCY: **Harrison** (*Holoship*)

BRUCE, ANGELA: **Ms Lister** (*Parallel Universe*)

BURDEN, HOWARD: Costume Design (*Seasons 3 to 6*).

BURRELL, MICHAEL: **Pope Gregory** (*Meltdown*)

BURWELL, LOIS: Make-Up Design (*Psirens, Legion, Gunmen of the Apocalypse, Rimmerworld, Out of Time*)

CALVERT, JENNIFER: **Loretta** (*Gunmen of the Apocalypse*)

CAMPBELL, HELEN: Production Team Member (*Kryten, Better Than Life, Thanks for the Memory, Parallel Universe*), Assistant Floor Manager (*Queeg*)

CARRIVICK, NIGEL: **The Captain** (*Better Than Life*)

CAVE, DON: Prop Buyer (*Season 4*).

CHARLES, EMILE: **Young Lister** (*Timeslides*)

CHICK, BRIDGET: Production Team Member (*Season 6*)

CLARE, RON: Technical Co-ordinator (*The End, Future Echoes, Balance of Power, Waiting for God*)

CLARKE, GEORGE R: Production Manager (*Season 1*)

COLEMAN, NOEL: **Cat Priest** (*Waiting for God*)

CORMACK, JAMES: **Thomas Allman** (*The Inquisitor*)

CORNES, LEE: **Paranoia** (*Confidence and Paranoia*)

COWLEY, ANDREW: Technical Co-ordinator (*Season 2*)

CROSS, MELVYN: Camera Supervisor (*The End, Balance of Power, Season 2*)

CURTIN, MAIREAD: Production Team Member (*Seasons 4 and 5*)

DALTON, SIMON: Property Master (*Season 6*)

D'AURIA, PAUL: Graphic Designer (*Season 4*)

DAVIES, JANE: Casting (*Seasons 4 and 5, Psirens, Legion, Gunmen of the Apocalypse, Emohawk – Polymorph II, Rimmerworld*)

DAVIS, JAMES: Visual Effects Designer (*Demons and Angels, Legion*)

DAY, SIMON: **Number Two** (*Holoship*)

DE EMMONY, ANDY: Director (*Season 6*)

DEVEREAUX, STEVE: **Jimmy** (*Gunmen of the Apocalypse*)

DEVITT, MATTHEW: **The Dog** (*Parallel Universe*)

DISTEFANO, DONA: Assistant Floor Manager (*Seasons 1 to 3*)

DOBSON, ANITA: **Captain Tau** (*Psirens*)

DOCHERTY, JOHN: **Inquisitor** (*The Inquisitor*)

DOHERTY, SOPHIE: **Kochanski's Room Mate** (*Stasis Leak*)

DORNAN, JILL: Vision Mixer (*Seasons 1 and 2*)

DREW, BILLY: Production Team Member (*The Last Day*)

DUBOIS, MARIO: Unit Manager (*Season 1*)

FALLON, MIKE: Props Buyer (*Future Echoes, Balance of Power, Me², Season 2*)

FERGUSON, CRAIG: **Confidence** (*Confidence and Paranoia*)

FOLAN, FRANCESCA: **Hologram Camille** (*Camille*)

FOX, DAVE: OB Cameraman (*Backwards, Marooned, Timeslides*), Camera Supervisor (*Polymorph, Body Swap, The Last Day*)

FRIEDMAN, MARIA: **Waitress** (*Backwards*)

FRIEND, MARTIN: **Einstein** (*Meltdown*)

GAFFNEY, SIMON: **Young Rimmer** (*Polymorph, Timeslides, Dimension Jump*)

GALLERY, NEIL: Production Team Member (*The Last Day*)

GAN, NINA: Make-up Designer (*The Inquisitor, Terrorform, Quarantine, Demons and Angels, Back to Reality*)

GIBBONS, IRENE: Unit Manager (*Season 5*)

GIBSON, JEZ: Video Effects (*Season 5*)

GILLESPIE, DAVID: **Selby** (*The End, Balance of Power*)

GREEN, RON: Gaffer (*Seasons 5 and 6*)

GREENHALGH, LEN: Vision Supervisor (*Kryten, Parallel Universe*)

GREENWOOD, KALLI: **Mrs Rimmer** (*Polymorph, Dimension Jump*)

GROGAN, C P: **Kochanski** (*The End, Balance of Power, Stasis Leak, Psirens*)

HADLEY, KENNETH: **Hitler** (*Meltdown*)

HAINSWORTH, RICHARD: **The Medical Orderly** (*Stasis Leak*), **Bodyguard** (*Timeslides*)

HAMILTON, CHRISTINA: Production Assistant (*Season 3*)

HARGREAVES, JOHANNA: **The Esperanto Woman** (*Kryten*)

HARRIOTT, AINSLEY: **GELF Chief** (*Emohawk – Polymorph II*)

HAWKINS, JUDY: **McGruder** (*Better Than Life*)

HAWKS, TONY: **Dispensing Machine** (*Future Echoes*),

The Guide (*Better Than Life*), **The Suitcase** (*Stasis Leak*), **Compere** (*Backwards*), **Caligula** (*Meltdown*)

HEDGES, MARK: Prop Master (*Back To Reality*)

HICKLING, LIZ: **Simulant Lieutenant/Rogue Simulant** (*Gunmen of the Apocalypse, Rimmerworld*)

HIGGINSON, JULIE: **Girl Android** (*The Last Day*)

HILLE, ANASTASIA: **New Kochanski** (*Back To Reality*)

HILSON, ZOE: **Temptress** (*Psirens*)

HITLER, ADOLF: **Himself** (*Timeslides*)

HODGE, DAVE: Camera Supervisor (*Backwards, Marooned, Timeslides*)

HOLT, SUZANNAH: Location Manager (*Psirens, Legion, Gunmen of the Apocalypse, Rimmerworld*)

HORRILL, SPRINGER: Properties Buyer (*Season 6*)

HORROCKS, JANE: **Nirvanah Crane** (*Holoship*)

HOYE, NICHOL: Production Team Member (*Season 5*)

HUTCHINGS, GRAHAM: Videotape Editor (*Seasons 4 to 6*)

INCH, ROBERT: **War** (*Gunmen of the Apocalypse*)

INGRAM, MARK: Production Team Member (*Gunmen of the Apocalypse, Emohawk – Polymorph II*)

JACKSON, MIKE: Camera Supervisor (*Future Echoes, Waiting for God, Confidence and Paranoia, Me²*)

JACKSON, PAUL: Executive Producer (*Seasons 1 to 3*)

JANSEN, SUZANNE: Make-up Designer (*Season 1*)

JEFFERY, JEFF: Technical Manager (*Seasons 5 and 6*)

JENKINS, TINA: **The Newsreader** (*Better Than Life*)

JONES, BETHAN: Make-up Designer (*Seasons 2 and 3*)

JONES, KELVIN: Unit Manager (*Season 2*)

JUDD, JUSTIN: Producer (*Season 6*)

JULIAN-JONES, CANDIDA: Associate Producer (*Season 4*)

KEMP, FIONA: Assistant Make-up Designer (*White Hole*)

KENNEDY, GORDON: **Hudzen** (*The Last Day*)

KING, TRISHA: Lighting Director (*Queeg*)

KLAFF, JACK: **Abraham Lincoln** (*Meltdown*)

KONSTANTINOU, RINA: Stage Manager (*Season 6*)

KOOL, NICK: Visual Effects Designer (*Quarantine, Rimmerworld*)

LAWRENCE, DAVID: Production Team Member (*Legion, Rimmerworld*)

LENAHAN, JOHN: **Toaster** (*Future Echoes, Waiting for God*)

LILL, DENIS: **Simulant Captain/Death** (*Gunmen of the Apocalypse*)

LOVETT, SONIA: Vision Mixer (*Polymorph*)

McCARTHY, MARIE: **Nurse** (*Back To Reality*)

McCULLEY, ROBERT: **McIntyre** (*The End*)

McDONALD, MAC: **Captain Hollister** (*The End, Me², Stasis Leak*)

McEWAN, ANNIE: Make-Up Design (*Emohawk – Polymorph II*)

McGUINNESS, PAUL: Visual Effects Designer (*Holoship, Psirens*)

McINTYRE, STELLA: Prop Buyer (*Seasons 3 and 5*)

McKINTOSH, STEPHEN: **Thicky Holden** (*Timeslides*)

MACHIN, ALAN: Sound (*Me²*)

MANZANERA, PHIL: **Dave Lister's Hands** (*Psirens*)

MARCUS, STEPHEN: **Bear-Strangler McGee** (*Gunmen of the Apocalypse*)

MARK, CLAYTON: **Elvis** (*Meltdown*)

MARSH, MATTHEW: **Captain Platini** (*Holoship*)

MARSHALL, ALAN: Visual Effects Designer (*Terrorform, Emohawk – Polymorph II*)

MASSON, FORBES: **Stan Laurel** (*Meltdown*)

MAY, JULIET: Director (*Holoship, The Inquisitor, Terrorform, Demons and Angels*), SSS Esperanto Director (*Back To Reality*)

MAYES, KEITH: Sound Supervisor (*The Last Day, Seasons 4 to 6*)

MILNE, GARETH: Stunt Co-ordinator (*Backwards, The Inquisitor, Terrorform*)

MONTAGUE, PAUL: Designer (*Seasons 1 and 2*)

MONTGOMERY, JANE: **Number One** (*Holoship*)

MOONEY, KARL: Video Effects (*Season 6*)

MOSES, CHRISTINE: Production Assistant (*Seasons 4 to 6*)

MOTOR CITY DIVA: Disco Music (*Balance of Power*)

NAPROUS, GERARD: Stunt Co-ordinator (*Gunmen of the Apocalypse*)

NETTLETON, JO: Assistant Make-up Designer (*White Hole*)

PALMER, ANNA: **Customer in cafe** (*Backwards*)

PARKER, DAVID: OB Lighting (*Better Than Life, Thanks for the Memory, Stasis Leak*)

PARKER, JANE: Production Team Member (*The Last Day*)

PARRISH, BELINDA: Make-up Designer (*Holoship*)

PASCOE, JUDY: **Mechanoid Camille** (*Camille*)

PEMBER, RON: **The Taxman** (*Better Than Life*)

PENNELL, ANDRIA: Make-Up Design (*Seasons 4 to 6*)

PETERS, JEREMY: **Pestilence** (*Gunmen of the Apocalypse*)

PINKS, JACKI: Costume Designer (*Seasons 1 and 2*)

PRESTON, KATE: Production Team Member (*Kryten, Better Than Life, Thanks for the Memory, Parallel Universe*), Production Secretary (*Stasis Leak, Queeg*)

POWELL, DINNY: **Famine** (*Gunmen of the Apocalypse*)

PURDY, PAUL: Prop Master (*Holoship, The Inquisitor, Terrorform, Quarantine, Demons and Angels*)

QUARSHIE, HUGH: **Computer** (*Emohawk – Polymorph II*)

RATH, WENDY: Sound (*Me²*)

RHATIGAN, SUZANNE: **Kochanski Camille** (*Camille*)

RIDINGS, RICHARD: **DNA Computer Voice** (*DNA*), **Crazed Astro** (*Psirens*)

ROBSON, SAMANTHA: **Pete Tranter's Sister** (*Psirens*)

ROCKET: OB Cameraman (*Better Than Life, Stasis Leak*), Camera Supervisor (*Seasons 4 to 6*)

RUDLIN, HELENE: Production Team Member (*The Last Day*)

RUTHVEN, LOUISA: **Ski Woman** (*Timeslides*)

SALKILLD, GORDON: **Gordon** (*Better Than Life*)

SANDERS, SIMON: Vision Mixer (*Seasons 4 to 6*)

SCOTT, JULIAN: Production Manager (*Season 4*), Associate Producer (*Season 5*)

SEAL, SAM: Videotape Editor (*Terrorform*)

SHARIAN, JOHN: **New Lister** (*Back To Reality*)

SHAW, GILL: Costume Designer (*Season 5 and 6*)

SHERSTON, CRESSIDA: Production Co-ordinator (*Season 6*)

SIMS, MARTIN: **GELF** (*Emohawk – Polymorph II*)

SKEAPING, COLIN: Stuntman (*The Inquisitor*)

SLATTERY, TONY: **Android Actor** (*Kryten*)

SMILLIE, JAMES: **Justice Computer Voice** (*Justice*)

SMITH, ARTHUR: **Pub Manager** (*Backwards*)

SMITH, JANET: Unit Manager (*Season 3*)

SMITH, TONY: Technical Co-ordinator (*Season 3*)

SPALL, TIMOTHY: **Andy** (*Back to Reality*)

SPENCER, MIKE: Vision Supervisor (*Seasons 4 to 6*)

SPICER, JOHN: Technical Co-ordinator (*Confidence and Paranoia, Me²*)

STANILAND, ANNA: Production Assistant (*Season 2*), Production Manager (*The Last Day*)

STARK, KOO: **Lady Sabrina Mulholland-Jjones** (*Timeslides*)

STAVES, LESLEY: Costume Assistant (*Me²*)

STEED, MAGGIE: **Dr Hildegarde Lanstrom** (*Quarantine*)

STEEL, MARK: **Ski Man** (*Timeslides*)

STEELE, BRUCE: Video Effects (*Season 5*)

STOCKBRIDGE, SARA: **Handmaiden** (*Terrorform*)

THOMAS, DAI: Consol/Console Operator (*Season 5, Psirens, Legion, Gunmen of the Apocalypse, Rimmerworld*), Lighting Assistant (*Emohawk – Polymorph II, Out of Time*)

THORNBER, ALISON: Production Assistant (*Season 1*)

TILLER, STEPHEN: **Pythagoras** (*Meltdown*)

TUCKER, MIKE: Visual Effects Designer (*Back to Reality, Out of Time*) (wrongly credited as Mike Turner on *Back to Reality*)

TYLER, PETER: Model Photography (*Gunmen of the Apocalypse*)

VON DOHLEN, LENNY: **Cop** (*Back to Reality*)

WADDELL, KERRY: Stage Manager (*Seasons 4 and 5*), Production Manager (*Season 6*)

WALKER-LEE, FRANCINE: **Handmaiden** (*Terrorform*)

WALLACE, SIMON: Floor Manager (*Season 6*)

WARRINGTON, DON: **Commander Binks** (*Holoship*)

WAX, RUBY: **American Presenter** (*Timeslides*)

WESTAWAY, LOUISE: Production Accountant (*Season 6*)

WHEELER, DUNCAN: Props Buyer (*The End, Waiting for God, Confidence and Paranoia*)

WHIPPEY, JEM: Sound Supervisor (*DNA, Terrorform, Back to Reality*)

WHITE, GORDON: OB Lighting (*Better Than Life, Stasis Leak*)

WICKHAM, STEVEN: **GELF Bride** (*Emohawk – Polymorph II*)

WIDDOWSON, PERRY: Videotape Editor (*Demons and Angels*)

WILLIAMS, MARK: **Petersen** (*The End, Balance of Power, Stasis Leak*)

WILLIAMS, NIGEL: **Legion** (*Legion*)

WILLIAMS, SABRA: **Lise Yates** (*Thanks for the Memory*)

WOODEN, ED: Videotape Editor (*Seasons 1 to 3*)

WORTHINGTON, TONY: Sound Supervisor (*Seasons 1 to 3*)

ZAHL, ANN: Associate Producer (*Season 2*)

SECTION SIX:

THE
SPIN-OFFS

Back in the first edition of this book we foolishly suggested that Red Dwarf, given its time slot, was not likely to generate a wide variety of spin-offs. Hardly prophetic words as it turns out, what with a plethora of Dwarfish items finding their way into the specialist stores. There has been, however, one notable casualty: Fleetway Editions declined to renew the contract for *Red Dwarf Smegazine*. A sad day for our bank managers.

As before, we begin our overview with:

THE NOVELS

1) RED DWARF – INFINITY WELCOMES CAREFUL DRIVERS

| First published | (Soft cover) | 1989 Penguin Books |
| | (Hard Cover) | 1991 Chivers Press |

2) BETTER THAN LIFE

| First published | (Hard cover) | 1990 Viking Books |
| | (Soft cover) | 1991 Penguin Books |

Despite their experience at script writing, when Rob Grant and Doug Naylor decided that they would attempt to write a novel, both were initially unsure if they would be able to tackle the entirely different kind of writing involved in producing such a book.

Surprisingly, landing a deal for an actual *Red Dwarf* novel proved to be quite difficult. BBC Books themselves expressed some early interest in publishing the *Red Dwarf* spin-off, but Grant and Naylor feared that, under the BBC imprint, the book might be considered to be merely the usual novelization or straightforward adaptation of the TV episodes rather than a proper novel in its own right. Eventually, after the end of series two, they approached Penguin Books and, armed with a speculative first chapter and outline of the structure plus eight bottles of Sancerre, Grant and Naylor were able to persuade editor Tim Binding that the series was fantastically popular and that the project was well worth going ahead with.

Red Dwarf – Infinity Welcomes Careful Drivers was faithful to the spirit of the TV series, but only certain elements were retained exactly as they had originally appeared on the screen; ideas were expanded, altered – either slightly or radically – or dropped altogether and a number of totally new concepts were introduced. If it seemed as if Grant Naylor was trying to proffer an improved and perhaps definitive version of events, it was because that was exactly the case. While this revised approach to *Red Dwarf* is a treat for the reader, it tends to make life difficult for anyone wanting to make any kind of sense of the continuity. Perhaps the simplest option is to locate the printed adventures of the *Red Dwarf* crew in one of the infinite number of parallel universes that the TV series claims exist, or more properly into one of the six – the more conservative estimate of extant alternate dimensions – suggested in the books themselves.

The enormous success of the first novel, published in paperback form only, earned its sequel, *Better than Life*, the prestige of a hardcover first edition in the Viking imprint. Once again, the content of the book diverged significantly from its small screen counterpart; because the books vary so much from their television progenitor it is worth, if only for the sake of completeness, detailing the plots here.

RED DWARF – INFINITY WELCOMES CAREFUL DRIVERS

In the latter part of the twenty-second century it has proven essential for man to look beyond Earth for valuable resources and to exploit the rest of the solar system – rich in mineral wealth. Technology too has advanced, to such an extent that death is no longer the impediment it once was; computers are able to project simulated holograms derived from the brain patterns of the dead. Unfortunately for the rank and file, the process is expensive in terms of both money and energy; only the most essential members of the populace are resurrected as these impalpable beings.

After celebrating his birthday, with a bold attempt to complete a Monopoly Board pub-crawl around London, Liverpudlian Dave Lister wakes up in a McDonalds wearing a lady's pink crimplene hat and a pair of yellow fishing waders, with a passport in the name of Emily Birkenstein. And, if that wasn't bad enough, the burger bar just happens to be located on the Saturnian moon of Mimas.

Completely broke and without a work permit, Lister is forced to steal taxis in a reckless attempt to earn enough money to buy a ticket home. Unfortunately, the small amount he saves not paying rent – by living in a left luggage locker – is either squandered on consolatory drink or forcibly taken by muggers. One fateful night, however, Lister has a brainwave. After picking up a fare wearing a false moustache and claiming to be Christopher Todhunter, an officer in the Space Corps, he decides to enlist.

Upon joining the Space Corps, Lister is posted aboard the mining ship *Red Dwarf* as a technician third class, the lowest rank in the Corps. However, Lister is not at all concerned with his lack of status, he doesn't intend to be around for long anyway; his plan is simple, the minute they get to Earth he'll jump ship and go AWOL – unfortunately he had reckoned without a four-and-a-half-year round trip. Lister's bad luck doesn't end there; his bunk mate for the duration is none other than Arnold Rimmer, the badly disguised man he'd once taxied to a plasti-droid brothel. Rimmer is not exactly the most popular man aboard the vessel, he can count his friends on the fingers of one hand and still have five digits spare and his idea of a good night out is to spend it not ageing in a Stasis Booth. It had taken Rimmer six years to achieve the lowly rank of First Technician and so become the leader of Z Shift – an eleven strong team responsible for routine maintenance, cleaning and sanitation – a squad from whom he commanded no respect whatsoever, least of all from the newest recruit, Dave Lister.

After several months of the same routine, life aboard *Red Dwarf* becomes mind numbingly boring for Lister; even the excessive drinking with Petersen, Selby and Chen in the 'Copacabana Hawaiian cocktail bar' seems to lose some of its appeal. But one night he meets Third Console Officer Kristine Kochanski and immediately falls head over heels in love. A glorious, magical, passionate affair follows – lasting until Kochanski goes back to her old boyfriend, just over a month later.

Devastated, the lovelorn Lister concocts a scheme to avoid the rest of the voyage; buying a healthy pregnant show cat on the Uranian moon, Miranda, he is quickly summoned before the Captain for breaking quarantine regulations. The captain, an American woman with the unfortunate name of Kirk, gives Lister two choices: hand over the cat or spend the rest of the trip in stasis and forego three years' wages.

Three million years later the ship's computer Holly revives Lister from Stasis and informs him that his unavoidably ex-tended sentence was due to a leak of Cadmium II radiation which wiped out the rest of the crew and had until very recently been contaminating the ship. Lister promptly cracks up. A probability study conducted by, the now erratic, Holly reveals that Arnold Rimmer is the best person to keep Lister sane; Lister isn't at all convinced by the findings, but the computer proceeds to restore Rimmer as his holographic companion anyway.

Although, in Holly's not entirely reliable opinion, the likelihood of humanity still being around is slim, Lister elects to return to Earth, undertaking the journey in Stasis. The newly resurrected Rimmer doesn't relish the idea of spending the next few million years alone in space, nor does he fancy being turned off – death may have thwarted his chances of promotion but it's all he's got. Fortunately, circumstances provide a reprieve from his potential solitary existence.

Upon opening the radiation seals, Holly has discovered a non-human lifeform; the task of investigation falls to Lister and Rimmer. Travelling down hundreds of floors of supplies they first find ten floors completely devoid of their original contents and then discover a city comprising igloo-shaped buildings, constructed from some of the missing supplies. In this strange town they meet what looks exactly like a man wearing a neon pink suit, but in fact he isn't a man at all, he's a cat, the Cat – the last surviving descendant of Lister's pet, Frankenstein. Safely sealed in the cargo hold her kittens had bred and bred. It was a case of survival of the fittest and over the course of time the cats had evolved; Felis Erectus was born followed, eventually, by Felis Sapiens.

Though by nature the Cat is a self-centred egotist, Lister elects to take him into Stasis for the voyage home. They never reach the booths. While the Cat is reluctantly saying goodbye to his home-made collection of immaculately tailored suits and Lister bids farewell to his bunk mate, *Red Dwarf* breaks the light barrier; images from the future appear before the crew. A shocked Rimmer believes he has witnessed the death of his companion, but an aged Dave Lister materialises and reveals that it is in fact one of his six grandchildren that will die. Following instructions from his older self, Lister hastens to the medical unit where he sees another future echo of himself, complete with twin babies. Realising that it will be interesting to find out how he will eventually get them or, more accurately who with, Lister decides to wait around and see.

Eons earlier the *Nova 5*, a space ship on an advertising mission for Coca-Cola, had crash landed on an unnamed world. The responsibility for the accident lay solely with the ship's service mechanoid, Kryten; taking enormous pleasure from his cleaning duties, the conscientious mechanoid had given the onboard computer a good wash with soapy water. The only survivors had been the Captain, Yvette Richards and two other female officers Kirsty Fantozi and Elaine Schuman.

A distress call from Kryten is received on *Red Dwarf*. The encouraging message, with its prospect of some female company at last, prompts Lister, Cat and Rimmer to get kitted out in their finery and mount a rescue, but it's all in vain – the girls have been dead for nearly three million years. It takes a while to convince Kryten of this fact but when it does finally sink in the inconsolable, guilt-ridden android activates his shut-down disc.

In the week that follows, the wreckage of the *Nova 5* is transported aboard the *Red Dwarf* – complete with the essential supplies that were still contained on the ship. While Lister endeavours to repair Kryten, Rimmer discovers that, although the personality discs of the crew are all corrupted to some extent, the *Nova 5*'s Hologram simulation suite is fully operational. He takes the opportunity to create a new hologram anyway – a duplicate of himself. Now that he has found the perfect companion he doesn't have to put up with Lister anymore; Rimmer decides to move in with his double.

Once repaired and functional Kryten explains that the *Nova 5*'s quantum drive duality jump could get them back to Earth in the space of three months – providing there was enough uranium 233 available for fuel. Reading up on the subject, Lister discovers that the fuel can be synthesised from the abundantly available thorium 232. Lister, the Cat and Kryten set off along with 12 skutters to do some thorium mining on a nearby moon while, on *Red Dwarf*, the two Rimmers oversee the remaining

84 Skutters in the job of welding back together the two halves of the *Nova 5*. Neither task runs as smoothly as it ought to. The Cat puts in around fifteen minutes' work per day – between naps and meals. Kryten on the other hand is a great help as long as his duties require nothing more responsible than making tea and sandwiches. Back on *Red Dwarf* the two Rimmers are beginning to fall out – even he doesn't like himself very much – and succeed in breaking the *Nova 5* into three pieces before finally restoring it to its proper, single piece construction.

Returning after three months' solid mining, Lister is shocked to discover that the Rimmers have actually completed their work and the *Nova 5* is in one piece; though arriving at its current state has been at the expense of most of the skutters. By now the Rimmers actively loathe each other; the copy believes the original has been changed for the worse, by his association with Lister. It's just as well that it's only possible for one hologram to make the trip back to Earth and Lister must decide which one. Leaving the choice to fate he tosses a coin; the original Rimmer loses. Lister, however, erases the copy but not before coaxing, from the first Rimmer, the hugely embarrassing tale of the time he sent back his gazpacho soup to be warmed.

Earth: two years later. Dave Lister has at last found happiness in the peaceful American town of Bedford Falls; the others are doing well for themselves too. Rimmer is the third richest man on the planet, his wife, Juanita, is the most beautiful woman – true, she is unfaithful and temperamental, but he loves her anyway – and, thanks to a time machine developed by his company, his friends include Julius Caesar and Napoleon Bonaparte. Elsewhere, on an island off the coast of Denmark, the Cat has all the fish, milk and scanty-armour clad Valkyries he could ever need.

Despite having everything he ever wanted from life, Lister is convinced that something is amiss. It's all too good to be true; his wife – supposedly a descendant of the original – is identical to Kristine Kochanski, his two sons change each other's nappies and Bedford Falls is indistinguishable from the town of the same name featured in his favourite film *It's a Wonderful Life*. His suspicions are confirmed by the painful messages that appear on his arms, spelling out 'DYING' and 'U=BTL' – for the past two years, he realises, he has been living in a fantasy.

Searching out his crew mates, Lister assures them that their lives are unreal, but it takes the arrival of Kryten for the truth to be fully discovered. The mechanoid explains that all was set for the voyage home in *Nova 5*, or would have been if the Cat hadn't gone missing. He was eventually found linked up to Better Than Life – an illegal, addictive game, which utilises hallucinogenic brain implants to create an authentic, yet totally imagined environment. Lister had gone in to pull the Cat out; Rimmer had gone in to pull them both out; they had all become game heads. Kryten had reluctantly burnt the messages into Lister's arms to make him aware of his situation and had then gone into the game himself.

Now, fully cognisant of their potentially fatal predicament, all they have to do is get out of the game and leaving the game is the easiest thing in the world – all the player has to do is want to. But, as its name suggests, the game is 'Better Than Life'.

BETTER THAN LIFE

A couple of years have passed, the crew are still trapped within the game; Kryten too has succumbed, the temptation of infinite numbers of dirty dishes to wash proving irresistible to a cleaning mechanoid. Lister continues to lead a contented existence with Kristine Kochanski, in the fictional town of Bedford Falls. For the Cat a life of eating, preening, cruelty to animals, and, of course, constant sex with his economically dressed Valkyries remains indispensable. While in Rimmer's fantasy the Brazilian Bombshell Juanita had been passed over for the more homely charms possessed by Helen.

Meanwhile, back in reality, Holly's condition has deteriorated – he has become computer senile. To ease his loneliness he finds a companion in the shape of Talkie Toaster – a cheap novelty belonging to Lister, with a degree of artificial intelligence and an obsession with making toast. Reading Holly's manual – which the computer can not now understand – the Toaster discovers a way to intensify his intelligence, while at the same time reducing his operational lifespan; because of his eagerness to be clever again and his current lack of brain power Holly agrees to undergo the intelligence compression process. The procedure is successful – after a fashion. The computer's IQ rises to twelve thousand three hundred and sixty-eight, but his running time is drastically reduced to three point four five minutes. To conserve his precious remaining moments Holly shuts down the *Red Dwarf*'s engines, then himself.

In the game, salvation is at hand from an unlikely source. Rimmer's psyche decides to make things unpleasant for him, bankruptcy soon follows, his 'Solidgram' body is repossessed and he is sent to prison in the form of a soundwave. Fortunately Rimmer manages to escape in the body of Trixie La Bouche, a prostitute. In turn he finds the others and his presence corrupts the fantasies of both Lister and the Cat. With nothing left to lose they finally decide to leave the game – along with Kryten who had eventually managed to drag himself away from the washing up.

Aboard *Red Dwarf* life is perfect – too perfect; not only have Rimmer, Kochanski and Petersen survived in Stasis, but there are ice cubes in the ice-making compartment of the fridge. Lister surmises correctly that the game is not quite finished. This discovery induces Better Than Life's designer, Dennis McBean, to make an appearance and offer the crew the opportunity of a replay; they decline the invitation, this time it really is Game Over. Life is rather less than perfect aboard the real *Red Dwarf*. The years spent in the game have taken their toll on Lister and Cat and their wasted bodies are put into medi-suits to recover.

Much to Holly's annoyance he is temporarily switched back on in order to reveal why the ship is operating on emergency power and not moving. Rimmer and Kryten realise that having the ship up and running would be quite convenient, as a rogue planet is on a collision course with it and is due to hit *Red Dwarf* in about three weeks – the length of time it will take to start up the engines.

Bemoaning the lack of a blast-off button, Rimmer begins work on his half of the procedure. Determined to complete the task well within the allotted time he succeeds only in destroying forty skutters in the piston towers. The only alternative now seems to be to abandon ship.

Kryten thinks it only fair that Holly is brought back on line for his remaining minute or so – quite a fortuitous move as it turns out, for the computer has a plan.

Using the shuttle craft, *Starbug*, a thermo-nuclear device can be fired into a nearby sun, creating a solar flare that will knock a planet out of its orbit and drive it into the rogue. Lister sees it as playing pool with planets and, believing Holly to have devised a total mis-cue, elects to take the shot himself.

Accompanied by Rimmer in *Starbug*, Lister sets off to save *Red Dwarf* and surprisingly his eccentric trick shot actually works. Unfortunately the small shuttle craft encounters the slip stream of one of the planets, the force of which causes it to crash-land. On the frozen world Lister is without warmth and his food supply consists of little more than a tin of dog meat and a pot-noodle. Not all his luck is bad though, Rimmer's remote relay fails and the hologram is returned to *Red Dwarf*. On the mining ship time is behaving oddly – in one part of the ship it's Monday, in another Friday. The source of the trouble is found to be a black hole; although the newly re-started engines are set on full reverse thrust the *Red Dwarf* is being pulled inexorably into it. Holly is reactivated again but can offer no help on this occasion as his terminals are operating in different time zones. The toaster, however, claims to have a solution to their problem which he will reveal providing everyone eats a great deal of toast.

Meanwhile Lister is having problems of his own; the ice has melted and the planet seems intent on killing him.

Wearing a makeshift metal suit he survives a downpour of acid rain, he leaps over gaping earthquake-induced chasms and finally avoids suffocation in a torrent of oil before realising – after seeing Mount Rushmore – that the planet is in fact Earth.

Millions of years before, the rest of the solar system had been colonised; Earth had been abandoned and converted into an enormous garbage dump. Eventually a methane explosion had set off a chain reaction which tore the planet out of its orbit and sent it off into deep space.

The planet seems appeased by Lister's promise to make amends for his ancestors' transgression and with the help of the planet's current inhabitants – a colony of eight-foot cockroaches – the last human being begins to set his world to rights.

Travelling at the speed of light *Red Dwarf* enters the black hole; many of the ship's propulsion jets are destroyed, but enough survive to maintain light speed and carry the vessel through the omni-zone – where the gateways to the six other universes converge at the centre of a singularity – beyond the event horizon and back out into the universe.

With *Red Dwarf* safely navigated through the black hole it only remains to find and rescue Lister. Rimmer and the Cat set off in the transport craft *White Giant* while Kryten and the Toaster take *Blue Midget*. It doesn't take long before the remains of *Starbug* are discovered, along with acres of farmed fields. An impatient Lister is there too. Instead of spending a few weeks on the planet as the others had thought, thanks to the time dilation effects of the black hole, he has been waiting for thirty-four years. During the time spent on his home planet Lister has come up with an idea: they'll tow Earth back to its rightful place in the solar system.

A message from Kryten is greeted with a certain amount of

surprise; apparently he and the Toaster have found Lister too. The real Dave Lister warns that his double is in fact a polymorph, a shape changing genetically engineered mutant which feeds on emotions; he instructs them to initiate the auto destruct on *Blue Midget* and abandon ship. Unfortunately, by now they are in space en route to *Red Dwarf*, and the polymorph is showing its true colours. Before the creature is able to strangle Kryten, Talkie Toaster decapitates it with a toasted metal ashtray.

Back on *Red Dwarf* Lister is puzzled over why the polymorph didn't feed and was so easy to kill; taking no chances he decides to go ahead with the destruction of *Blue Midget*. He was right to be worried: the polymorph had reproduced itself, and the second mutant was attempting to find a shape in which to escape from the shuttle craft before it exploded. In the form of a light beam it sped across space back to the *Red Dwarf*.

As Lister prepares to eat his first shami kebab in thirty-four years the polymorph attacks – first as part of his meal, then as his boxer shorts. In the guise of a rat it feeds off Lister's fear and then completes its meal transformed into a hideous armour plated creature with rather a lot of teeth.

The now fearless Lister decides to take on the polymorph single handed. His ship mates, opting for discretion, choose to sit it out on 'Garbage World' until the emotion deprived creature starves to death – they get no further than the supply deck. Imagining that the shape changer is lurking in the shadows, Kryten and the Cat fire off heat-seeking laser bolts from their bazookoids, but the heat that they actually locate is emitted by the Cat himself. Managing to evade the bolts of energy, Cat succeeds in trapping them in a lift. But his luck ends there and, under the pretence of being a beautiful woman, the polymorph is easily able to flatter the narcissistic animal and steal his vanity.

As Arnold Rimmer, the mutant blames Kryten for the Cat's fate and is consequently able to make a meal of the android's guilt. Finally, by entering the hologram's personality disc it is able to feast on Rimmer's anger.

The emotionally crippled crew are unable to concoct much of a plan to combat the polymorph. The Toaster, volunteering to become their leader, only provokes Kryten into putting him in the waste disposal. Lister, fearless as ever, is still convinced that a direct approach is best. The mutant is easily tracked down, but assumes the form of a lamp post, against which the bazookoids prove ineffective.

Eventually, when the polymorph begins to transform, Lister launches himself against the creature, but is easily tossed aside. The others attempt to run away; seeing his only escape in an old lift shaft Kryten inadvertently unleashes the heat-seeking bazookoid bolts and this time they find their intended target and the polymorph is destroyed.

Dave Lister is dead, the result of a heart attack. His body is placed in a coffin – along with a chicken vindaloo, eighteen cans of lager and a photograph of Kristine Kochanski – then blasted into space.

Reactivated to be given the sad news Holly, once again, has a solution: the casket must be retrieved then taken through the black hole into the omni-zone to a planet in universe 3 – a universe where time runs backwards.

Lister wakes surprised to find himself restored to life, albeit a life that is in reverse. A newspaper message instructs him to meet the rest of the crew in thirty-six years' time. In the meantime he has his past to look forward to and somehow Holly has arranged for it to be spent in the company of Kristine Kochanski.

The plot of *Red Dwarf – Infinity Welcomes Careful Drivers* borrowed extensively from the original television episodes 'The End', 'Future Echoes', 'Me²' and 'Kryten', though not necessarily in that order. The concept of the Total Immersion Video from the 'Better Than Life' episode was also used for the first book's cliffhanger ending. The idea was carried through into the second novel where the game was revealed to be a later version than the one featured on television. The book *Better Than Life* also contained elements from 'Marooned', 'Polymorph' and 'Backwards'; in the case of the latter episode it was merely the concept of an Earth on which time runs backwards that was utilised. The fourth season's 'White Hole' was previewed in the novel, but in this earlier version the spatial phenomenon's actions were undertaken by its complete opposite – a black hole. The third book in the sequence is in preparation and will perhaps reveal not only how Lister went about creating the universe, but how and if Holly is able to increase his life span beyond its remaining few seconds. Although Rob Grant and Doug Naylor only signed a three book deal with Penguin the next novel is not necessarily the last as both of them are keen to continue the saga in this format.

THE LAST HUMAN

What with publishing deadlines and stuff, you can guarantee that some time between us sending the revised programme guide update to the printers and it reaching the shops, the long delayed third *Red Dwarf* novel *The Last Human* will finally see the light of day, making our book look out of date. Typical.

THE RED DWARF OMNIBUS

Basically, a slightly edited compilation of the first two novels, with the pilot script and a bit of Dave Hollins – Space Cadet thrown in for good measure.

RED DWARF – THE TALKING BOOKS

Appropriately enough, it's Chris Barrie who does the talking on these Laughing Stock releases. The standard two-cassette version of *Infinity Welcomes Careful Drivers*, abridged by Tim Binding, has loitered around the audio charts since its release. The full version is available in a six-tape pack; though you might find it harder to track down, it's certainly worth it if you're too lazy to read the book yourself. *Better Than Life* is now available too.

PRIMORDIAL SOUP

Not a recipe book, but a collection of scripts; the most significant at the time of publication being the yet to be broadcast 'Psirens'. The others, all selected by Rob and Doug, were 'Marooned', 'Polymorph', 'Justice' 'Dimension Jump' and 'Back to Reality'.

RED DWARF SMEGAZINE.

As *Red Dwarf* began its fifth season in February 1992, it also became one of those rare programmes to be awarded the distinction of its own magazine. Like the programme itself (and like this book!), *Red Dwarf Smegazine* (originally titled *Red Dwarf Magazine*,) got its start in Manchester, where the misnamed London Editions were the first to spot the potential of the programme. Work began in late 1991, but by the time the finished product saw print, the company had merged with London-based Fleetway (home of, amongst many others, Judge Dredd and Roy of the Rovers), and the magazine came out under the new label of Fleetway Editions.

Red Dwarf Magazine featured a blend of factual and humorous articles, along with comic strips which both adapt episodes and tell new stories. Interestingly enough, these strips show Rimmer (and any other holograms which happen to turn up in them) in black and white. This is the result of a request by Rob Grant and Doug Naylor, who confess that they would have liked to have done this in the series, had the effect been a little easier to achieve.

The Smegazine sold reasonably well, but editor Mike Butcher believed the potential readership was much higher and after 15 issues elected to relaunch the magazine in a revamped Volume 2. Sadly, it seems that sales didn't increase significantly enough to persuade Fleetway to renew their contract and the final issue Vol 2 #9 appeared in December 1993, the same month that saw the demise of Dan Dare's Eagle, also from the Fleetway stable.

Given the popularity of the series, quite why the *Smegazine* never realised a readership comparable to, say, *2000AD* is impossible to say. On the plus side the *Smegazine* boasted some fine artwork by the likes of Colin Howard, Glenn Rix and Paul Crompton as well as some great articles by a couple of handsome and well-endowed writers (modesty forbids us mentioning names). Negative aspects were, in our opinion, the odd-ball comic strips based on concepts very peripheral to *Red Dwarf* as seen on TV; and to be fair, there is a finite number of times the same small group of people can be interviewed on the same subject and still find something fresh to say.

THE FREEBIES

During the course of its relatively short run the *Smegazine* had a number of exclusive free gifts stuck to its cover by various means. In order of appearance these were:

Badges

RDM#3 (May 1992) boasted a 'Smeg Head' badge which featured the immortal insult on a black background and laid out over a red ellipse, in much the same way as the series' logo itself (this issue's cover warned jokingly of a 'potentially lethal emission of cadmium II' should the free gift be removed from its stuck on position, the intention being that the badge itself would obscure the warning; unfortunately, the printers 'corrected' this mistake by moving the badges to a more 'suitable' position before distribution)

Ace Rimmer's catchphrase 'Smoke me a kipper, I'll be back for breakfast' was attached to the cover of RDM #6, again in red and white on a black background.

One further badge, featuring the magazine's logo (or, put another way, the series' logo with the word 'Magazine' underneath it), was produced by Fleetway; however, this wasn't actually presented with the magazine but rather was issued as a promotional giveaway for comic conventions and the like.

Postcards
These appeared with the advent of volume 2; the first issue's pair of cards featured Duane Dibbley and the crew of Red Dwarf V, whilst Vol 2 #2's brace had Lister and Starbug.

Stickers
Volume 2 # 6 came complete with stickers of Duane Dibbley 'The Man From U.N.C.O.O.L', 'Robo-cak' Kryten, 'How's it hangin' dudes?'with the original Holly and 'The Boys from the Dwarf'.

Starbug Key Ring
Not quite as exciting as it sounded when announced in the previous issue, but amusing nonetheless. Basically a piece of transparent plastic with a picture of Starbug on one side and on the reverse the witty line, 'My other spacecraft is the Red Dwarf.'

THE CLOTHES.
If you're the sort of fan who's keen to express his or her loyal appreciation of *Red Dwarf* to the world at large, what better way than to dress up in some of the tasteful items of attire available from Wimbledon based firm BMS. These include Baseball Caps, Jackets, Surf Jams, Sweat Shirts and of course T-Shirts. In the time it's taken you to read this paragraph BMS have no doubt produced two more T-Shirts featuring characters and quotes from the series. Consequently, it would be a futile exercise for us to attempt to include a complete list. (Too idle? Us?) If you really need to know you can contact BMS via PO Box 10, London, SW19 3TW.

That's nearly it. There are, however, just two more items of clothing to mention in this section – and again both are T-shirts, albeit ones which were produced long before BMS came onto the scene.

The two shirts in question feature different drawings of Craig Charles as Dave Lister, placed against a black background; both bear the legend 'Smeg Mania' on one side whilst on the other 'Who the Smeg are You Looking At?' appears

Both were commissioned by Craig himself, and used as giveaways to studio audiences for early recordings of the show. Although it was possible at the time to obtain these through selected retail outlets, they were issued as a very limited edition and are for the most part, no longer available. Again, all you ardent collectors out there are going to have a bit of trouble with these!

THE GREETINGS CARDS

There are 24 of these photographic cards available from Portico – naturally, they come complete with red envelopes.

TONGUE TIED (The Record)

The debut single single from the Cat (Danny John-Jules) as featured originally in 'Parallel Universe'. Released by EMI in both 7" and 12" versions as well as on cassette and CD, canny marketing meant that in order to obtain all the mixes of Tongue Tied and the Red Dwarf theme the record had to be purchased in more than one format.

The single peaked at no. 17 in the charts and might well have risen higher had Danny not had to cancel his scheduled appearance on Top of the Pops.

Uniquely, the video reunited Danny with Craig Charles, Chris Barrie , Robert Llewellyn and *both* Hollys, Norman Lovett and Hattie Hayridge; also featured were 'Queeg' actor and 'Parallel Universe' choreographer Charles Augins and Clayton 'Elvis' Mark. The promo video along with other related bits and pieces was set for commercial release but was dropped for reasons unknown. Readers of *Red Dwarf Smegazine*, however, were able to send off for a copy in plain packaging.

Both the video and the record sleeve featured a female Cat character called Kit (shades of Red Dwarf USA).

THE VIDEOS

Of course, no matter how many T-shirts you wear and how many books you read, there is still no real substitute for actually watching the programme. Fortunately for *Red Dwarf* fans, BBC Video have realised this, and taken it upon themselves to release the show's classic episodes on tape.

The first set of two videos was released for the 1991 Christmas market, each featuring three episodes from the tremendously popular third season. Each was named after the first of those episodes, these being 'Backwards' and 'Time slides' respectively – and before you go flicking back to the episode guide in Section 3, we can assure you that yes 'Timeslides' was the fifth story in that particular season. However, having obviously decided that it was a much better cover title than that of the fourth episode, 'Body Swap', the Beeb swapped the two episodes around to make it so.

One other interesting point about the video release is the 15 certificate which the censors attached to tape 1. As the other *Red Dwarf* videos released to date have all been granted the more liberal PG rating, it does not seem unreasonable to assume that the cause of this was the third series' Alien spoof 'Polymorph', which apart from containing a pre-titles warning to squeamish viewers (see Section 1) also contained the show's only use of a certain four-letter word beginning with t. However, this is not the case – and it will probably come as a surprise to most of you to learn that the higher rating was actually 'necessitated' by one single line in the episode 'Marooned', in which Dave Lister talks about losing his virginity at the age of twelve. How dare he!

In any case, *Red Dwarf III* was obviously a success, and as such it was quite logically followed up, in March 1992 by . . . *Red Dwarf II* – that is, *Red Dwarf* Series 2, renamed for the sake of conformity. Again, the series was released on two tapes, each containing three episodes – this time in the right order. The only drawback to this release seems to be that, due to the lack of colour photographs from this season, shots had to be taken from television monitors to provide the video covers. As a result, these look somewhat less than professional, although obviously this couldn't be helped. *Red Dwarf I V* hit the shelves in October and November 1992. The two tapes entitled 'Camille' and 'Dimension Jump' featured the fourth series in the order in which it was originally screened and not in the preferred repeat season sequence.

Incidentally, there was an opportunity to send for an exclusive *Red Dwarf VI* T-Shirt with this release, which we ought to have mentioned in the entry for clothes.

After being rescheduled a time or two *Red Dwarf I* finally appeared in Summer 1993. To overcome the problem arising from the lack of early photos artwork covers were provided by Bruno Elettori. The episodes appeared in their original broadcast sequence and Byte One was entitled 'The End', so no surprise there; however, tape two was named after the fifth episode of the series, 'Confidence and Paranoia'. Apparently BBC Video decided against calling it 'Waiting for God' just in case people confused it with another BBC sit-com. Can't think which one . . .

The blurb on the video cases reminded us that the episodes had never been repeated by the BBC, so naturally, everybody rushed out and bought these rare gems – then of course the BBC repeated them.

July '94 saw the release of 'Back to Reality' the first half of season five, though no prizes for spotting that *Red Dwarf V*'s order on video differed from the first TV run. Anyone who bought their copy from Woolworths recieved a free official metallic *Red Dwarf* badge (subject to availability) and very nice it is too. The second part of season five appeared in August entitled 'Quarantine'. And no doubt Red *Dwarf VI* will appear in due course. Meanwhile you can have a good old chuckle at the *Red Dwarf Smeg-ups* tape.

THE POSTER

Before you ask, no we're not getting a backhander, but the only place we could find this was Woolies (not that we actually looked that hard). This large poster features the *Red Dwarf* logo, a photo of the crew, and the caption 'In space no one can hear you smeg'. If you want our opinion that's probably just as well.

RED DWARF CALENDAR 1995

Published (if that's the word) by Scandecor, this colourful item features not only photos of the cast but lists all 365 days in 1995.

THE MUSIC

Budding musicians can recreate the sound of their favourite programme in their own front rooms, because Howard Goodall's excellent theme to *Red Dwarf* is also available as sheet music.

Contained in a four-page booklet, which is fronted by the familiar logo on a tasteful blue circle, the music should be easily available from any of the normal outlets for such things. It is copyrighted by the Noel Gay Music Co. Ltd., and published through International Music Publications under order reference 17542.

KRYTEN MODEL KIT

Produced by Sevans models, this 1:6 scale kit (that means it's 30cm high) is a pretty accurate version of the mechanoid. Apparantly, if you ordered it through *Red Dwarf Smegazine* you received a free groinal attachment! There is a possibility the Sevans will be releasing further models in the series – in the meantime however, why not take a Sevans Captain Scarlet, paint it emerald green, add a bit of plastacine to the nose, draw a letter H on the forehead and, hey presto, a series three Rimmer.

THE MAKING OF RED DWARF

Glossy and full of pics, this Penguin tome by Joe Nazzaro is recommended if you like 'Gunmen of the Apocalypse'.

THE MAN IN THE RUBBER MASK

Sticking with Kryten, Robert Llewellyn has written a book about, amongst other things, his experiences as the popular bog-bot, particularly his time spent working on *Red Dwarf USA*. It's published by Penguin and it's great, so go out and buy it. Oh, you already have.

THE RED DWARF QUIZ BOOK

Yet another book from Penguin, who've obviously realised they're on to a good thing.

THE FAN CLUB

The Official Red Dwarf Fan Club can now be contacted c/o Steev Rogers, 12 George Brown Way, Beccles, Suffolk, NR34 9JU.

Steev (who obviously changed the spelling of his name to avoid being constantly mistaken for Captain America) tells us that members not only receive a brilliant quarterly magazine (which is actually published 3 times a year), but also have the chance to attend the club's annual Dimension Jump conventions and meet cast and crew from *Red Dwarf*. You could meet us there too, if only we got invited!

THE PROGRAMME GUIDE (original edition)

No. 8 in the Sunday Times bestseller list. Nuff said.

THE OFFICIAL COMPANION

Whoops, nearly forgot to mention this publication from Titan Books, again! Written by Bruce Dessau this thin volume was rushed out in time for Christmas 92. It features a lot of photos, one or two of which haven't been seen before.

THE REST

This is really a category for all the other bits that aren't commercially available but are worth picking up if you see them. Items such as the glossy synopsis sheets that used to be given out at Shepperton recordings, posters and promotional material for the various books, the autographed cast photo card, etc.

RED DWARF – USA

All right, so you can't go out and buy it and chances are, if you don't attend the right convention, you won't even get the opportunity to see it. Anyway, after careful consideration, we decided that rather than put it in either the History or the Programmes section, the US pilot episode of *Red Dwarf* should be classed as a spin-off.

American TV producers first noticed that *Red Dwarf* had the potential to be adapted into a series made especially for US television as far back as season two, when the British show aired on PBS. However, the sweeping changes – to both the characters and the format – they insisted upon, were enough to deter Grant and Naylor from making any deals.

Following *Red Dwarf's* successful run in the Los Angeles area in 1991, further approaches were made to Grant Naylor Productions, with a view to producing a version of the saga originating in the USA. It was a bid from Universal Studios that seemed likely to yield the most desirable end result. And so, on the completion of *Red Dwarf V*, Rob Grant and Doug Naylor flew to California to assist in the making of a pilot episode. They were accompanied on the trip by Robert Lllewellyn, who was to be the only member of the British cast to reprise his role. His Kryten make-up would again be applied by Andria Pennell. Incidentally, Chris Barrie was offered the Rimmer part, but declined the invitation.

Although essentially close in structure to its British antecedent, the studio executives insisted on a few changes in order that the show might appeal more readily to an American audience. Instead of being a complete slob, the new Lister, played very agreeably by Craig Bierko, was more in the heroic leading man mould. Consequently, had the series gone ahead, the intention was to include a romantic interest for our hero in every episode, a far cry from the enforced celibacy of the original. Incidentally, an early notion of Grant and Naylor had been to include the pleasure GELF Camille as a regular character, but this idea was quickly abandoned.

The changes to Rimmer were less radical: instead of a letter H to denote his status as a hologram, a red circle would be present on his forehead. The familiar music and logo would also disappear, the latter replaced by pink digital lettering. The script, by Linwood Boomer, was adapted from 'The End', with several ideas from the books and other episodes slotted in. Boomer's task was primarily to give the jokes more of a Stateside flavour.

RED DWARF (The Pilot)

Created by Rob Grant and Doug Naylor. Developed and written by Linwood Boomer. Music by Todd Rundgren. Produced by Todd Stevens. Directed by Jeff Melman. Cast: Craig Bierko (Lister), Chris Eigeman (Rimmer), Jane Leeves (Holly), Robert Llewellyn (Kryten), Hinton Battle (Cat), Elizabeth Morehead (Christine Kochanski), Michael Heintzman (1st Officer Munson), Lorraine Toussaint (Captain Tau).

By the latter half of the twenty-second century, humankind had colonised the outer fringes of the solar system. After a night of excessive drinking had caused Dave Lister to wake up on one of the moons of Saturn – a long way from his home town of Detroit – he had little option but to join the 5000 strong crew of *Red Dwarf*, a beat-up Class 5 Miner/Freighter with a cargo capacity of 47 cubic miles. Although assigned to Rimmer's menial work team, Lister isn't disheartened. Not only does he have his dream of owning a farm with various animals, including two pigs, but he's also found love aboard the mining vessel, in the attractive shape of Christine Kochanski. Lister's work mates are a couple of skutters who are none too keen on Rimmer either and, to express their disapproval, they have learnt how to form an offensive gesture using the middle one of their three digits.

While in the process of being dumped by Chris, because of his reckless and carefree attitude to life, Lister encounters the robot Kryten 2XB 517P, who is newly arrived aboard *Red Dwarf* and en-route to the Captain. The two strike up an instant friendship and Kryten is introduced to Lister's cat Frankenstein, which he'd rescued from being cooked in a Titan restaurant and now keeps hidden in his bunk room. Kryten reveals that the cat is in fact pregnant, and not putting on weight because of the amount of beer it drinks.

It isn't long before the unquarantined animal is discovered and Lister and Kryten are summoned before Captain Tau. A security camera has exposed the android taking the cat to a new hiding place, but Kryten refuses to reveal her whereabouts. However, the strain of defying a direct order causes him to overload and explode.

Lister too refuses to spill the beans and consequently is sentenced to stasis. Just as he is about to become a non event mass with a probability of zero, Kochanski arrives to tell him she loves him – Lister says he'll talk after all, but it's too late.

Three million years later Holly 6000, the ship's computer, revives Lister and informs him that the rest of the crew have been killed (by a lethal dose of Cadmium 2, if you hadn't guessed). However, Holly informs him that he needn't be entirely alone. One of the crew's personality discs remains undamaged and using a holographic projection unit a new hologram can be introduced to replace Munson, the ship's previous one. Much to everyone's disappointment the intact disc is that of Rimmer, who was last seen being carried out of an exam, wearing a straitjacket. Kryten too is still around, albeit in pieces.

From the shelf where his head has been stored for the last three million years, the android has contentedly passed the time by reading a conveniently placed fire exit sign.

Holly detects one further presence aboard the vessel. But before introducing the others to the Cat, she explains his origins by means of a series of computer generated, animated images. Yet although an entire race of Cat People had evolved from Frankenstein's kittens, a civil war had wiped them all out except the one about to become the final member of the *Red Dwarf*'s new crew.

Despite his companions, Lister is understandably far from happy, but then something happens to give him renewed hope. He is visited by his future self accompanied by Kryten, the Cat and, best of all, Christine Kochanski. The visitors have some important information to impart to Lister, but the huge amount of power needed to facilitate their presence requires them to be brief. Unfortunately, Rimmer's eagerness to discover what awful thing fate has in store for him prevents them from revealing much, not even the reason for the hologram's absence – though the Cat helpfully suggests that it's not so much awful as disgusting.

Though learning little of his destiny, the knowledge that Chris is to play a part in it is all the encouragement Lister needs. Filled with a fresh sense of optimism he engages *Red Dwarf*'s powerful engines and sets off into infinity, keen to get out there and do some 'space stuff'.

Although not entirely happy with certain aspects of this try out episode – some of the casting in particular – the studio executives still saw enough promise in the project to give it a second chance, this time with Grant and Naylor in charge of the production. Rather than completely refilm the pilot, Rob and Doug decided to make a promo video utilising scenes from the already filmed episode alongside newly made segments spotlighting the new cast members. Strangely, however, the Kryten footage was from the UK episode 'Terrorform'. The two characters recast were Rimmer and the Cat; Anthony Fuscle was Rimmer (with the familiar letter H restored) and Terry Farrell played a very different kind of Cat – a female one to be specific. Craig Bierko and Jane Leeves reprised their roles as Lister and Holly respectively.

Had it proven successful the resulting series would have aired on NBC, the largest of the US network. But, sadly the promotional film too was unable to secure a deal for a full season of episodes. Terry Farrell went on to land the role of Dax in *Star Trek – Deep Space Nine* and Jane Leeves appeared as Mancunian Daphne Moon in the *Cheers* spin-off *Frasier*.

Since Universal's involvement ceased, other companies have expressed an interest in making *Red Dwarf* for American TV. However, as with some of the early proposals, the changes requested were more than sufficient to put Grant and Naylor off. So, for the time being at least, it seems that *Red Dwarf USA* is dead. Blimey, we're still ending on a depressing note.

Other Books In This Series:

DOCTOR WHO – THE PROGRAMME GUIDE

Jean-Marc Lofficier

This indispensable handbook first appeared more than a decade ago, and immediately established itself as the single most important reference work about *Doctor Who*.

Since then it has been updated four times. This new edition contains all the important information about every *Doctor Who* story.

Each story entry includes the storyline, the full cast list, technical credits, and details of the novelisations, video cassettes and audio cassettes of the story.

An additional section gives details of the New Adventures that have been published since the TV series finished in 1989.

ISBN 0 426 20342 9

BLAKE'S 7 – THE PROGRAMME GUIDE

Tony Attwood

The perennial appeal of *Blake's 7* is reflected in this programme guide, which has been through three printings in hardback and paperback editions.

This latest edition has been revised, expanded and updated. In addition to a synopsis and cast list for each television story, and an alphabetical encyclopedia of the *Blake's 7* universe, the book contains the latest information about the actors and writers, the merchandise, the story continuations that have appeared since the programme ended, and about the fans' network.

ISBN 0 426 19449 7

DOCTOR WHO – THE SIXTIES

David Howe, Mark Stammers & Stephen James Walker

The Sixties is the definitive record of *Doctor Who*'s early years, from the broadcast of its first episode on 23 November 1963, to its change into colour with the beginning of the Jon Pertwee era.

Illustrated throughout with colour and black and white photographs, most of which have never been published before, this is a meticulous record of the beginning of a cultural phenomenon. It is also a lovingly assembled history of the art of television in a decade perhaps less jaded than our own.

'. . . for the science fiction fan who's always wanted one book about the series, but who has been put off by the plethora of titles available, this is the one to get.'

Starburst

'This will probably rank as the ultimate book on the subject . . .'

Doctor Who Magazine

ISBN 0 86369 707 0

Also available:

DOCTOR WHO – THE SEVENTIES by Howe, Stammers & Walker

THE PRISONER

Alain Carrazé & Hélène Oswald

A spy story? A science fiction thriller? A critique of modern society? Or all of these things, and more?

Patrick McGoohan's startling television series broke new ground in the 1960s; and time has only emphasised the magnitude of McGoohan's achievement – and increased the programme's popularity.

This book, the most comprehensive study of the programme yet published, contains over 250 photographs as well as an episode-by-episode breakdown of the entire series, complete with script extracts.

ISBN 0 86369 557 4

THUNDERBIRDS, STINGRAY, CAPTAIN SCARLET – THE AUTHORISED PROGRAMME GUIDE

John Peel

In 1956, Gerry Anderson's small film company was commissioned to produce 52 episodes of a puppet series for children – *The Adventures of Twizzle*. There followed a decade of ageless, innovative and increasingly sophisticated science fiction programmes.

This book provides an overview of Gerry Anderson's works, and concentrates on his three most popular and enduring creations. Each series is described in detail, with a story synopsis, technical credits and background information, as well as photographs from the series' archives.

ISBN 0 86369 728 3

Other telefantasy books:

DOCTOR WHO: THE HANDBOOK – THE FOURTH DOCTOR

David Howe, Mark Stammers & Stephen James Walker

Doctor Who is the world's longest-running science fiction series, and Tom Baker was the longest-serving of the actors who portrayed the title role.

This volume covers the reign of the fourth Doctor, from 1974 to 1981, when the programme achieved its highest ratings in Britain, and became a sensation in the United States.

As well as interviews with Tom Baker, the book includes an in-depth study of the production processes and location work used, and an episode-by-episode guide to the era.

ISBN 0 426 20369 0

Also available:

DOCTOR WHO: THE HANDBOOK –
THE SIXTH DOCTOR by Howe, Stammers & Walker
DOCTOR WHO: THE HANDBOOK –
THE FIRST DOCTOR by Howe, Stammers & Walker